Still the rice
Grows green

Asia in the Aftermath
of Geneva and Panmunjom

The coast of Red China as seen from Kinmen.

STILL THE RICE
GROWS GREEN

*Asia in the Aftermath
of Geneva and Panmunjom*

JOHN C. CALDWELL

 HENRY REGNERY COMPANY
Chicago, 1955

Contents

PROLOGUE 1

BOOK ONE: A BRIGHT LIGHT SHINING 5

Being the story of the men and women of Free China living and fighting on the guerrilla islands and on the mainland of China.

BOOK TWO: OF MEN AND DREAMS 83

Being the story of men on Formosa who have risen from corruption and defeat to build good government.

BOOK THREE: THEY WILL NOT FIGHT 185

Being the struggle of Korea's people in the bitter aftermath of a truce which leaves the land divided.

BOOK FOUR: THE FAR EAST IN FERMENT 255

Being the struggle between those who have given up hope and those who still fight on, and an account of the part that America must play if right is to conquer.

MAP OF FORMOSA 309

MAP OF NATIONALIST ISLANDS ALONG FUKIEN COAST . . 310

FACTS ABOUT FORMOSA 311

ACKNOWLEDGMENTS

Portions of some chapters in this book have appeared previously as articles in *The Freeman, The Christian Herald, The Nashville Banner,* and *The Nashville Record,* and in feature articles distributed by The Spadea Syndicate, New York.

Names of persons given are true names except in a few cases where individuals have relatives living in Communist China and North Korea and where true identities cannot be given because of the danger of reprisals.

STILL THE RICE
GROWS GREEN

Prologue

IF THE DAY be bright and clear, the pilot flying the lonely skies from Formosa westward to the China Coast sees the mainland of Enslaved China even before the lofty peaks of Free China recede into the haze.

First are the beaches, the mud flats, the myriad islands. Then, like a giant staircase, the mountains rise, green tier upon tier, to the horizon and on far beyond to the sterile heights of Tibet.

If one looks closely upon this unfolding panorama of China one sees alien gashes upon the land. Beginning at the very water's edge, trenches zig-zag across rice fields and hills, even cresting, here and there, to the very mountain tops. There are new trenches, lately dug by the men of Mao. There are older trenches, overgrown and weedy, built five years ago in defense against those who now rule the land.

And among the maze are even older diggings, the preparation of a decade ago, dug by ill-trained and poorly armed men in desperate hope that the Japanese invader could be stopped. If imagination takes over, still more and more futile trenches we see; those of the 1930's when Communist and Kuomintang first clashed in the green mountains of Fukien and Kiangsi. Too, there are those of still earlier times, when a young Generalissimo swept victoriously northward to victory.

So it is that the very face of the land shows the never-ending struggle of the people whose yearning has been for peace but whose lot has been war for as long as even the old men can remember.

1

So it is also, on Formosa, for hundreds of miles through the heartland of Korea, on Okinawa where signs of past war mingle with preparations for the new. The face of Eastern Asia, the landscape of an hundred off-shore islands mutely testify to bloody past and hopeless future.

Yet men and women live on and breed on in the shadow of the guns. Their rice fields are still green, though increasingly is the rice bowl not filled. Children come, in ever increasing numbers, for fertility never leaves the starving and the poverty-stricken. Many are destined some day to man the trenches. Untold thousands will never see their ancestral homes. For they are victims either of wars or of man's new solution to war—the dividing of ancient lands by the 17th or the 38th parallel. These are the men and women of the divided lands: Korea, north and south; China, free and Enslaved, Indo-China, Communist and for-a-time-free. And who knows where next?

Hearts and souls too, have been scarred by the drift of events. The yeast of Change, of uncertainty and broken moorings ferments in the hearts of the young. Some have a new-found faith, many have no faith.

In the tea fields of Formosa's mountains, the young farm girl sings as she works down the row, the song answered by the young man whose soul is also in torment. And shamelessly, these children of a great moral heritage lie down together between the rows, the meeting of their flesh watched and applauded by others who soon join in brief escape.

On the broad avenue which leads past the Chang Duk palace in Seoul, the Kims, the Paks and the Lees gather each evening as dusk falls. Their bodies released from ancient binding dress are for sale: to the lonely GI who must take his pleasure in the dark alley; to the officer, the foreign correspondent who has the luxury of privacy and a bed. And in the center of the city a raucous noise comes from the heart of the gutted Bangchang, the black-market rabbit warren of Korea. Carnegie Hall it is called, the new night club where the Korean officer comes with his girl, to drink expensive American whiskey, to dance to American music, to forget for a while that his ancestral home lies only fifty miles away, but in an alien land.

There are others, no less tormented, who work and study and hope. Empty minds and souls jam the tiny book stores in Seoul, in Tokyo, in Hong Kong and Bangkok to read of Utopias offered by "democrassie" and Communism. Thousands more diligently study English by choice, Russian by force, hoping that futures may thereby be affected.

Such is the face of Asia, physically marked by signs of war, past and planned for, even hoped for; spiritually in ferment, the new competing with the old, a bounteous picking of a strange fruit.

But still, everywhere the rice grows green. For part of the story of Asia in the aftermath of Panmunjom and Geneva is one of men and women who still have faith, who refuse to bend with the changing wind. It is a story found in the dreams of a guerrilla captain on a lonely outpost, in the hopes of men and women on Formosa, in the plans of a lady general, in the heroism of a little girl in Korea, in the courage of a band of lepers, lost in the backwash of war, but who would not give up.

Everywhere for those who seek it, faith and hope can still be found. Everywhere are those who keep the rice fields green and growing.

BOOK ONE

A BRIGHT LIGHT SHINING

Chapter 1

MANY years ago when I was a high school lad in Shanghai, I fell in love with a lighthouse keeper's daughter.
Her name was Bobbie, and she was beautiful in the
manner of those who come from mixed Oriental and Western
stock.

I would not claim that Bobbie was my first love. But she
was unquestionably the first and only daughter of a lighthouse keeper to enter my life. And therein, rather than in
her beauty, lay the charm and the attraction. In my romantic
day dreams I could see the two of us, tending the flashing
light that guided storm-tossed ships into Amoy's harbor. I
could see us as guardians of the South China Coast, keeping
the beacon lighted through winter storms and typhoons. Pirates would cruise about us, smugglers might tempt us, but
together on a lonely island we would keep the China Coast
lighted.

However, an engineer's daughter soon replaced Bobbie in
my heart. *Her* father was engaged in building a vast dyke
along the Yellow River, and surely this too was a noble project. Did not perhaps my future lie in doing good works, in
saving China's millions from the ravages of yearly floods?

And so it was that Bobbie and her lighthouse were soon
forgotten. A quarter of a century has passed now and I do

not know where she may be. But a few months ago, unexpectedly and dramatically, I did see—I actually visited—the lofty cliff where Bobbie's lighthouse stands.

I was on board a tiny Nationalist Chinese gunboat, an observer only, but feeling much a part of the motley crew of guerrillas, regulars and commandos, taking part in what was to them a routine raid on Communist shipping off the China Coast. Besides the officers and crew of Free China's gunboat P-6, we were three, for my host that day was a Chinese admiral, deputy commander of Free China's coastal forces. I had even been assigned an aide, Commander Yao Wei Tao of the Chinese Navy, who guided and helped me during a month's tour of the Chinese guerrilla islands that have been so much in the news of late.

We had chased and captured a Communist junk out of Amoy, and the pursuit had taken us far south of our home base on Kinmen Island, called Quemoy in newspaper reports. It had been an exciting and dangerous afternoon, for raids on shipping are risky affairs. Always our captain must be careful to stay out of range of the Communist coastal batteries; for in the excitement of the chase it was easy to stray too far towards the blue mountains that rise up from the Fukien Coast.

The P-6 was an ancient craft, built as a trawler for Japan's fishing fleet. Officers and crew members lived together in evil-smelling quarters. The day's laundry hung willy-nilly about the deck. Behind the wheel house were baskets of cabbage and spinach, for the P-6 had no refrigeration. The vegetables kept fresh in the wintry breeze which had increased in force all through the afternoon.

But even at sea on dangerous duty, there was hospitality on the P-6. After a long and successful chase, Lieutenant Chang Se Chek, the P-6's commanding officer, produced a rickety table; a tea pot and cups came from the galley. As we cruised along on the very edge of the civilized world, just beyond the range of Communist gunners, we drank tea and talked of the never ending twilight war along the China Coast.

It was then I noticed a tiny, rugged island, steep cliffs topped by the white of a lighthouse tower.

"Who does that island belong to?" I asked the admiral, as I had asked of a score of other islands. For along the Coast there are islands held by Free China's guerrillas, islands occupied by the enemy and the "vacuum" islands, those of shifting control or insufficient importance for either side to fortify.

"We occupy it," replied the admiral. "It is called Tungting Island."

Suddenly the memories of a quarter of a century came flooding back. Tungting Island! That was Bobbie's lighthouse I saw perched high on the cliffs. I remembered too, the briefing in the guerrilla general's headquarters a few days earlier, remembered that Tungting is the most southerly, the smallest, the most exposed of all Free China's holdings. Quickly I made my request. Could we visit the island; could I have the opportunity to talk to the guerrillas who garrisoned its cliffs?

Admiral Tang, Commander Yao and Lieutenant Chang conferred lengthily. They spoke in Mandarin which is not my native dialect, which I can follow only imperfectly. But it was clear that the admiral was worried about my security, by the danger of suddenly being cut off by the Communist gunboats which slip out from mainland harbors as night begins to fall.

The argument was going against me, so quickly I cut in, speaking to the Lieutenant in Foochow, my native dialect.

"Tell the admiral that I will take all responsibility," I urged. "He may radio guerrilla headquarters to that effect. I must go to Tungting."

And so it was decided. Messages cracked out, back to Kinmen to advise of our destination, to tell the commanding general that I would not be present at the feast that night; and a message went to Tungting on the horizon so that the garrison would know that it was a friend, not foe, approaching.

There is not a tree on Tungting's heights. Sheer cliffs rise three hundred feet from the pounding surf. As we approached the island I could see the zig-zag steps carved in the cliffs, leading from the tiny concrete jetty to the summit. The face of the cliffs bristled with machine gun nests, with rifle pits barely deep enough for a man to maintain foothold.

The afternoon storm had risen, the sea was roaring by the time we had approached to the limit of safety. It was still a half mile to the cliff's base, so the guerrillas sent a tiny sampan to take us ashore.

It was no mean feat to climb from a rolling gunboat into a bucking sampan. It was particularly difficult for the admiral who was a portly man. And once aboard, it was a marvel that we did not capsize. Waves roared over us, drenching us from head to foot. I felt that I was doing far more than duty required. And the admiral was doing something not called for on the part of men of his rank.

After a half hour we reached the tiny jetty; eager hands reached out to grasp our tiny craft, to lift us to safety. Twelve guerrillas stood at attention at the base of the cliff. They presented arms, and a little man stepped forward to introduce himself. Thus I met Captain Chang Yi Ming, commanding officer of the tiny guerrilla forces of Free China on Tungting Island.

The captain was overwhelmed at the honor accorded Tungting's defenders. As we climbed the steps to the summit he eagerly asked if the visit of an American newspaper correspondent did not perhaps mean that the United States was about to send aid to the guerrillas.

I explained that I hoped my visit would result in such aid, but that I was merely a representative of the American press, without official connections, seeking news of our brave allies.

It was a hard climb for me, more so for the admiral. We passed by the machine guns nestled among the rocks. Here and there a white rabbit incongruously hopped about, nuzzling the sparse patches of moss and lichens growing on the cliffs. Upon the sides of the sheerer cliffs I could make out the myriad nests of swifts, from which one of China's greatest delicacies is made.

Captain Chang noted my interest in the nests.

"We have little rice here," he remarked jokingly. "But we are rich! We can always have a feast of birds' nest soup—and sharks' fins too!"

At last we reached the summit and I saw Bobbie's lighthouse, its beacon darkened now; for the Nationalists keep the lights dark so that it will be difficult for shipping to enter enemy ports. Around the tall white tower was a courtyard, at its end the house where Bobbie and her family had lived in days gone by. Other smaller and newer huts were scattered about the two acres of level land.

Captain Chang ushered me into the old sitting room, clapped his hands for tea and began, earnestly and seriously, to "brief" me.

"We are responsible for keeping this lighthouse out of enemy hands," he began. "We report on shipping, we send agents to the interior, we gather intelligence from the fishing boats."

"What is the strength of your garrison?" I asked.

"We have just fifty men here," he replied. "And that crowds us a good deal."

Then I inquired of rotation, of food and supply problems, of how these men kept body and soul together in such utter loneliness.

Captain Chang explained that officers were supposed to be rotated every six months, enlisted guerrillas every two months; a supply ship was scheduled to come with rice and fresh meat once a week. But these schedules never quite worked out. He had already spent a year on Tungting. Most of his men had had a few days' leave on Kinmen. Sometimes the supply ship missed three or four calls. It all depended upon weather, upon the activity of the enemy.

"That is why you see a few rabbits," Captain Chang explained. "The general has told all of us that we must raise as much food as possible. We have tried rabbits, we have a few chickens, too." Then he smiled as he continued. "But our men get so lonely for something to love that most of them hate to see rabbits killed. Actually it is the 'enemy' that keeps us going. The fishing junks from the mainland come out and we trade them rice for fresh fish and vegetables."

"Tell me, Captain Chang," I asked, "What do your men do for recreation?"

"Oh, some of the men fish a great deal. We have regular classes, too. Almost all my men are literate now." Then the Captain added proudly, "And did you notice the place to play basketball, right under the lighthouse?"

There were thousands of questions I wanted to ask about the men who live on Tungting's peak, but there was little time, the storm was rising and darkness would soon come upon us. I was curious where the fifty men came from, what part of China they called home.

Captain Chang's answer surprised me. "Our fifty men come from twelve different provinces," he told me. And he ticked off some: Sergeant Chiang hailed from the fruitful red basin of Szechwan, 1500 miles away; Corporal Lin from nearby Fukien; Corporal Chen from Peiping.

"How long have these men been away from their families?" I asked; and then I added a question I would have hesitated to ask in the days before Communism. "Don't you have a serious morale problem, cooped up here for months with no family and women?"

The little captain answered me without embarrassment. "I

am fortunate. My family escaped with me to Formosa. But it has been nearly two years since I have been there. It has been that time since I had a woman. . . . Twenty-three of our men are married, most have families they have not seen or heard from for five, six years."

Then the guerrilla captain paused before continuing. "It is curious. Corporal Lin whose family lives within fifty miles of us worries more than those whose women are thousands of miles away. Occasionally the men who get leave will visit the "white-faced" girls who have an establishment on Kinmen. Do you know of it? There are many girls there; the price is controlled. But many of us never visit the place. You ask how we get along. I do not know exactly except we fill our days with work, with study. We are always tired—and we hope always for that day when we will go back."

That was by far the longest speech Captain Chang had made, and he seemed tired, as though the subject confused him a little. Quickly I changed the topic. As we walked through the courtyard I asked what military aid he needed most.

Chang's face was bright and animated as he answered: "Above all we need fast boats. You saw the only craft we have—a sampan! We have not much trouble defending the island when they attack us. Why once when they tried to land here all we had to do was throw grenades over the cliff! But we need boats to take us ashore quickly, to get our agents to the mainland." Then the captain stumbled a bit for words as he finished. "We need that kind you used in the big War— the Pee Pee boats, I think they are called."

I did not smile at the little slip of initials. I agreed that such boats would be most useful, and I promised that I would tell my people and my government how much use could be made of a few PT boats. I realized that I had asked an unwise question, or at best had worded it poorly; for the captain did not fully understand the relationship between press and government in America. It was inconceivable to him that an American newspaper man would come to Tungting Island without some official connection, that I could not become a vehicle for fulfillment of his needs.

And then it was time to take our leave. There remained for us the dangerous trip back to the gunboat in the rising seas, the long dark miles back to anchorage at Kinmen. Single-file we walked down the steep steps to the water's edge. There the honor guard was waiting, and as I stepped into the tossing sampan, a curious thing occurred. The twelve guerrillas snapped to attention. But instead of presenting arms, or even saluting, they began to clap.

It was more than the salt wind that brought tears to my eyes as I heard that unmilitary salute, as Captain Chang bowed and repeated: "Tsaichien"—till we meet again.

As I looked back up the cliff I noticed something on the white lighthouse tower I had missed. A plaque on the tower's side proudly proclaimed: "Built by A. M. Bisbee, in the Year of Our Lord 1871."

Tungting's lighthouse no longer brightens the way for ships harbor bound or breasting the waves on down-coast course. The light is dark now, but I could not but believe that Mr. Bisbee, whoever he was, would feel as I did—that a new and bright light still shown from Tungting's summit, a light that has not yet been dimmed by war and uncertainty and unbelievable loneliness.

I could not tell Captain Chang or the admiral either that in all probability that light would be extinguished. I could not have explained that my people who had fought eight years of revolution, who struggled four bloody years to preserve their union, who had already fought two great wars for freedom, now seemed more interested in appeasement, in dreaming of co-existence, in making deals with the enemy under cover of loud pronouncements about the massive retaliation that would follow if the bargain were broken.

14

And what of Bobbie and her lighthouse-keeper father? Their lives had become inextricably woven into that of the Coast. Did they choose to stay on, to become engulfed in the tragedy of China? Are they too somewhere behind the darkness that has fallen on the mainland? Do they perhaps live somewhere in one of the old treaty ports, hoping desperately for the time when the lights will be turned on again?

Chapter 2

TUNGTING ISLAND is the southern anchor, the most exposed of the fifty-odd Nationalist-held islands that drape themselves like a necklace for nearly four hundred miles along the bulge of China's Coast. It occupies the southernmost position in the vital Kinmen Island Command area, Kinmen being the most important of all Free China's coastal holdings.

The newspapers call this island Quemoy. It was here that two American officers were killed on September 3rd, 1954. Around this island war and rumors of war have swirled for months.

But the Chinese know it as Kinmen, which means "The Golden Gate" and tradition-conscious Chinese attach great significance to the name. For although unknown to the western world until suddenly thrust upon the front pages, Kinmen is of great historical importance to China. Three centuries ago one of China's great generals, the pirate Koxinga, launched from Kinmen an attack which drove the Dutch from Formosa. His fleet of 7,000 war vessels was the greatest ever assembled.

Today Kinmen, or Quemoy, is again a staging area but this time for advance westward across the narrow waters that separate it from China's mainland. From it have been launched major guerrilla raids and upon it the enemy has poured an estimated 50,000 artillery shells. It is an incredibly crowded seventy square miles, supporting a population of 41,000 civilians and 75,000 troops and guerrillas.

For Free China Kinmen has become a symbol of hope, the Golden Gateway for triumphant return to the mainland. For Americans it has become another spot for uneasy wondering, an island constantly in the news, always called by a strange name, and described in unrecognizable terms.

The United Press described it as a "sand spit"—its interior as flat. *Time* magazine stated that it covers 85 square miles but the *U. S. News and World Report* gave its area as 57 square miles. On different days, by different writers it is seven miles, ten miles, fifteen miles from the mainland.

The National Security Council, highest strategy body of the United States Government, has met in extraordinary special session to discuss the little island which is so variously described. John Foster Dulles flew to Formosa to ponder its defense.

Senator William Knowland has demanded that the island be defended. Senator Charles Potter of Michigan says that it should not be defended. For, according to him, "it is only lightly defended" as it is. Senator Kuchel of California made a speech about Kinmen Island, calling it a "foolish" island with a name he couldn't even spell. And of course the ubiquitous Drew Pearson has devoted several inches of his precious space to explaining its significance.

Captain Chang Yi Ming, commanding Kinmen's (Quemoy) most exposed position on Tungting Island would not have understood all the fuss, perhaps would not even have been able to recognize Kinmen as described by American war correspondents.

However, the importance of this island cannot be understood in terms of square miles, of distance from the mainland, or even in terms of the number of fighting men who defend it. It can only be understood if it is visited and seen, if one talks to its soldiers, its guerrillas, its civilians. For Kinmen can indeed be Free China's Golden Gate, can affect the future of all Chinese, free and enslaved, indeed can affect the future of all Asia.

Kinmen Island, in short, must be seen to be believed. It is more than an island. It is an idea and an ideal; in its future are wrapped the hopes and fears of millions. It was my privilege last December to visit Kinmen, and beyond it, to visit Tungting, Leihyu, Ta-tang, Erh-tang, and Matsu—the other bits of land, other "foolish" islands with unpronounceable names, around which Free China pins its hopes. I traveled by sampan and gunboat and junk, by jeep and by foot. I ate and slept and talked with the men who have staked their futures on the Golden Gate. And even I, who was born upon the coast near Kinmen, who had spent years among the islands, was unprepared for what I saw.

On the day before I left Formosa for Kinmen and guerrilla-land I filed a story which began: "Tomorrow I shall be on the very edge of the civilized world, on the China Coast, within a few miles of Communist armies. My undertaking will be dangerous. . . . The China Coast is not a pleasant place in winter. In the twilight war that rages along the coast one can never be safe. There are spies and counterspies. Men are betrayed or quickly killed in the darkness. . . . If I am lucky, I shall be eating the meager fare of the Coast—soft rice mixed with sweet potatoes, pickled jellyfish, or dried fish."

I wrote honestly, for I did not know much more about Kinmen than Senators Potter and Kuchel, or even (though I hesitate to make such a confession!) than Drew Pearson. I had prepared myself for danger and hardship. I had expensive medicines, for I expected to be far from medical help. I had a sleeping bag, for I did not expect to find a bed. I warned my wife not to worry if she did not hear from me for long periods, for surely there would be no certain communications from the China Coast!

Danger there was, and I found excitement too. But the real story was not one of artillery duels and raids as much as of unbelievable accomplishment and of contradictions, of the hopes and fears of men who live within sight of their homeland, yet might as well be thousands of miles distant.

It is no misstatement to describe the island as being on the very edge of the civilized world, the nearest Communist artillery positions just two thousand yards distant. Yet one travels to the island in a regularly scheduled airliner. Once a week a plane of General Claire Chennault's Civil Air Transport makes the run. (CAT also operates once weekly to the Ta-Chen islands and twice monthly to Matsu.) My plane was a plush job, with uniformed attendant, stateside reading material and typical airline refreshments.

But Kinmen-bound travelers note certain immediate differences between their trip and a run from New York to Washington. The Kinmen run is not listed in the CAT schedules. The exact hour of departure is shrouded in secrecy, is changed a half dozen times. Once in the air and away from the friendly coast of Formosa, the pilot begins an intricate flight pattern. He must fly low to escape Communist radar, must follow exactly a flight pattern that is changed every day, must take particular care as he circles to land on Kinmen's airstrip. The airstrip lies just beyond the range of Amoy's Communist antiaircraft batteries; a tiny error and the lumbering C-46 would be a sitting duck for the trigger-happy gunner who dumped thousands of shells upon the island in the fall of 1954.

And of course as the plane approaches the China Coast there is the hazard of enemy air attack. Unarmed, unescorted, any attack would be fatal. Even engine failure and ditching in an unfriendly sea could be disastrous.

These thoughts were going through my mind as I watched the smoky blue mountains of mainland China rise from the haze. Our plane was crowded: agricultural experts and government officials; guerrilla leaders, returning after special training on Formosa; a few Chinese army wives, their children who roamed the aisles as do children anywhere. There was no hint of anxiety on the part of anyone. But I was uneasy.

The plane's copilot came into the cabin, sensed my unrest and sat beside me. We talked first of his work. Still a young man, he had ten years of flying, had taken part in most of the spectacular ventures which have become commonplace to the men who fly for CAT: supplying beleaguered Nationalist garrisons during the last days on the mainland, evacuating cities surrounded by the enemy, flying Nationalist guerrillas out of Burma, dropping supplies to the men of Dienbienphu. All this plus the flying of regular schedules throughout the Far East make the men of CAT proud and unafraid. It is certainly one of the world's most unusual airlines, deserving indeed the motto on its schedules which says "The Orient's Own," a tribute to the vision of the man who founded it.

"Why, this kind of thing is nothing to some of our jobs," the copilot assured me. "There is really nothing to worry about. Notice how low we are flying? That's to escape radar. And we have radar stations of our own, on the guerrilla islands almost up to Shanghai. Every ten minutes we pick up a coordinated radar search report from all the stations. If all is clear, if there are no enemy planes in the sky we are cleared to land during the next fifteen minute period."

And there—just fifteen minutes—is the margin of safety upon which the lives of my fellow passengers depended. It did not seem much of a margin to me, though, for I had not yet savored of the boundless faith of men like Captain Chang Yi Ming on Tungting Island. Added to the fifteen minutes, this faith has proved a sufficient margin for over 100,000 people to live and work and prosper and to keep their hopes alive.

20

The signs of war become immediately apparent as the plane circles over Kinmen's landing strip. The island is neither a sand spit nor flat, as described by the United Press. Nor is it lightly defended as stated by Senator Potter. Magnificent beaches are marred by barbed wire; behind the barbed wire are trenches, pillboxes. The mass of tumbled black rock that rises over a thousand feet in the island's center is scarred by military roads, trails, concrete lookout posts, machine gun nests, artillery emplacements. And all around lies enemy territory: the radar-crested peak of Amoy three miles away; the promontories which mark the southern and northern limits of Amoy's spacious harbor reach out to encircle Kinmen, a giant nut within the jaws of a giant nutcracker.

As our plane rolled to a stop, unloading crews quickly appeared, for no plane is allowed to stay long on the ground, a tempting target for enemy attack. As I climbed down the ladder to the ground a guerrilla general stepped forward to greet me.

His first words, designed to make me feel safe, were: "Now Mr. Caldwell, don't worry about the Communist artillery. It is only the first shell that kills anyone here." And then he added, as an afterthought, "You see, we have so many places to hide."

For Communist shelling of China's Golden Gate did not begin last August and September when what the newspapers call "Quemoy's vest pocket war" broke into headlines. An estimated fifty thousand Communist artillery shells have fallen upon the island since it was first occupied by Chiang Kai Shek's troops in 1949.

Kinmen is not a pretty place. Shaped like a huge dumb-bell, it is fifteen miles long, four miles wide at its narrowest point. In summer it is lashed by typhoons, in winter by the cold winds that rage through the Formosa straits. Mountains scattered with huge black boulders rise to 1200 feet. Hundreds of acres of red and white clay hills are eroded into miniature bad-lands. A few lovely beaches tempt the visitor until he notes the grim warning "Beware, this area is mined." But I soon forgot about Kinmen's ugliness in the surprises that were in store for me.

It is twelve miles from the airstrip to Hopu, the island capital, and I traveled a three-lane highway, the last three miles paved. Magnificent lateral highways lead off to every nook and cranny, a total of two hundred miles of all-weather highways. Soon after I left the airstrip I noticed a huge, modernistic building facing upon a beach. I found it to be a newly completed 500-bed Chinese Army hospital.

I was surprised to notice a half dozen schools between the airstrip and Hopu. Later I was to find that there are fifty-three grade schools and one high school on Kinmen. Eighty-six percent of the children are in school. When the Nationalists occupied the island in 1949, there was one elementary school.

Little Kinmeners study a normal curriculum with two exceptions: every child studies guerrilla tactics, and drills constantly; all children learn how to be lookouts, know how and where to report suspicious movements upon the sea.

The hospital and Kinmen's miles of highways have been built without aid of one piece of modern machinery. There are no bulldozers, no road scrapers, no excavation equipment, for these are luxuries Free China cannot afford. She has done here as she did in building vast airfields during World War II: used the one great resource she has, the hands and strong backs of her people.

During my stay on Kinmen the ugliness of landscape was forgotten as I noted with admiration the adaptiveness of this people in solving crushing problems with the means and the tools at hand.

Kinmen is, I am sure, the only place in the world where a huge army is almost entirely billeted in civilian homes; where every soldier attends agricultural classes and, when not soldiering, is a farmer; where thousands of trees are planted by the troops and are tended with a wondrous and tender care; where the army operates an agricultural section in headquarters, on a par with our G-1, G-2 and G-3; where there are agricultural officers at all levels, from army through division, on down to company; where the guerrillas run a cigarette factory and a wine distillery producing wine famous from Taipei to Hong Kong.

On my first day on Kinmen I passed a tiny drug store and out of curiosity entered to see what things besides powdered tiger bones might be offered for sale. There was the same brand of aureomycin with which I had equipped myself at thirty-five cents a capsule, selling for less than a dime. My fears for want of medical attention were unfounded, for in addition to the 500-bed Army hospital, there is a downtown medical center for civilians, headed by a graduate of the University of Texas.

My first night on Kinmen, dusty after miles of driving over the island, I thought wistfully of a bath, wondering if I would have to find some unmined beach and dunk myself in the wintry ocean. As if my thoughts had been read, a guerrilla orderly popped up saying, in effect, "Sir, your bath is ready."

I was led downstairs, into a spotlessly clean bathroom, with flush toilets and huge tub. Clean towels were laid out, and on the side of the tub was a bar of Palmolive soap!

I found no need of sleeping bag; for in my private room in "The First Guest House of the Fukien Provincial Government-in-Exile," I slept upon a bed with clean sheets. I took my meals in an adjoining room, cooked and served by guerrilla orderlies, not magnificent but always of several courses and always delicious.

Flowers bloomed in the quiet courtyard outside, neatly trimmed hedges lined the walks. There was quiet and peace in the air, a quiet and peace which in a few hours made one

23

forget the ever-heard mutter of heavy artillery, the bark of machine guns, in the never-ending war that is waged across the narrow waters separating Kinmen from the mainland.

The war across the waters had been unceasing for five years, Kinmen coming upon its prominence largely because of the unexpected results of the major battle in that war. In 1949 the forces of Frec China reeled in defeat. City after city fell to the Communist armies; time and again Nationalist China's capital was moved until at last one move remained. The island of Formosa, separated from the mainland by 120 miles of water, might become a place where demoralized leaders and soldiers could have a breathing spell. Perhaps on Formosa the scattered remnants of Chiang Kai Shek's forces could start building anew.

But moving a sizable army across the Formosa straits posed problems. There was little shipping, and that which was available must be protected and covered. On all the mainland of China not one airfield remained in the control of Chiang's beaten armies.

And so it was that the high command gave the order that certain islands off the coast opposite Formosa must be occupied and held, to offer cover while tired men crossed to the safety of Formosa. Kinmen was among those islands, especially strategic because it lies off the harbor of Amoy, because it is large enough in area to accommodate many troops, because it is very close, not only to the mainland shore, but to the nearest point on Formosa.

No one expected Kinmen to be held for long; that was not even in the plan, if there were any real plans in Chiang's desperate hours. Remnants of various armies, those of defeated Tang En Po and of a half dozen other armies, crossed in junks and rafts and wooden steamers. Once ashore on Kinmen, the soldiers of Nationalist China did what little they knew how to do. They dug trenches, they built little pillboxes, they strung barbed wire along beaches, they planted a few mines. And perhaps here and there a man prayed to his Buddhist, Christian or Moslem God. For among the armies on Kinmen were men from every province of China. They could not even speak the language of the Kinmen islanders. And because time was short and money shorter, no barracks could be built. Soldiers of China, speaking a score of dialects moved in with the 41,000 islanders, most of whom even now speak only the dialect of south Fukien. They have lived together since those dark days of '49.

But the breathing spell was short indeed. Even while Nationalist remnants still crossed to Formosa, the jubilant and cocky Communists assembled their ships, briefed their leaders and began the assault upon Kinmen's western beaches. It was October, 1949, the 25th day, when the first Communists poured ashore near Mashan. They came first by the hundreds and then by the thousands. Some were killed by mines, others were delayed and tangled in trench and barbed wire. But within hours the men of Mao had breached Kinmen's hastily built defenses. Another typical Nationalist defeat seemed in the making.

But camped on the hills and in the villages near Hopu was an American-trained division, complete with tanks, laboriously ferried over from the mainland. American-trained officers were attached to that division. Here and there other officers, men like little General Li Liang Yung, with long American contacts, still had hope.

Orders went out to the American-trained division to attack. Nationalist tanks lumbered forward, later Nationalist planes came in from Formosan fields. Other beaten, untrained Chinese foot soldiers were infected by the sudden surge and will to fight. Charge after charge was made, thousands upon thousands of Communist soldiers died, or were wounded or captured. But still the enemy came on, all through the night of the 25th and the 26th of October. As fast as they came, they were killed; for by now the Nationalist armies had become suddenly invincible. The battle ended on the evening of the 26th.

I do not know how many Communists died in the battle for Kinmen. The men who took part in the slaughter are justifiably proud. Some told me thirty thousand died, some only nine thousand. But this I do know: the people who live in the villages on Kinmen's western side have a peculiar problem. Eight hundred wells are no longer usable, new ones have been dug each year. For it was still warm that October, and there were so many Communists dead that normal burial was impossible. The dead were dumped into the wells and rocks thrown upon their bodies. Today the wells remain sealed.

And in the center of Kinmen Island, surrounded by massive black rock hills, is a lovely cemetery, kept green and clean. In a memorial building a wall is inscribed with the names of Chiang's men who died during those October days. There are row after row of names, listed by rank, beginning with a major general, ending with the privates.

Kinmen is more than a military fortress, although for this reason alone it invites Communist attack and explains the Red boasts that it will soon be conquered. For also on Kinmen is the government-in-exile of Fukien province; the commanding general is concurrently the governor-in-exile of Fukien and its 12,000,000 people. With him is a provincial government staff, trained and ready to move across and take over when and if "D" day comes. Already the reforms that have strengthened Chiang's government on Formosa have been transplanted to Kinmen.

Perhaps even more significant, Kinmen, as a symbol that all is not lost, has a particular importance for the millions of Chinese who live "overseas," in all the lands and islands of southeast Asia. The island has had but one export. For two centuries its young men have gone forth to seek their fortunes in Malaya, Indonesia, Thailand and the Philippines. Over 100,000 overseas Chinese who claim Kinmen as their ancestral home have already given the island defenders tremendous financial and spiritual support. What happens on Kinmen may well determine what happens throughout Asia.

Of course the senators and other members of Congress who speak of foolish and lightly fortified islands do not know these things. The reasons for this lack of knowledge are part of the story of Asia in the aftermath of Panmunjom and Geneva.

It is doubtful if the members of the National Security Council, responsible for advising the President on matters of national security, know of Kinmen. For another part of the story is that of American intelligence, adept at locating artillery positions and able to ascertain the location and strength of an enemy army, but not yet proficient at understanding psychological factors, the importance of a human export from a tiny island.

Perhaps Americans can understand Kinmen if we can imagine that our country has been defeated in war, our government pushed off the mainland of North America to exile in Cuba, or Puerto Rico. Then imagine that somehow we have been able to retain control of a few offshore islands, including Staten Island. Enemy guns bristle along the Jersey coast, are trained on the island; other guns pound it from the tip of Manhattan, from Long Island. A vast fanatically-led army is poised to strike, backed by airfields roaring with jet planes. Yet because we would not give up, we have held our Staten Island, supplying it with difficulty, using it for a base of operations, as a listening post, as a demonstration to those living on the mainland that the American way of life is not dead.

With this comparison in mind it is possible perhaps for Americans to understand a little of life on China's Golden Gate, around which war has been raging, which may quite possibly be lost even before these words are in print.

For Kinmen Island, as strong as it is, can be taken if the enemy wishes to stage all-out attack. The tragedy of Kinmen is that, did we but understand its importance, it could be saved, could perhaps become that Golden Gate about which the Free Chinese wistfully talk and dream.

The night before I left Kinmen I sat in my room in "The First Guest House of the Fukien Provincial Government-in-Exile." Old family friends had joined with Kinmen officials in a last bull session. Chang Chow, ex-general in Chiang's army, now magistrate of Kinmen and responsible for many of the good things accomplished there, was talking about his island.

"Kinmen is the West Berlin of the Orient," he said. "We are surrounded by unfriendly seas, and we never forget that the Communists are nearby. But there is one big difference between our Berlin and Europe's Berlin. We have never had anything like an airlift to keep us going. Indeed, our Berlin is unrecognized and unknown to the Free world."

Chapter 3

"Would you like to see the 'battlefield' today?" Magistrate Chang Chow asked me one morning while I was still on Kinmen. It would have been most impolite for me to have said no, regardless of personal interest. For from Admiral and General down to private, the Nationalists are proud of the last great battle in which their armies were victorious.

So it was that we traveled north from Hopu by jeep, along the magnificent north-south defense highway. We saw the battlefield, the sealed wells, the shells of buildings hit and never repaired. We visited also the defense works along all the shore that faces directly upon the mainland.

From a hidden howitzer position under twenty feet of concrete I watched Communist soldiers lounging on the beach across the waters. I walked and rode on sunken roads and pathways, made beautiful by the lovely flowers of the yellow sesbania trees planted along the roads after the general had read about them in *Harvest* magazine, published by the U. S. Information Service in Formosa.

There were few men in the great concrete works along the beaches. I asked General Chen what would happen if there were a sudden attack. How could he get his men into position quickly? For I had noticed that the regulars and guerrillas of Kinmen were short on motor transport.

"Come," said the General. "I'll show you how I can move my whole division into position in twenty minutes."

We walked a hundred yards. There I saw a doorway and steep steps. The General apologized because there was no electricity. At the steps' bottom was a concrete boulevard, lighted dimly here and there from hidden vents far above.

"You are forty feet underground now," the General told me. "It would take a direct hit from a very heavy gun or bomb to harm anyone here."

We walked for a long way, with light gradually brightening ahead. There were more steps, and suddenly the brightness of sunlight again. I do not know how far we had traveled underground. I do know that we were now in a village, the village where the General's division was quartered.

Perhaps General Chen exaggerated when he said he could move his men to the front in twenty minutes. But he certainly could move quickly and in safety.

I expressed frank amazement. I marveled at what I had seen that day. General Chen was grateful for my interest. As we parted he said, "Mr. Caldwell, you have still not seen our real strength. It lies not in these concrete positions, in my sunken roads, my underground supply line. It lies in the spirit of the men, soldiers and civilians. That is our real strength on Kinmen."

Is it not strange that America, which speaks so loudly of the brotherhood of free men, should devote so much praise to the men and women of Berlin, while the men and women of Kinmen lie somehow outside the pale? Is it because these people are of a different color, of different cultural heritage? So it must seem perhaps, to men like General Chen.

I saw increasing evidence of the spirit of which General Chen was so proud during the rest of my stay on Kinmen and its neighboring islands. I saw increasing evidence that the Free Chinese have not only spirit, but an ability to meet difficult problems in a unique manner.

I could begin to understand the amazement of a forestry expert who had visited Kinmen shortly before I arrived, who said to me: "Why such care of trees has never been known in the history of tree culture! After a rain the whole landscape is filled with soldiers and guerrillas, working the soil, tending the trees with all the care we would lavish on the rarest flowers."

From general on down, Kinmen's defenders keep themselves engaged in a prodigious variety of projects. Reforestation of Kinmen's eroded hillsides is but a part of the work (3,700,000 seedlings planted in 1954). The planting of trees provides work, keeps the soil in place and eventually will provide camouflage. However, other strange activities, having a more direct bearing upon daily living, have been necessitated by difficulties of communication and supply, the certainty of eventual Communist attack.

Ta-tang and Erh-tang are two small islands in Amoy's outer harbor. Under the muzzles of Communist guns, the islands can only be reached by night. There are two thousand troops crowded on Ta-tang's cliffy heights, for the island is important. Communist shipping entering or attempting to enter Amoy harbor can be easily spotted, reported, attacked. Three years ago the commanding general told the Ta-tang commander that his men must grow as much food as possible, and so one sees tiny vegetable patches in every nook and cranny, sometimes practically hanging from the walls of the cliffs. And everywhere, too, one sees chickens.

In an effort to solve his food problem the commanding officer had brought a few chickens over. For reasons I could not ascertain, the chickens flourished. They laid eggs bountifully, reproducing in such numbers that chickens seemed always available for the pot.

I talked to a young private from Ta-tang, asking him how long he had been stationed on the lonely island.

"Nearly three years," he replied.

"Of course you are rotated, or you get leave sometimes, don't you?" I asked. It seemed inconceivable that any soldier would stay on the island for three years and not lose his mind.

"No, sir, I have had no leave." And then sensing my amazement he added: "I like it here."

To my further questions he said, quite simply, "You see I like chicken very much."

However on Kinmen it takes more than chickens to solve the economic problems created by 75,000 fighting men superimposed upon 41,000 civilians who, themselves, have a hard time making ends meet. Kinmen has always been poor. It lacks water for rice production; most of its surface is made up of rocks, red clay, sandy wastes.

And so it was that the armies on Kinmen became the only modern armies to have an agricultural section in headquarters. When he is not fighting or training, the guerrilla or soldier farms or learns to farm. Agricultural classes are held in every section, on even the smaller islands. Civilian and soldier study together; farm shoulder to shoulder. Hundreds of acres of waste land have been reclaimed and are now dotted with the vegetable crops of the soldiers.

It is a common sight to see soldiers and farmers working adjacent fields, attending the same agricultural classes and demonstrations. And surely the Kinmen soldiers are the only fighting men in the world belonging to 4-H clubs!

Near Hopu there is an agricultural experiment station, operated by the army and under the direction of a fellow townsman of mine. Chen Shi Ho, a graduate of one of China's best universities, has traveled a long way from his home in nearby Foochow. Many years ago his family moved to North China. He attended a university in Peiping and was just finishing when the Japanese invaded China. Mr. Chen is one of the millions of Chinese whose patriotism has been forgotten in the rush of stories about those who went over to the Japanese, to the Communists, to any new master.

His government refugeed far into the interior and Mr. Chen followed. From Peiping he traveled by rail to Shanghai. Then by ship he moved on, ever under the suspicion of the Japanese, to Hong Kong. From Hong Kong he worked his way to Indo-China, thence across the jungles into Yunnan province, thence back eastward to take up the job his government had for him in an experiment station in China's Southwest.

Then, when the mainland fell, Chen's travels started again. From Southwest China he went to Chungking, then back down to Shanghai, which had already fallen. It was impossible to reach Formosa from Shanghai; so Chen walked southward some thousand-odd miles to the Hong Kong boundary. Like thousands of other Free Chinese, he slipped across the border to freedom, to a job with the government—and now to Kinmen within a few miles of his birthplace.

The problems that face Mr. Chen and his Chinese army agricultural experiment station are difficult ones. How can more food be coaxed from the sterile soil? What new seed varieties are needed, can thrive on Kinmen? How to get more water on an island that has no real stream, where many wells are sealed with the bodies of enemy dead?

Sometimes ancient superstition makes agricultural progress difficult indeed. The Chinese love pork, and that is true of men in or out of uniform. Kinmen's hog population, never large, was cut down with disease, caused by too much inbreeding. And so it was that one day, through the generosity of Uncle Sam, a strange passenger debarked from one of General Chennault's ubiquitous planes. A giant Berkshire boar had arrived to bring new blood and many piglets to Kinmen.

But neither Mr. Chen nor the American experts back on Formosa had reckoned with an ancient Kinmen custom. When there is a death in the family, little Kinmeners wear white shoes in mourning. Berkshire hogs have white feet.

Obviously there was bad business. The siring of white-footed piglets could only bring bad luck.

And so for a long time the Berkshire led a lonely life. But time and patience can wonders perform. Mr. Chen bred the Berkshire to experiment station sows. He kept very interesting charts, showing how much more they weighed than less blooded strains given the same amount of food.

Soon farmers began to take notice; one after another began to break with superstition.

I met the Berkshire boar one day, while Chen Shi Ho and I were visiting agricultural projects. The boar was traveling down the highway in a wheeled cart.

Jokingly Chen said: "There goes the luckiest male on Kinmen. He has the highest travel priority. He goes forth pulled in a cart, or even by boat. He has visited and is allowed to go to islands where I have never been. That boar has not only a life of travel but of varied female conquests!"

But for human males, life on Kinmen is neither traveled nor varied. The guerrillas, because of special training needed, because of secrecy involved in operations, are being moved into barracks as such can be built. The men of the regular army, however, still live, as they did when Kinmen was first occupied, with the civilians of the island.

Imagine if you will, your home city, garrisoned with troops from a dozen different lands and living in your very homes!

I visited in many Chinese homes on Kinmen and in most of them twelve soldiers lived. At first the soldiers had a difficult time. Inevitably there was friction. The Kinmeners could not speak Mandarin, or Cantonese or the Shanghai dialect. Suddenly alien men, speaking these and other dialects, were thrust into their homes.

Mrs. Li, living in a little village on Kinmen's eastern shore, comes from my home town; I could visit with her, could hear her story. Her living room is no longer a living room. Twelve soldiers sleep there, six on a side facing the ancient ancestral tablets. The soldiers sleep on the floor. All furniture has been removed, for there is no room for chairs and tables in a room

34

where twelve men must live. And too, always ready for instant use, tommy guns hang on the walls above each bed. In one corner there is a mortar. In the center, between the two neat rows of pallets on the floor are ammunition boxes. And especially incongruous in the ancient house, an army field telephone hangs from the wall in one corner. For the men who live in Mrs. Li's home must be always on call.

Perhaps a figure or two will show just how crowded the Li home is. The average housing space per person on Kinmen is eight square feet. My family of four, living in a modest suburban home, enjoy 125 square feet each. And we consider ourselves crowded, have spent many a Sunday afternoon house-shopping.

"How in the world do you get along here?" I asked.

Mrs. Li did not gloss over her problems.

"We had a hard time at first," she told me. "Most of our boys are from the North. They could not understand us, nor we them. There were problems about food, too." And then she paused and pointed to the courtyard where a Chinese GI was tossing her three-year old daughter in the air amidst much giggling and merriment.

"But you can see now that we are friends—good friends. We all understand that as bad as it is here, it is much worse over there." Then to explain a bit further, Mrs. Li added: "You see my husband is a fisherman. Each day when the seas are not too high he goes out to fish near Tungting. There he meets with fishing boats from the mainland. He talks to those men and women. Their lives are hard indeed!"

And that is perhaps why the Free Chinese have been able to accomplish so much, in spite of difficulties—because everyone knows what it is like "over there."

Men outnumber women on Kinmen by nearly ten to one, yet there has been no case of rape in two years. Only a few, the officers, can bring their wives to live with them. The Chinese are realistic: They have provided a giant house of prostitution in Hopu, equipped with dispensary, full-time doctor, reading room, ping pong tables—and a nursery for the unfortunate mistakes that occur. I visited the house on a Sunday afternoon. There are seventy-five girls there, but few were busy. The price is cheap, thirty cents for an enlisted man, who draws his partner by lot; seventy-five cents for the officer who can make a face to face choice.

Yet even though it was a Sunday, as near an off-day as the men of Free China have, there were few patrons, no mad rush to the flesh pots. Men come to the "white faces" to be sure; and the girls are even taken to outlying islands. But I could not but feel that this was no great part of Kinmen's life.

Fighting and training, farming, road building, planting trees on Kinmen's barren hillsides keep men busy. For their free time, there are basketball courts, tiny reading rooms and PX's. Mobile units show motion pictures at night in villages and in the country. The men keep busy, terribly busy, and their free time is filled with simple pleasures.

But the reason why there is little friction where vast trouble could be expected, why lives are disciplined is because, like Mrs. Li who puts up with a dozen permanent guests, the people know what it is like "over there." Not only can the beaches and mountains of mainland China be seen from Kinmen. The face of the enemy is clearly visible. And spirits are high because beneath that face feet of clay are clearly showing.

Chapter 4

I FIRST saw the physical face of the enemy from a gun position on Liehyu, or Little Kinmen Island, which lies off the southwestern tip of Big Kinmen. From Liehyu's southern end other little islands stand out like stepping stones across the mouth of Amoy Harbor. Chief of these are Ta-tang and Erh-tang, the islands where the soldiers enjoy chicken every day. Ta-tang can be loosely translated as "The Big Little Island"; neighboring Erh-tang is "The Second Little Island." Then there are several more "tangs"—Little Tang, Third Tang, even Fourth Tang. All are garrisoned by men of Free China; all look out upon the enemy, all are under easy artillery range from Amoy's major batteries.

It was a hazy day, and the general who commands the division on Liehyu and all the Tangs thought it might be safe for me to visit the advance outposts.

"If visibility were very good," he told me, "I could not allow you to go to the advance posts. Those Reds are trigger happy. We never know when they will shoot. If they saw anything at all unusual, they might let go."

I could very well understand what the general meant. Every village in Liehyu is battered and scarred, roofs gone here, gaping holes in the walls there. I noticed too, that the houses of Liehyu had no doors or windows on the Amoy side. These

37

had all been filled with rocks, so providing a little protection from shell fragments.

As we drove over Liehyu (for even this tiny island, ten square miles in area, has its highway system) with the general whose name is also Chen, he told me that he had once commanded an armored division on the mainland. He has armor still, a few ancient tanks. But he confided that as far as other motor transport was concerned, the three jeeps in our caravan, plus three trucks was it.

"And on any given day I can count on at least two of the trucks not running," he added wryly.

But fortunately distances are short, the troops are billeted with the villagers, and when Liehyu is attacked, its defenders will not have far to move.

The last few hundred yards were crossed on foot, as it would be unsafe to drive within full view of Amoy. Three jeeps in a line would provide a tempting target. So we slipped single file through waist-high grass, entered a tunnel and emerged in a gun position overlooking the magnificent panorama of Amoy Harbor.

Across from me, startlingly close through the field glasses, a Communist soldier relaxed against a rock near the radar tower which sits upon the crest of Amoy Peak.

Far below I noticed a small group of Communist soldiers, lined up on the beach, stiffly at attention. An officer stood before them, and I could imagine the pompous words that might be coming from his lips. Suddenly the whole group melted into the landscape.

It was a peaceful scene, water calm, air motionless. Five hundred yards away, in a watery no-man's land, on one of the smaller Tangs completely ringed with concrete pillboxes, Nationalist guerrillas walked about, or fished from the top of their fortress perch.

Suddenly the calm water broke into a froth, as if a school of fish were jumping in precise line; moments later came the ripping chatter of a machine gun burst, the sound delayed across two miles of water.

A non-commissioned officer in our lookout position made a few notations in his log: "Communist machine gun fire across the sea; no damage, no casualties, fire not returned."

Farmers, working in their cabbage patches below us hardly raised their heads.

Thus I came closest to the actual physical presence of the Communists who rule the land of my birth. But I saw his real face a hundred times: on gunboat patrol, when I interviewed captured crewmen of a junk out of Amoy; from scores of refugees, from guerrillas back from mainland assignment; from the few letters that come across, from leaflets washed across one day in tiny bamboo tubes and picked up on Kinmen's beaches.

And the face of China's rulers is frightened and weak. Tyranny and torture have backfired, have not been enough to shatter the will and morale of the people. I cannot claim to have walked the streets of Shanghai and Peiping and Canton as did Clement Atlee. I cannot verify Mr. Atlee's finding that Communist efficiency and good government have even eradicated all the flies from the mainland.

However, though I do not know of the fly population, I can report one bit of information Mr. Atlee and his friends missed. I have been told by reliable witnesses that there are no dogs on the mainland. On Kinmen, on Liehyu and on Matsu there are dogs; they howl at the moon; they roam the streets, are loved and petted by the children.

But just across the waters is a dogless land. For the Communists consider the dog a typically capitalistic pet, not able to work, consuming food that should be consumed only by those who contribute to the people's society. I pass on my observation about the dogs, not because the presence or absence of dogs is of great import. As a matter of fact, I know there is at least *one* dog in China. Children are taken to the zoo in Chengtu, so that they may see this capitalistic creation. And I report on the dogs merely because it is an interesting bit of information, one of the less important differences in the villages of Free China and those on the mainland.

Regardless of reports on the fly or dog population, there is increasing evidence that the Communist giant has feet of clay, the most convincing evidence coming from the Communists themselves.

One day I received a briefing at guerrilla headquarters. As Chinese are wont to do in naming organizations, they have given the Kinmen guerrillas a flowery designation: the Patriotic Anti-Communist Liberation Army of South Fukien.

The guerrilla general and his aide had maps and charts to explain their operations. But most interesting was a series of captured Communist documents. There were Red intelligence reports, letters and diaries, wanted posters offering rewards for mainland guerrillas. Some were old, others had come into Nationalist hands within the past weeks and months.

One document, a mimeographed Communist intelligence report on Fukien province, stated that during the past year there had been some 5,000 military engagements in the province. Another booklet, prepared as a guide for anti-sabotage units, complained bitterly of the fact that "the people of Fukien seem uneducated and unfriendly; they give food to the guerrillas who hide in the mountains by day and attack us by night."

I was interested in the reports on my home province. How could it be that there had been 5,000 guerrilla-Communist engagements in one province, within the space of one year? I asked the general if this were not a mistake.

"Yes, in a way," he answered. "We do not have enough active and organized guerrillas to have been engaged in that number of battles. What this means is that villagers, peasants, fishermen—just plain people—have been fighting the Reds at every turn."

Later from fishermen, from guerrillas just back from mainland assignment, I heard of the hatred which gives the rulers of China reason to complain about the "unfriendly" attitude of the people. There are vast sections of coastal China, mountainous areas of Fukien, Chekiang and Kwangtung where the Communists do not even attempt to maintain control. There are other areas where no Communist official can travel without guard, where even a small unit of troops is liable to attack. In nearly every city it is unsafe for officials and soldiers to be abroad at night.

The 5,000 Fukien engagements reported by the Communists included actual military contacts, attacks and murders of officials, just plain bushwhacking that goes on constantly. Guerrillas are often engaged; just as often peasants and villagers, sick with hatred, strike out blindly at a small Red unit, at a lightly guarded Communist official.

The Communist press itself admits evidence of increasing difficulties. During the summer and fall of 1954 the Communist press moaned about the continued activities of "reactionary elements." A force of 140,000 to 150,000 well trained and organized guerrillas were reported active in Kwangtung Province. Authorities in Yunnan, in China's Southwest, complained that it had been necessary to kill over 200,000 reactionary and dissident elements during a one year period.

Another news story told of efforts of Communists in the Yangtse Valley to organize vast "tiger" hunts. Special recognition was offered for loyal comrades who could take part in controlling these savage beasts. The interesting point to this story is that the Yangtse Valley is one part of China in which tigers are rare. It seems obvious that, in peculiar double talk, the Red authorities were attempting to drum up interest in an anti-guerrilla campaign.

The Communists rarely speak of guerrillas, seem loathe to admit that they are faced with opposition of trained men, operating under military discipline. More often the Communist press and radio talk of "dissident" elements, "reactionaries," uneducated peasants. But in so doing they admit a grave weakness. For a regime that cannot control its farmers cannot maintain control of the country. From the very beginning the Chinese Reds have aimed their biggest propaganda guns at China's rural population; their greatest initial successes were achieved because their promises of rural and land reform were attractive.

Yet it is among the peasants in South China that the Reds are meeting the greatest resistance. Thousands of farmers have quit the land, going into the mountains to join guerrilla units. Land reform has backfired, peasants everywhere are finding themselves so harrassed by additional taxes, special levies, food collections that they speak longingly of the "good old days" under the Nationalists.

Communist propaganda often labels Chiang Kai Shek "that bandit Chiang." And all along the China Coast there is a wry saying: "Bring back that bandit Chiang!"

Peasant revolt has taken concrete and sometimes dramatic form. During the fall of 1953, again in 1954, the peasants of Fukien and Kwangtung provinces rebelled against the Communist Government's effort to control prices and production. Tons upon tons of the precious cabbage crop were dumped into the creeks and rivers rather than be sold at government prices. Rice is held out, hidden so that the government agricultural people cannot collect it. Farmers sometimes harvest in the dead of night hoping thus to keep the amount of their yield secret. Acres of land once in production lie idle, because farmers either refuse to till it or are no longer there to till it.

As I traveled among the guerrilla islands from Tungting northward, I heard over and over again an expression in my native Foochow dialect that best expresses the plight of the people of China. Rendered phonetically it is "Ki-kwee, Ki-kwee" and it means "very miserable." I talked to a family on Matsu Island, just over from the mainland city of Santuo.

"How are you getting along over here?" I asked.

"We are miserable. My husband was killed by the Communists. My son is a guerrilla, and he must support six of us," was the reply.

"But if you are so ki-kwee here, why did you come over?"

Quickly the reply came. "Oh, but we were *really* ki-kwee over there," the Chinese woman explained. "Here at least we can eat. We can buy a few things. We can talk freely. We can go to the market freely."

"And what is it like over on the Tai-lu [mainland]?" I asked.

"For those who have work, there is just barely enough to eat. For those who do not have work there is only that which can be taken from the streams or the fields. To buy a suit of clothes requires the earnings of a year."

Father Linus Lombard of Massachusetts, coming out of Red China during the summer of 1954 reported that "there is systematic starvation for those who do not belong to the Party." I found ample evidence from coastal refugees to support his statement. For those who have work there is food, just enough to live on. For those who are not favored, there is systematic starvation. Ration cards are denied. Travel is impossible, so a family cannot openly move elsewhere to find work. Indeed so stringent are travel regulations along the coast that one cannot even spend the night other than under one's own roof without a special pass and permission.

While visiting one guerrilla island I learned of an old family friend, of the efforts made to break his will and body. It is a typical story, worth telling because it also illustrates one of the problems faced by China's Red masters.

I shall call the man Dr. Chen, which is not his real name. He has attended two of America's best known universities. For years he served as head of a famous Christian institution

43

in China. He was beloved by Christians and non-Christians. Government officials sought his advice; the little people on the street considered him their friend.

But since Dr. Chen was a Christian, had studied in the United States, was widely known as pro-American, he was considered an enemy of the People's government. However the Communists were afraid to kill the doctor, for his influence after death might be even greater than while he lived. So they imprisoned him. He was beaten, tortured and brainwashed. After months of imprisonment it was reported that Dr. Chen was dead; but soon there was talk among the people, talk which frightened the authorities. And so Dr. Chen was released, broken physically but still alive and still in possession of his soul and mind.

Dr. Chen is a Ph.D. He speaks three or four languages, can converse brilliantly on almost any subject. But he has refused to take part in government programs, will not teach in a Communist school, refuses to recant. Afraid to kill him, the authorities are now attempting to starve him.

Dr. Chen is now a goat herder in the hills of central China. He sells a little milk to the poor, occasionally butchers one of his goats. He has refused as yet to be starved. He is a living rebuke to the regime, a symbol of hope to thousands who know his story. The Communists are caught in a trap. As long as Dr. Chen lives, there will be many who will not believe the anti-American campaign. If he should die there will be many who will not forget what Dr. Chen stood for.

It is, in part, because of men like Dr. Chen that the Communist attack against the United States has sadly backfired, has contributed to the rising tide of opposition against the regime. The anti-American theme runs through all the propaganda broadcasts, the leaflets, the special indoctrination courses, the news gatherings where Red functionaries interpret the day's or the week's news for the people. During 1953 and 1954 the main theme was America's defeat in Korea. I read Communist leaflets floated over to Kinmen in tiny bamboo boats. One leaflet was devoted to a statistical breakdown of American losses, the number of tanks, guns, ships and men. The theme ended upon a plaintive note: Why do you ally yourself with imperialistic America which has already been defeated?

The men of Chiang who defend the guerrilla islands are undoubtedly puzzled by some of "imperialistic" America's actions but they know that America is not as yet defeated. The people of the mainland may also be puzzled. But when they hear stories of American brutality, of pilots who drop germs, they remember also the Dr. Chens of China, who brought back learning and progress from the United States. The people of Coastal China have seen America's best face; they can neither believe that she is defeated or corrupt. And if their masters insist on linking this America with Chiang Kai Shek, perhaps Chiang will yet win out; for among the old and uneducated there still is a deep seated belief in America's strength and goodness.

The Communists have not been able to supplant America with Russia. While it is foolish as yet to hope that the Red Government has shown any indication of breaking with Moscow, among the common people there is a loathing of Russians, a hatred that surpasses anything in China's history.

Matsu Island is not far from Foochow where a considerable group of Russian technical experts is stationed. The Russians are universally spoken of as the "Tai-taos"—the big heads. Originally billeted within the city, they have now been moved to an airfield on Nantai Island. They are not allowed to go about the city freely because there have been too many unpleasant incidents. The Russian advisors live in virtual isolation from the people they are supposed to help.

I talked one day to the crew of a fishing junk, out that morning from Amoy. They spoke of all the things so much in the minds of Chinese: the difficulties of getting enough to eat,

45

the impossibility of buying consumer goods any more, the police restrictions. I asked finally if Russians were living in Amoy.

The grizzled old Captain answered me, speaking with such loathing and disgust as I have never heard from a Chinese.

"Yes," he answered. "There are 'Tai-taos' in Amoy. And only last week I saw Russian women. That is a terrible thing, to see Russian women in China. For if they bring their women it must mean that they will stay a long time."

The Communists, so clever in many ways, are becoming desperate and making mistakes. From the mainland they wage a ceaseless propaganda war against the Chinese on the guerrilla islands. Leaflets are sent over, loud speakers blare of the Utopia waiting to be enjoyed by the persecuted people living under Chiang Kai Shek's imperialistic regime. But then tactics are suddenly changed.

A People's court will be held on the beach in full view of a guerrilla-held island. Loud speakers announce the name of the victim, and it is usually a person with relatives living on the island within earshot.

The court proceedings, finally the execution, are held so that the Free Chinese can see and hear. That this alternating of brutality with promises of life in paradise does not make sense never occurs to the Communists. Such proceedings do not cause Nationalists to desert, but merely add to the growing hatred that fills all Chinese who have seen the face of the enemy.

Father Lombard and the other Catholic missionaries who came out of Red China in 1954, believe that the vast majority of the people would welcome a Nationalist invasion. As Father Lombard put it,—"they cannot wait until the day of that invasion comes."

There can be little question but the vast majority of the people south of the Yangtse will whole-heartedly support the Nationalists. Disaffection even reaches throughout the ranks of the Communist armies, especially the locally-recruited and trained Security Forces responsible for guerrilla fighting and defense of much of the coast.

Shortly after the first anti-Communist Chinese prisoners of war arrived from Korea, a group was taken to Kinmen. The group visited Liehyu Island and one by one, began to tell their experiences, speaking over loud speakers from the very same lookout post I visited.

Magistrate Chang Chow who was present that day told me of the remarkable drama that took place.

"As the POW's began to speak," Chang Chow told me, "a strange thing happened. One by one we could see Communist soldiers leave their trenches, their gun positions, their posts at the radar station. Soon there were soldiers visible from the beach to the top of the peak. They listened in obvious rapt attention as they heard the stories of their estwhile comrades.

"Suddenly we saw a cloud of dust on the highway from Amoy City. A Russian jeep roared up, Communist officers jumped out. Of course no one could hear what words were spoken. But I can tell you there was a lot of arm waving; there must have been a lot of shouting.

"It took those officers ten minutes to get their men back into position. As one who has been a commanding general, I can imagine the fear that must have been in the hearts of the Communist officers. And I could not but wonder what would happen if one of our raiding parties should strike at a time like that."

After five years the Communist government that was at least tacitly welcomed by the majority is now cordially hated. Executions, torture, brutality have become liabilities yet must be used to keep the people in check. Farmers hate the government because they have less than at any time in their unhappy history. The landowners hate the government, those who are still alive, because they have been robbed and ridiculed. The merchants hate the government because their meager earn-

47

ings are taken, either in direct taxes or in the interminable "loan" and bond drives from which they cannot escape. The soldiers are beginning to hate the government because, as one young prisoner of war told me, "I became sick of useless bloodshed, of seeing the good people of my own village, even some of my relatives, tortured and ridiculed and executed."

It is useless, as sometimes is attempted, to define in percentage, the opposition of mainland people to their government. I have heard it said that ninety per cent of the people of mainland China would support any liberation army; others tell me that seventy-five per cent would be a more accurate figure. Mainland opposition varies according to geography and length of Communist rule. Given long enough time the Reds seem able to break the will to resist. Even the Nationalist government admits there are no guerrillas in Honan province, long under Communist rule. Certainly opposition is great south of the Yangtse Valley, and this is where Free China will have to strike should it some day be allowed to attempt a return to the mainland.

It is from Shanghai southward that the Red rulers face their greatest problems, and it is this that the Free Chinese call their "invasion coast." There are reasons why the coastal Chinese have been slow to appreciate the benefits of the People's government. South China has been under Communist rule for a *shorter period* than the north; its people are more volatile, more inclined to fight back. South China has been the cradle of revolutions, has sent forth its adventurous sons to populate all the nations of Asia. South China has produced pirates and smugglers, among whom General Koxinga, who once made Kinmen his base, was the greatest.

South China also was the cradle of Christian endeavor, and this too has a bearing on the spirit and resistance of the people. One day I talked with a refugee family from Futing, a city in northern Fukien province. We spoke in the Foochow dialect, and I heard in terms I could understand the story of one family's escape. The husband had been killed and it was the wife who told me of their experiences, in particular of the reasons they left Futing.

"Our children were forced to go to Communist schools," the woman began her story. "Or if the government so decided, they had to work. We had so little food that the children were ill. We could not travel anywhere and my husband made his living as a traveling tailor, visiting the hill villages around Futing. But even to spend one night away from home he had to have a special permit which required days to get. We became sick of torture, of killings. We were always afraid of a visit from the secret police for they suspected my husband of evil things just because he had traveled much."

And then, exhausted by her long speech, the woman from Futing added: "And for over a year we were not allowed to go to church."

That too, is part of the story of China, a story of religious people, Christian and Buddhist, and their fight against Mao's Utopia. That fight has contributed to the fear on the enemy's face, to the heaviness in his feet of clay.

Chapter 5

"MISSIONARY KIDS," we are often called, we who were born of American parents in China, Korea, India or Africa, our parents among the thousands of missionaries who for over a century have served God in the far corners of the world. Wars and revolution, frequent illness, gaps in formal education—this was part of our lot. But our heritage is rich, impossible to forget. We who came from the good earth of China have become the worst of the "Old China Hands," a breed notorious for its ability to forget unpleasantness and hardship, for its nostalgic longing to go back again.

But the Communists have accomplished what revolutions, illness and hardship never did. Our parents have been driven out of China. The work of a century and more is ended. And, we wonder, of what good was all the sacrifice? Is there anything left of the foundation they built? Have the millions spent by America, the pennies of Sunday School children, the dollars of the rich, the donations of foundations, have they all gone for naught?

Such thoughts were in my mind when I went back to the China Coast where my own family labored for a half century. One day I flew in a lumbering PBY amphibian plane along the coast so close that I could see Haitang Island, my father's sea girt district where once there were over thirty prosperous churches, a school and a hospital. "The most Christian spot in China," father used to call Haitang. But that was ten years ago. What of those churches, the school and the hospital today? Is there anything left of the spiritual impact of these physical evidences of Christianity, an impact that once was felt all along China's Coast?

I did not have time at first to seek out Christians, or even to ask of church life on the guerrilla islands or on the mainland; for I was busy with visits to military installations, my days filled with gunboat raids and interviews with the fascinating cross-section of all China that now lives on Kinmen. But it was Christmas week, and one night after I had retired early to my room in the Fukien Guest House I heard unmistakably the sound of Christmas hymns. The singing came from close by, an odd yet thrilling accompaniment to the distant mutter of artillery.

The next day I visited the church that stood within two blocks of the Guest House, began an exciting hunt for what I call "the lost Christians of the China Coast."

The pastor of the church was away in Formosa. I was able that day to talk only to his wife, using an interpreter since she spoke the Amoy dialect.

"Of what denomination is your church?" I asked.

The old lady seemed confused by my question. Her answer was surprising. "I don't know what you mean," she replied. "We are just Christians here."

The furnishings in the church gave no clue to denomination. There were rude, hand-made benches, a simple pulpit with a tiny wooden cross. In a corner was a stack of packing cases, filled with recently arrived Bibles—a gift of Madame Chiang Kai Shek, the old lady told me.

News travels fast on a guerrilla island. Two days later five young men called upon me. They addressed me as "reverend"; they made a startling request. I was asked to preach the sermon, the next day.

"But I am a newspaper man," I explained. "My father was a missionary here for many years. But I cannot preach. If I could, my Chinese is not good enough."

The young men, two in business, one a civil servant, the other an army dental officer, had heard that an American had visited their church and presumed that I must be a missionary.

From the men I heard the story of Ho Pu church, learned the location of other churches. The church I visited was built in 1924, established by English missionaries of the Church of England, now called the Church of Christ in China. Missionaries had last visited Kinmen in 1947. By 1949, when Kinmen was occupied by Nationalist troops in the retreat from the mainland, church membership had dwindled to fifty. Today the church has 350 members. Among the growing membership are men and women of four denominations, refugees from the mainland. Mr. Shih, leader of the group calling on me, is himself a Methodist from Foochow. Refugees from the Dutch Reformed churches of southern Fukien, the Methodist churches throughout the province, the Congregational churches in Changlo, Ingtai and far up the Min River, from Baptist congregations in Kwangtung province—all had gravitated to the Ho Pu church. Nominally Protestant Episcopal, it has now become truly interdenominational. There was good reason why the pastor's wife could not understand my talk of denomination!

There is only one ordained minister on Kinmen Island. Yet the church has grown in membership and influence, without help from the outside world. Another little church which I visited at Hsi Mi in the northern part of Kinmen is now considered a branch of the Ho Pu church. Hsi Mi is within artillery range of the mainland. Here and there are the marks of heavy artillery—gaping holes in walls and roofs, watch towers pock-marked with shell holes. Thousands of guerrillas are stationed in the town, and the church is used as a guerrilla mess hall. Services are still held; simple services, for the most part devoted to hymn singing; for the minister from Ho Pu is not able to visit Hsi Mi often.

My visit to Hsi Mi was brief; I had no opportunity to talk to regular members. The information I got came from a refugee hut near the church. I heard Foochow, my native dialect being spoken in the hut and went in to visit. The man of the house was a refugee from Hsiapu, north of Foochow. Two sons were guerrillas.

Wistfully, the wife asked me: "Could you by any chance be a Catholic?" I replied in the negative. It was then that she told me about the little church next door, which her Catholic family was now attending, because as she said, "There is no place else to go."

Across from Kinmen, on battered Little Kinmen, I found another church, a lovely brick building with white spire that might have been transplanted from New England. But a direct hit from enemy artillery on Amoy had removed the roof, gutted the interior. The Christians on Little Kinmen are small in number, between fifty and one hundred the commanding general told me. They must worship in their homes now; they have no regular pastor.

"They are very earnest, fine people," the general said, and Magistrate Chang Chow quickly agreed. As I continued my search for Christians, hoping especially to find members of my father's churches, it became apparent that the Christian population was respected, had an importance out of all proportion to its numbers.

For wherever and whenever I asked about Christians the answers were immediate. "Why, so and so is a Christian," or "There are such and such number of Christians on this island, that island."

And so as the days passed I located more Christians, more churches, began too, to get a little news of those who have stayed behind the mainland.

On lonely, isolated Matsu Island are six Christian families,

—four Congregational and two Methodist. On White Dog Island are seven families, all Methodist refugees from the Haitang and Lungtien districts of my father's parish. Among the thousands of soldiers and guerrillas are other Christians. Far to the north on the Ta-chen Islands there are two churches, without pastors and of origin and denomination I could not ascertain.

But the greatest tribute to Christianity along the China Coast came in a guerrilla general's headquarters. As I sat and sipped tea, the general told of raids and battles, of hopes and plans. On the walls of his office was a chart, showing the population groups which could be counted upon when the forces of Free China are allowed to invade the mainland.

Very neatly done, the chart showed the number of dispossessed former landlords, the guerrillas presently active in the mountains, the unemployed—but heading the list was the statement "450,000 Christians."

The statement was surprising for several reasons. As the general finished his briefing I said, "But general, your figures are wrong. There are not that many Christians in Fukien Province, or even along the whole coast."

"Yes," replied the general. "You are right as to actual church members, particularly now that so many have been liquidated, driven underground or so watched and hounded that they are helpless. But we include the thousands who have studied at some time in missionary schools, the other thousands that have received treatment in American missionary hospitals. Most of these people we count also as our friends, and there are so many they cannot be located or persecuted."

From this conversation and from others, came the realization of an important factor in the eventual freeing of China. Time and again I was asked about the whereabouts of missionaries who had once lived and worked in Fukien. In a ten minute ride in a sampan, from Matsu Island to the seaplane which was to carry me back to Formosa, the two boatmen talked only of one thing: Dr. Gillette, the Congregational medical missionary who had operated a hospital at Pagoda Anchorage for years. In my brief hours on Matsu I was asked about Dr. J. E. Skinner, for over fifty years active in a remarkable medical work; about the Congregational missionaries who had been stationed in Changlo, on the coast near Matsu.

One day on Kinmen a handsome guerrilla captain came to see me, asking for the American who spoke Foochow.

"You must be either the son of Mr. Caldwell or Mr. Hayes of Futsing," he said. "Few Americans can speak Foochow dialect as well as members of those families."

Captain Song Hsi was his name, and he had walked fifteen miles across the rugged hump of the island to see me. He was graduated from the Ming Gnie Middle School in Futsing which my father founded with an initial gift of $25,000 from the First Methodist Church of Des Moines. He had been a member of a rural church father started on the Lungtien Peninsula. Captain Song is one of a colony of 275 guerrilla families from the Futsing region, just settled on Kinmen. He told me of other Christians in the colony, but they had been moved from pillar to post so often that no organized religious life had been possible.

The tremendous interest in the missionaries, so often expressed by men like Captain Song, is, I was assured, reflected among the older people still on the mainland. As I have noted in a previous chapter Communist propaganda is actually backfiring because it always links "capitalistic, brutal America" with "that puppet bandit," Chiang. Except for the young, except for leftist college students, the people of the China Coast simply do not buy that. To them, America is still the most powerful country in the world, the land that sent the Skinners, the Gillettes to help them. As far as the common folk

55

are concerned, if Chiang and America are working together it is a good sign indeed; it probably means that Chiang will come back, that Communism will be defeated.

I would not exaggerate the numbers of Christians I found. Among the 200,000 soldiers, guerrillas and civilians on the Free Chinese islands I found five churches and one pastor. Unaffiliated Christians number several thousand. I would like to, but cannot say that I was able to get encouraging news of a vast revival among the Christians on the mainland. Many churches have been forced to close their doors. Ming Gnie School in Futsing, like other missionary institutions, has been taken over by the Communists. But there are scores of underground congregations, there are still even many churches that operate openly. Among the Methodist churches in Fukien, many are now served by women pastors. Even district superintendents are sometimes women, perhaps because the authorities are more loathe to terrorize women, perhaps because much of the trained male leadership has been liquidated.

To me the exciting story is that there are even five churches among the islands, that there are even a few thousand Christians among the guerrilla families. For the churches that exist, the Christians still practicing their faith have done so without encouragement, spiritual or financial, from the outside world.

But most significant is that a non-Christian guerrilla general considers the Christian and Christian-related population of tremendous strategic importance, that even those educated in mission schools and treated in mission hospitals are considered friendly to the Free Chinese cause. Many of us who have lived long in China have suspected that American influence might still be strong.

Over two years ago I wrote *China Coast Family*, the story of my family's fifty years of missionary work on the Fukien coast within sight of Matsu and just 100 miles north of Kinmen. I wrote of the bandit in a mountain village who accepted

my father's effort at mediation between bandits and government forces, with these words: "I trust the missionary, for he
is an American."

And I wrote in *China Coast Family*,—"I am sure there are
men still living along the China Coast who would say it. As
long as that is so, and if we will act on it before it is too late,
China is not lost to us."

Matsu Island was my last stop in guerrilla-land. As my seaplane circled to take me back to the safety of Formosa, I could
see many old landmarks along the coast of what is the cradle
of Protestant Christian work in China. The mouth of the Min
River up which the first missionaries, a Methodist and a Con-
gregationalist, sailed in 1847 was clearly visible; and Sharp
Peak, the island summer resort where we used to spend the
months of summer heat. Standing out clearly in the sparkling
winter sky was Kushan Peak, and Kuliang, the summer resort
above Foochow. As I saw these landmarks so familiar from
childhood days I was once again proud of my heritage, of the
part my family played in the building of a Christian society
in China. Certainly the sacrifices made were not in vain, for
the foundation built at such cost and sacrifice, with the offer-
ings of hundreds of thousands of American Christians, are still
there, awaiting men and women who will come to begin building anew.

Christianity is not strong enough on the China mainland to
conquer Communism, but it is a factor of importance, which
added to all the other factors make China's liberation far from
hopeless. The religious faith of China's Christians can never
be stamped out, and China's Red rulers must know it. That
faith contributes to a continued belief among hundreds of
thousands of people that America is not the villain it is painted
as being. No, religious faith alone will not drive out the enemy. It is just one more problem the enemy must worry about;
it is a factor in the eventual liberation of a half billion people.

The liberation of Communist China will come about

through a combination of faith and will and force of arms. And among those who bear arms, the guerrillas will be most important. There are Christians among them too. There are rich men and poor men, guerrillas who fight from distant mainland bases, guerrillas who strike from Kinmen and Matsu and Ta-chen. The story of the guerrillas, their missions, their training and way of life is also a story of faith.

Chapter 6

"MEN of Iron in Wooden Ships," my friend Fred Sparks, Pulitzer Prize winning NEA correspondent has called the Free Chinese guerrillas. In the ceaseless war that rages along the Coast all men, even women and children, have a part. I have already noted that the children of the guerrilla schools study the tactics used by their fathers, learn to spot the approach of Communist raiders. Women too, are active, as civil defense workers, in special sewing classes producing clothing for their men and for the guerrilla dependents who come out of occupied China penniless. There are women fighters and leaders, too, women like Two-Gun Annie—Wang Pai-mei—who strikes out from a base off the Chekiang Coast.

Among their number, the guerrillas include a cross section of all China. There are educated men and uneducated fishermen; there are opportunists and intensely patriotic men who live only for the day of return to the mainland. There are ex-pirates and ex-bandits, dispossessed landlords and ruined merchants.

In the years that have passed since Communist victory on the mainland, there has been ceaseless action along the coast, scores of little raids, many big raids. Islands have been wrested from Communist control, some permanently, others to be lost through Red counterattack. Today nearly fifty islands are in Nationalist hands. From tiny Tungting in the south, the islands stretch northward for nearly four hundred miles to the Ningpo Coast. The Free Chinese islands divide into three natural groups, most important of which is the Kinmen group of five major islands. One hundred and forty miles to the north is the Matsu group, which includes the White Dog Islands, tiny Turnabout Island—a total of a half dozen islands. Still further north the Ta-chen holdings begin, extending for nearly 150 miles along the coast of Chekiang Province. In addition to these islands, actually held by Free China, there are numerous "Vacuum Islands" extending almost to the mouth of the Yangtse. There are Fenghuang, Nanlung, Peilung, the whole Tungpan group, Tachang and Laitoyu—islands inhabited by hundreds of people, but held by neither side, or lightly held and evacuated when attack seems imminent.

Sixty-five thousand civilians live on the islands. Two provincial governments-in-exile exist, ready to move across and set up operations when L-day, Liberation Day, comes. The regulars, the men of Chiang Kai Shek's armies, number in the tens of thousands, to be counted now in armies rather than in divisions.

Free China's navy too, is active. Five naval bases are in operation from Kinmen northward. The ships are small, ancient Japanese trawlers converted into gunboats, a few destroyers, destroyer escorts and mine layers. Ceaselessly the navy patrols the coast, watching the shipping that attempts to enter Communist ports, fighting short but fierce battles with Communist ships that slip out of mainland harbors, carrying food to the residents of the Vacuum Islands.

But the brunt of the fighting falls upon the shoulders of the Chinese guerrilla. It is he that must go far inland, on sabotage missions or merely to collect information or to transmit orders. While the regulars come from every province of the mainland, the guerrillas are generally local men, residents of the adjacent coast. While the guerrillas are billeted with Kinmen and Ta-chen families, the regulars more often live apart in training camps. While the regulars have been separated from families for years, the guerrillas often have wives and children living nearby. For the Chinese wisely decided that the guerrillas, to be effective, must be able to live and fight with the knowledge that their families are free from danger of arrest and torture. And so hundreds of wives and children have been brought out from the mainland, to live in dependent colonies in the Ta-chens, on White Dog, on Kinmen and now even in Formosa.

On the islands the guerrillas now approach 100,000 in number, perhaps half of them already intensively trained. As I have already noted, their counterparts exist in all but one of China's mainland provinces. No one can say exactly how many men still fight on there. The Communists themselves admit to 400,000; the Nationalists claim 550,000.

The guerrillas operate under the Continental Operations command of the Free Chinese department of National Defense. On the islands they are under the command of the commanding general whoever he may be. Yet they enjoy a certain autonomy. On Kinmen, main training base, the men live and work in vast camps, in dialect groups. I saw 5,000 men from north Kwangtung province in a massive demonstration of fighting power. I visited another unit, all men speaking the Foochow dialect. Further north there are other contingents, speaking the dialect, knowing every footpath of a specific coastal area.

Knowledge of the coast is of tremendous importance to the guerrillas. They must know the local dialect, must know every water buffalo path, must know who is reliable and who will help. This knowledge is important in hit-and-run raids, sabotage operations; it will be even more important when the guerrilla divisions go ashore, the advance waves in a battle for the mainland.

As the guerrillas are specially trained, so also they must rely on special and unusual financial operations. For they have unusual problems, among these that of housing, clothing and feeding their dependents.

So the guerrillas add to their war chest through some unorthodox and unmilitary operations. A guerrilla unit that captures a Communist ship of any type has the right to keep and sell the cargo. This creates some unusual situations. As I have mentioned, I went to Kinmen equipped with aureomycin, costing me thirty-five cents a capsule in Nashville, Tennessee, and found the same brand on sale locally for the equivalent of ten cents. A shipful of wonder drugs had just been seized by a raiding party.

But it is the wine distillery and cigarette factory which contribute most to the guerrilla treasury; for the guerrillas have a monopoly on both items. Four brands of cigarettes are made, bearing such brands as "Kinmen Tiger" and "Overcoming Difficulty."

The wine distillery illustrates the complicated financial goings-on one finds on Kinmen (this includes the issuing of its own currency). The island produces very little rice. But the poor soil will grow a grain known as kaoliang which is an important crop because it helps prevent soil erosion. The farmers are encouraged to grow kaoliang which they can then barter for rice imported from Formosa. Finding itself with tons of surplus kaoliang, the guerrilla command decided to build a distillery.

At this point in the Golden Gate's turbulent history there appeared on the scene the island's most unusual guerrilla. For Allen Yeh, manager of the wine distillery, is a guerrilla in the sense that he plays an extremely important part in financing operations.

Allen Yeh speaks perfect English with a British accent. He was born in Malaya, is a graduate of Hong Kong's best college.

"Why in the world did you come to Kinmen?" I asked. "Do you like it here?"

Allen Yeh's answer carried with it a further clue to the importance of Kinmen.

"This is my ancestral home," he said. "My people came from Kinmen. I was needed here, and it just happened that when I arrived a distillery was under discussion."

Did he know anything about the making of wine? No, Allen's education was in the liberal arts. He is more poet than brewer. But he has been able to improvise and invent, and he is using that surplus kaoliang. Allen Yeh has problems: The Yeh brew must be bottled in whatever empties his scavengers can find. It generally appears in empty soy sauce bottles, but occasionally a beer or Coca-Cola bottle shows up.

Allen Yeh has added another link in the chain reaction of rice-for-kaoliang-for-wine. Every month he has tons of mash which he feeds to a large collection of hogs. The spectacular growth of the mash-fed hogs threatens to put the Berkshire boar out of business. After all, why take the chance with white-footed piglets when native hogs can be raised to tremendous size, and perhaps with a delicate, winey flavor?

The story of Allen Yeh illustrates a facet of Kinmen's importance which U. S. policy makers might well take note of. The island has had one export in all its history—its young men and women who have gone forth to *Nan Yang,* the countries of Southeast Asia, to become business leaders, merchants, bankers, educators. Over 100,000 Kinmeners live overseas. The fact that Free China has been able to hold and strengthen the island has been an important factor in the battle for the allegiance of Asia's 10,000,000 overseas Chinese. In the center of the island is a huge statue of Chiang Kai Shek, symbolically facing westward towards the mainland. The statue was paid for, was even built, by overseas Chinese from Thailand, Vietnam, Malaya, Singapore and Indonesia. Delegations of overseas Chinese from six countries have already visited Kinmen.

The loss of China's Golden Gate would be a severe blow to Nationalist China's uphill fight to keep the overseas Chinese on its side.

Yes, Allen Yeh is a guerrilla, even though he does not carry a gun, will never learn how to blow up a railroad bridge or how to kill a Communist sentry quickly and silently. There are many others like him, business men, agricultural experts, all playing an important part in Free China's mainland operations.

But wars will not be won by wine masters, nor by breeding better pigs or planting trees. What of the fighting guerrillas, the men who come in actual contact with the enemy on raids far into the interior? Here too, I found men of varying backgrounds, educated and uneducated, a cross-section of China. One of the leading guerrillas is an old family friend, who owes my father a debt of gratitude, for he was once a pirate who got too big for his britches. Not content with simple piracy, he started a full-scale revolution on the coast just north of Kinmen. The short-lived revolution ended in the pirate's capture; but father pleaded that there was good in the man, that the death sentence should be commuted. And so it was that Pirate Ung lived to become guerrilla General Ung, based upon Kinmen Island.

The story of Ung Ding Buong is important, casting light upon the loyalties of the pirates who have been the scourge of South China for generations. The meeting with Ung on Kinmen was accidental, but in a way it was no surprise. A year and a half before I visited guerrilla-land I had written these words in *China Coast Family:* "I often wonder about Ung Ding Buong,—about all the outlaws of the Fukien Hills and Seas, who in the past refused to knuckle under to tyranny. Are the Ungs, the Lings, the Lu Hing Bangs causing their Communist rulers trouble today? Given arms and direction, and above all understanding, will not perhaps these sturdy people provide a deadly obstacle to the solidification of Communist rule? Is there not here an opportunity worth a small investment?"

Ung Ding Buong, with a dark history, can perhaps be labeled an opportunist, although why opportunism would lead him to choose Free China when most of the world considers its cause lost is an interesting question. But what of more typical guerrillas, not tainted by a history of piracy and trafficking with the enemy? The story of a man I shall call Captain Shih sheds light on the thinking, the ordeals, the assignment of the other "men of iron" who sail to the mainland on wooden ships.

My meeting with Captain Shih was also accidental and it took place, not on Kinmen but on Matsu Island. I must confess that my visit to Matsu was for romantic and personal reasons. For it lies off the mouth of the Min River. Many years ago when I was a small child, my dad visited Matsu, looking for the eggs of the many sea birds that nest among the islands. As a child I often saw the island. Later, when I was a student in the Shanghai American School, I saw the island each time the steamer took me to and from Shanghai.

Matsu is one of a group of small and cliffy islands taken by the Nationalists in 1952 in a successful testing of combined guerrilla, regular army and sea operations.

It is not possible to land a plane anywhere on Matsu, or on the neighboring White Dog Islands. Once every two weeks one of General Chennault's air liners flies in, a converted PBY, and, weather permitting, lands off the beach with supplies and VIP personnel.

I was signally honored when I flew over to Matsu. The PBY had been equipped with exactly thirteen seats. The commanding general of the Matsu garrison was also returning that day. Always before it had been understood that when the general flew there could be only twelve passengers. The thirteenth seat must always be left empty. After all, the trip was pretty risky anyway. The battered old seaplane must skim low over the water in order to escape the enemy radar, planted around the mouth of the Min River, leading to the important harbor at Pagoda Anchorage. The plane was, of course, always unarmed.

But when the general learned that I was myself a son of Foochow, when he learned that my father was the great tiger hunting missionary, he allowed me to take the thirteenth seat.

The Government Spokesman's Office at Taipei which planned my trips did not assign an aide or interpreter to me for the Matsu visit. The seating capacity of the PBY was small, and after all, I was going "home" where I could speak the dialect of the people.

And so it was that news spread quickly on Matsu that there was an American on the island who spoke the Foochow dialect. It was unusual news, too, for other than an occasional American pilot who might step ashore on the beach for a few hours, I was the first American to visit Matsu since my father climbed its cliffs in search of birds' eggs nearly forty years earlier.

I ran into Captain Shih quite by accident, for I had no plans for Matsu other than to walk about and talk to people. I was standing on a hill top, looking westward trying to pick out old landmarks around my birthplace. It was a bit difficult to orient myself to looking from the sea toward home. And so I turned to the Chinese officer nearby and asked him which was the Mui-hua beach.

From mountains and beaches our conversation turned to politics and war and guerrilla operations. And thus I learned the story of Captain Shih, a typical fighting guerrilla.

It had been only a few months previous that a lookout on Matsu had spotted an object bobbing in the water. Since refugees from the mainland sometimes swim to the guerrilla islands, or float out on logs or tiny rafts, the sentries are always watchful, always report any strange and unusual object.

So it was that one morning a Matsu lookout reported an unusual object bobbing on the water. For, Captain Shih, clinging to a log, was approaching Matsu after floating miles and for hours from the mainland.

But let Captain Shih tell his story, in his own words.

"I was one of a special sabotage squad," he began. "We were twelve, all men of the Min Nan area, and it was our job to land near Haikow, work our way inland and then sabotage the highways and especially the bridges along the coast.

"We landed without difficulty; then proceeded quite a way inland, to the highway near Putien. We had just begun our operations when we ran into very bad luck. I think it was purely by chance, but perhaps we were betrayed—one cannot always know. But we suddenly ran into a Communist patrol where we least expected it.

"I am not sure exactly what happened, who was killed, who was captured, who perhaps may still be alive. We were surprised and could not fight effectively. I know several of the men were killed on the spot. Only by luck I escaped into the tall grass along the highway. For hours I crawled along like a wild hog, working my way into the higher mountains. They looked for me for quite a while, but you know that country is pretty wild.

"I kept my gun but even so I was afraid of tigers. There are so many tigers in those hills, and I knew I wouldn't have much chance in that tall grass. I was especially frightened that first night and climbed a tree so that I would be safe from the animals.

"We have a large mountain area inland from Putien that is under our control, and it was towards that area that I must go rather than towards the coast, because I knew the Communists would put on a special watch all along the coast, expecting naturally that the survivors of my group would try to get back to one of the islands.

"I became terribly hungry in that first day or two. You know the Communists have one terrible weapon. It is one we also have. We can never be absolutely sure on the mainland who is safe, who are our friends. But then neither can they be sure. Anyway, I was afraid to contact anyone for food at first. So it was that I went for two days without food until I was able to steal a little rice and some cabbage which I ate raw.

"After three or four days of walking, sometimes during the day in the wooded country, sometimes also at night, I reached what I thought was the border of the guerrilla-held area. There I walked boldly up to a farm house and asked for food. The people were frightened at first. But after I talked for a while, they fed me, and I found that I was in fairly safe territory.

"You know we are not well organized in these areas. Some of the guerrillas are really Tu Fei's [bandits]. Some are patriots, indeed most of them are. After another day or so I was able to make contact with the people in charge. They gave me a pretty tough time, too. One of the terrible things about China today is that no one trusts anyone else. They questioned me for many hours before they could be sure that I was not from the other side. I cannot blame them at all for that. There are many betrayals taking place in China now. Friend is turned against friend, even son against father.

"But at last they accepted me, they fed me, and I began to plan a way to get back. We have an underground, but it again is not as well organized as it should be. We know that the Communists have also placed their men in our underground just as we have men in every Communist division. So we have to be careful.

"I gave up my gun; I got the roughest sort of clothes, the kind that the woodchoppers in the mountains wear; and after several weeks I began to move slowly back toward the coast.

"It was only about two hundred li from the mountain place to the coast, but even that short distance took me nearly three weeks to travel. Sometimes I rested with "friends" for several days at a time while the message went out to other friends that I should be expected. Sometimes I had to hide in the mountains all night, or as the case might be, all day. But I was fairly well fed—as well fed as the poor people are able to feed themselves these days.

"When I at last got near the coast the danger was very great, for the Communists are terribly frightened of an invasion. The coastline is filled with special agents, with the secret police. Every fishing junk is watched carefully. When a junk leaves it is searched from stem to stern, each passenger is noted, even the children. The captain must place his 'chop' in a special book, must say exactly where he is going to fish that day and exactly when he is returning. When he returns he is again searched, his crew counted, and I might say most of his catch taken by the greedy soldiers. Each member of the crew has a special pass, with his picture on it, so it is most difficult to make a substitution.

"We do it sometimes, of course. We Chinese are pretty good at forging things. But at best it is a pretty risky business and many of the fishermen are unwilling to take a chance.

"I tried for a long time to see how I could get back to Matsu or White Dog by boat, but at last I was forced to give the idea up. My continued presence with the friends who were keeping me was risky. I could not go out, day or night. Eventually someone might even notice that the family was buying a little more food than usual.

"You know the Communist secret police even take notes on such things: the amount of dried fish a family buys. If there is a sudden change in food purchase, there may be a midnight raid.

"And so I decided I had only one chance to get back. I must wait until there was a good off-shore wind, at night, and try to float back. My friends were fishermen, and they were able to locate a big log. You know even that is a difficult matter because fuel is so valuable. But they found one that would hold me and then carefully concealed it among the rocks. I knew where it was, and I only had to wait until the wind was right.

"That was in late October, and already the water was chilly. I wondered if I would be able to stand the cold for many hours. I wondered too, what would happen if the wind changed."

Then Captain Shih smiled boyishly, as he continued.

"But luck was with me. The wind came, a good brisk one. It started early in the evening. I was able to get into the water and started just before midnight. The tide was going out; that gave me several extra miles. By daylight I was well off the shore and could even see Matsu.

"It was terribly cold. And it was the loneliest time of my life out there in the water between our side and the other side. I kicked now and then until I became tired. Slowly my fine 'ship' moved toward Matsu."

And that, told simply, without any heroics, was the story of one man's ordeal, of a mission that failed and yet was signally successful.

Chapter 7

WHO arms and trains these men and women of guerrilla-land, men and women who have kept the Communist armies off balance all along the coast from Shanghai to Hong Kong? What more could they accomplish, given more American assistance? Can they hold out on their tiny island strongholds? This latter question may even be answered before these words are in print. The Communist build-up along the guerrilla coast was under way when I visited the islands in December, 1953. All through August and September of 1954 the build-up had continued; artillery fire was poured on Kinmen and Little Kinmen in such volume as the islanders have not experienced in five years.

The answer to the question of whether Kinmen and the less important islands can hold out (if these little Berlins scattered along the China Coast still exist as outposts of Free China when these words are read) rests in the answer to the first question: Who trains and arms the men?

Not the United States, at least not officially. One of the great anomalies of American policy is that the fighting men of the China Coast islands are considered outside the American defense area. The two American officers killed on Kinmen on September 3rd, 1954, were there as observers. The military advisory group on Formosa, charged with training

Chiang's armies, has not been allowed to work among the Nationalist guerrillas. Observers have gone to Kinmen and to the Ta-chens. They have not participated in planning the defense of the islands. And the simple fact is that Kinmen, especially, has not received the military assistance or the arms to enable it to hold out against determined Communist attack.

Only one American group is allowed to operate openly among the islands. That is the Joint Commission on Rural Reconstruction, of which I shall report more in detail. JCRR being a Sino-American operation, does work on Kinmen and in the Ta-chen Islands. Chinese and American agricultural specialists have visited the islands regularly and helped to make of Kinmen a show window of Chiang's progress, a show window clearly visible and understood by the enslaved millions just across the waters. The Berkshire boar, the Kankrej bulls from India, bred to native cattle and swine, thus producing sturdier animals for the Kinmen farmers, were sent to Kinmen by JCRR. Chen Shi Ho's army agricultural experiment station has received JCRR help.

All of this is to the credit of the United States, has helped to make Kinmen the potential Golden Gate to the mainland. And it is also to the credit of the United States that the guerrillas have received some assistance, but it has been given in supposed secrecy and has been of such limited character that it will not insure the island garrisons against annihilation.

As soon as one arrives on Formosa, one hears of Western Enterprises, Incorporated. Better known as WE, this is Central Intelligence Agency's vehicle for arming and training the Free Chinese guerrillas in "secrecy." I write of WE and its operations because it has long since ceased to be any secret. The British, all Free Chinese, and the Communists too, know full well what WE does. Its operations are worth while, yet also are childish. If America is really to develop partisan warfare, if it is to have an intelligence service in the Far East that can compete with the British, it will have to improve.

Western Enterprises, Inc., as the name might imply, is supposedly a bona-fide American business firm, doing import-export business in Free China. Yet when its 150-odd ex-marines arrived in Taipei, their method of achieving "cover" was surprising. WE people, wives and children, too, lived to themselves in special compounds, with their own PX and Commissary establishments, their own clubs.

Quite naturally WE immediately began to excite curiosity, to cause comment. Since when was there sufficient business in Formosa to cause the establishment of an operation of such size? Why did businessmen have to live to themselves? Why, when one discussed, or tried to discuss business, did the supposed businessmen profess complete ignorance? Also it was strange that WE's businessmen had planes of their own, took frequent trips to the off-shore islands!

I mention CIA's Formosan "cover" because its cover is equally transparent in other Far Eastern countries. In one capital city, CIA men have set up a ship chandlering concern. It did not take long for local businessmen to discover that the Americans knew nothing about chandlering ships. It took but a very short time for the enemy to know exactly who was to be watched in that city.

No one of course, not even the Congress, knows how many men CIA has in the Far East or in any other area. But one can nearly always spot a CIA operator. Time and again I have met old friends or acquaintances in the Far East and quite naturally I asked what the individual was doing now.

The CIA operator immediately gets a silly smirk on his face, with obvious pride mumbles something about something, and the identity of another American intelligence agent is immediately known. I would say that the identity of nine out of ten American intelligence agents is known. The exact opposite would apply to the British.

Another rumor I pass on because if it be true, it is a serious indictment of American operations. It is widely reported that

73

Central Intelligence Agency was behind the troubles between President Syngman Rhee and the Korean National Assembly during the summer of 1952. It is alleged that CIA attempted to have Rhee ousted by buying off members of Korea's congress. Such activity *might* be appropriate in Guatemala. In Korea, or elsewhere in the Far East it is dangerous and stupid and indicates abysmal lack of understanding of local politics.

But our present interest lies in what CIA, that is Western Enterprises, has done to train and arm the Nationalist guerrillas,—men of iron like Captain Shih.

The story can only be gotten in bits, and then largely from privates and non-commissioned officers in the guerrilla ranks; for WE maintains the utmost secrecy as far as other Americans are concerned. The degree of secrecy is almost ludicrous. I ran into a WE man on a lonely guerrilla island. There we were, two lone Americans, far from home. But as we passed down the narrow cobble-stoned street the WE man did not deign even to notice me. Naturally, the Chinese were somewhat surprised.

In fact, the WE approach to public relations has made it difficult to tell the story of what is going on, what might happen along the China Coast. Fred Sparks, of NEA, arrived in the Ta-chen Islands during Christmas of 1953. Fred is as honest and reliable a reporter as represents the American press. Yet his whole trip was almost ruined because of WE. The Chinese commander, not knowing who Fred was, welcomed him, thinking he was another WE man. Arrangements were made to take him through the islands, allow him to interview guerrillas and refugees. Suddenly the bottom dropped out of all plans, and Fred Sparks found himself shunned.

Less than a half mile away, the Americans at WE headquarters had discovered the presence of Mr. Sparks. They immediately told the Chinese commander that he was not of the elite, that care should be taken in handling him. When Fred sent a message to WE headquarters, asking for an interview, a Chinese came back saying that the Americans were all gone.

But that night, it being the Christmas season, Sparks heard the sounds of drunken Americans singing from the nearby hill, not the voice of one American, but of many.

WE has done its utmost to keep all Americans from visiting any guerrilla-held island. Once the American gets through the WE road blocks, he is quite likely to meet with further trouble on the islands. Only if one has the support of the highest Nationalist officials is it possible to get the story of the China Coast.

And that story is of tremendous importance to the Western World. Mainland guerrillas included, there are a minimum of a half million men available even now to strike fear into the heart of the enemy. There are men like Ung Ding Buong, who know every cove and mud-flat from Wenchow to Swatow; men like Captain Shih who have the courage and the knowledge of terrain so important if China is to be free again.

Within the limitations of curious American policy, WE does a good job. The training areas of the guerrillas on Kinmen are veritable arsenals. I walked through barracks after barracks, watched on the edges of parade grounds while the men maneuvered. I visited the homes of the guerrilla dependents from my home part of Fukien province; I watched them working out tactical problems on the hillsides.

WE's American instructors train the guerrillas in the use of every type of modern small arms. Each guerrilla keeps his arms by his bedside. In each section of each barracks are the store rooms in which the bigger pieces of every fighting unit are kept at the ready. Rifles, machine guns, sub-machine guns, mortars, large and small, grenades—all these are in the hands of the men.

The guerrilla must learn how to land quickly from the prow of a ship, how to kill quickly and silently in the dark. Special sabotage units, similar to the one which Captain Shih led, learn how to destroy bridges and railroads. Still others must become proficient as messengers, as radio operators.

The training of the men is extremely hard, from dawn until dark. Their discipline is the best that I have ever seen among Oriental soldiers, their physical appearance excellent.

What have these men been able to accomplish to date with American aid? And what more could they accomplish?

It is difficult to separate guerrilla activities from the activities of Nationalist regulars, for both participate in major engagements. Therefore it would be better to ask what have the Nationalist forces along the China Coast been able to accomplish.

Since 1950 these men of iron have captured literally scores of small Communist craft. They have been able to maintain a semblance at least, of contact and supervision over thousands of mainland guerrillas. They have engaged in scores of minor raids. They have recaptured Matsu and White Dog Islands. They took part in a 10,000 man assault on Tungshan Island in which they badly mauled two Communist divisions but finally were forced to retreat.

In 1952 alone the Nationalist attacks ranged from the taking of small islands off the Chekiang coast to a strike inland against the Penghu station on the Canton-Kowloon railroad. The battle of Vanjih Island, an ancient pirate lair near my birthplace, resulted in 1,035 Communists killed and 794 prisoners. The recapture of Nanping and Chungping Islands off the Fukien Coast resulted in 300 Communists killed and wounded, including one brigadier general.

Of special significance have been the number of prisoners and the ease with which the prisoners were taken. During the battle on Tungshan Island, eight hundred Communists surrendered during the first hour of battle. Total captured personnel was so great that it was impossible to move the prisoners back to Kinmen. Much to their disgust, the men who surrendered had to stay behind and rejoin their comrades.

It has never been understood in America that the Communist surrenders in Korea were not isolated events. The same willingness to surrender has been evident, over and over again in China. It is a matter of the greatest significance in any discussion of Chiang's chances of retaking the mainland.

So much for what the men of iron have accomplished. What more could they have accomplished and what more can they do to harrass the enemy?

Writing in the August, 1954, issue of *Readers' Digest,* Fred Sparks gives an idea of what could be accomplished by what he calls "Operation Bleed." With South Korean participation, all of China's Coast line, her holdings in North Korea, could be kept in a continual state of turmoil—if the guerrillas and the regulars had the support, the weapons they need.

There are few landing craft available to the Chinese guerrillas. Remember the pitiful request of the guerrilla leader on Tungting Island? He wanted a couple of PT boats. There are few small planes, no helicopters, not enough naval support vessels of the type that can beat into shallow harbors quickly.

From time to time anti-Nationalist American newspapers, of which there are many, make fun of Chiang Kai Shek and his puny efforts since President Eisenhower "unleashed" Nationalist forces in 1953. No great battles have been reported, no landings attempted. But considering their resources, the men of Free China have actually been extremely active. President Eisenhower's "unleashing" was a hollow gesture, not accompanied by any definite policy decision. American policy towards China is still negative. Formosa is to be protected but no offensive Nationalist action is encouraged.

Even since Kinmen burst upon the front pages in the fall of 1954, there has been no positive policy decision. The National Security Council met in extraordinary session in Denver to consider last fall's "vest pocket war." No stepped-up aid was announced; Kinmen's defenders were given no assurance that they would receive help if the Communists attacked the island in force.

And the truth is if the island is attacked in force, it can be taken; China's Golden Gate and perhaps its golden opportunity will be lost. For the aid given to date has not been sufficient to make Kinmen or any other Nationalist-held island invincible. The small arms and the training given to the guerrillas is but a drop in the bucket.

But how is it that the weary, defeated Nationalist armies were able to beat off Communist attack in 1949, yet might not be able to prevail today? In 1949, there were no elaborate defense works, no highway system, no well organized supply line to Formosa. Now the men of Free China are well entrenched, thoroughly dug in, with highways that make it possible to move troops quickly to any part of the island.

But Communist China has weapons now it did not have in 1949. In particular, the Reds have an air force, and Kinmen is vulnerable to air attack. Lying outside the defense line established by the United States, it has received little artillery of the type needed, none of the planning and advice needed. Its antiaircraft artillery is ancient and obsolete.

If the Communists attack in great force, first pounding the island by air, dropping paratroopers while amphibious forces land along the beaches, it is doubtful that the island can hold. Even Kinmen's regular artillery is inadequate; it is far inferior to the modern weapons provided the enemy by Russia. Two or three divisions of paratroopers dropped on Kinmen, preceded by massive air attack which its defenders have no way of beating off, and the island will be lost.

What is true of Kinmen is even more true of the other island outposts. Nowhere is there adequate air defense. If Red China wishes to take the risk, if it chooses to throw its air force into the attack, Free China's outposts will be lost.

Of course, a simple announcement by the United States that Kinmen's defenders will receive aid would forestall attack. But the United States has as yet made no such announcement. Indeed all the available evidence indicates that the National Security Council in its September, 1954, meeting decided that the guerrilla islands were not to receive help.

On what basis does the National Security Council make such decisions? In general, military policy decisions have their basis in the intelligence reports funneled into Washington from the agents of the Central Intelligence Agency all through the world. CIA through Western Enterprises has had its men on Kinmen, in the Ta-chen Islands, even occasionally on Matsu and White Dog. While training Chinese guerrillas, it is also their function to report upon Red China, its armies, its problems.

The average Western Enterprise agent is an ex-marine, youngish, combat hardened, thoroughly proficient in his trade, which is fighting. He does not speak Chinese, knows little about China, cannot read captured enemy documents, cannot interview refugees. The enemy almost invariably knows his identity.

If China's Golden Gate is lost, it will be in large part because American intelligence has failed to grasp the significance of the many forces at work there and on the mainland. A high United States diplomat in the Far East, talking of American intelligence methods and potentials, told me, "Our men are pretty good at locating enemy armies, airfields and artillery positions. The physical forces of the enemy they can understand and can evaluate. But beyond that our intelligence is a bust."

It is likely that Central Intelligence has never noted the significance of the fact we have noted elsewhere, that Kinmen has exported 100,000 men and women to other Asian countries, and of the fact that Nationalist holding of the island has therefore meant increased prestige for Free China all over Asia. It is almost certain that CIA has not understood the strength of Christianity on the mainland, the deep pro-American feeling that still exists. The presence of a Berkshire boar on Kinmen would have no significance to an average American Intelligence agent. The name of Koxinga, who made Kinmen a place of great historic importance to China, would be unknown to a Western Enterprise man; for it is doubtful if the ex-marines who made up our intelligence forces have ever read Chinese history.

If Kinmen be lost, it will be an indication of faulty U. S. intelligence, of a failure to understand the nonmilitary forces at work in Asia, forces which are fully as important as the number of men and planes and tanks possessed by the enemy.

The loss of Kinmen or Ta-chen or Matsu will not mean that Formosa will also be lost. The armies of Red China will still have a hundred miles and more of water to cross. Nor will the continued presence of Free Chinese troops on the islands mean that the Communist mainland is menaced, that a landing can be made to drive out China's Red rulers.

Kinmen is a vitally important Free World position, on the very edge of the civilized world. It is a monument to Free Chinese initiative, has certainly been made into a show window of progress. Furthermore, everything done there has been accomplished against terrific odds.

But Kinmen has no significance unless it is backed by similar accomplishments, by similar good government on the island of Formosa. It would be useless for the United States to keep West Berlin out of enemy hands if the government of West Germany were hopelessly inefficient, weak and corrupt. So would it be useless to give aid to Kinmen if Free China had failed to make progress, had failed to learn from its disastrous mistakes of the past.

The full potential of the islands in guerrilla-land can only be understood in terms of Formosa, of the men and women who crossed over in utter defeat and humiliation in 1949.

What has Free China been able to accomplish on its island stronghold?

On September 22, 1954, Clement Atlee, the world's newest authority on Far Eastern affairs, stated: "Personally speaking, the sooner we get rid of Chiang Kai Shek and his troops the better it will be."

If Clement Atlee be correct, it is useless to talk of Golden Gates and guerrillas and liberation of the mainland.

However, it should be remembered that Mr. Atlee has never visited the island he so cavalierly dismisses. And Formosa, too, must be visited to be understood. For there too is a story that must be told and understood if the people of Asia are to remain free.

BOOK TWO

BOOK TWO

OF MEN AND DREAMS

Chapter 1

T HE legend of a saintly official in the mountains of Formosa, or Taiwan, as it is known to Chinese, the story of an odoriferous farm project, these two, taken together, tell in part the story of the men and women who bolster the lonely outposts along the China Coast. First the story of a smelly project.

Tourists complain and hold their noses because of it. Old China hands complain too, then wax nostalgic when away from it. For our purposes we may call it night-soil, the human waste of Asia-without-sewers. It is bartered and sold like a commodity, sloshed through the streets in ox-drawn and sometimes mechanized "honey-carts." For millions in Asia it is the only fertilizer available and affordable. It is a menace to health, polluting vegetables and water supply with the bacteria and the viruses of a score of diseases. Partly because of it, ninety per cent of the people suffer from intestinal parasites and diseases. Sold and bartered, hauled through the streets, stored in stinking pits, it has almost caused international incidents. I knew a junior diplomat in Korea who argued and fought over the price of his output. I saw a drunken American official fall into a pit and come out stone sober in five seconds flat.

As far as the night-soil problem is concerned, a new day has come to Formosa. Those clever Chinese, with an assist from Charlie Wilson's General Motors and from Ralph Glea-

85

son, a soft spoken American Agricultural Expert from South Carolina, are solving the age-old problem.

I saw the dawn of a new day in Asia when I visited a Taichung night-soil disposal project in central Formosa. My guide, one Mr. Hsu Ping Woo, better known as Tommy, was rather irreverent about the whole matter. He called it the S-project and referred to the long suffering Mr. Gleason as the American S-pert.

Huge GM trucks, equipped with tanks and hoses roam the streets of Taichung each morning, collecting the night's production. The trucks transport the stuff into the country, to huge settling basins, holding 2,500 tons. The night-soil stays there from ten days to three weeks, depending upon the weather and temperature. By then it has become pure as a lily, sterile and devoid of germs without losing any of its potent fertilizing power. From the big basins, trucks haul the sterile stuff to smaller basins, scattered through the country and easily available to the farmers who use it.

The Taichung Project has cost $851,000—Formosan dollars —to date, or about $32,000 U.S. Of this the Taichung city fathers have put up all but $106,000 NT (The Free Chinese dollar is known as the New Taiwan Dollar—NT, for short).

Taichung has a three year night-soil project, plans to buy four more trucks, will build more settling basins. Already other Formosa cities are clamoring to start their own projects. It is possible that the Taichung project may become a model for all Asia, could lead the way to better health in a half dozen nations.

There is one aspect of the business that still defies solution. Mr. Hsu looked guilty, as if he must personally shoulder the blame when he told me a fact my nose had already verified.

"Mr. Caldwell," he said, "no matter what we do with it, it still smells."

But because the men of Formosa, with a small assist from America, have tackled and solved an age-old problem, the rice will grow still greener on many a Formosan farm, without endangering the health of the farmers.

It was on the same day that I saw the Taichung project that I also heard the story of Magistrate Wu Feng. Tommy Hsu and I were driving through the magnificent mountains surrounding Sun-Moon Lake, on the border of aborigine country. Tommy told me the story that is now often retold to young and old throughout the island, a story that has become an unofficial guide to official activity.

The mountains of Formosa are inhabited by wild tribes, non-Chinese aborigines, who came to the island centuries ago from Indonesia and Southeast Asia. These, the Indians of Formosa, speak their own dialects, have their own distinctive customs which included for many years the taking of human heads. The story of Magistrate Wu Feng is part fact, part legend, for it occurred many years ago, before Formosa was lost to the Japanese.

Magistrate Wu represented Imperial China in the Formosan mountains. He ruled his mountain tribes people for many years, and he ruled justly. The mountain people loved and respected him. But neither respect nor love had been sufficient to change one mountain custom. The elders of the tribe still insisted on ceremonial head-hunting. Magistrate Wu had threatened, he had pleaded but to no avail. The Chinese governor in Taipei, representing the Emperor in far away Peking, had at last written Wu that unless the head-hunting ceased, Wu was to be relieved.

So it was that Magistrate Wu called a meeting of the tribal chiefs. He would present a plan, would tell the mountain people again that head-hunting must end.

Wu was an old man, tired and discouraged as he entered the meeting hall to address the chiefs. For although he had a plan to present to his people, he could not be certain of its success. Magistrate Wu addressed the tribes people who faced him.

"Honorable Chiefs," he began, "I have often talked to you about your problems. I have tried to rule with justice. But you still have not obeyed the edict of the all-powerful Emperor that head-hunting must end. I am here tonight to tell you that it must end. But I understand the customs of centuries are hard to put away, and so I shall allow you to take one more head."

The magistrate quickly outlined his plan. On the morrow, before the moon came over the mountain and after full darkness had settled upon the hills, the tribesmen were to go to a crossroad near a mountain village. At eight o'clock a man dressed in white would approach from the west. That man would be the last sacrifice to ancient custom.

The chiefs retired to prepare for the morrow. A representative of each tribe was selected; ceremonial dress was required; a feast must be prepared. And even before the shadows began to fall on the appointed evening, the selected tribesmen were gathered among the bamboos at the crossing of the trails.

Just as the moon came over Sun-Moon Mountain, a figure appeared, dressed in white, walking slowly towards the crossroad. The tribesmen waited in tense excitement. At the appointed moment they rushed from the bamboos, uttering the war cries of centuries past. Quickly a tribal chief slashed off the head of the white-clad stranger. Then yelling in a frenzy of excitement, the tribes people carried their trophy up the winding mountain trail to the shores of Sun-Moon Lake.

There upon a white beach was a great fire. Around it gathered all the peoples of the tribes. The feast had been spread, but would not be eaten until after hours of celebration, after ancient rites had been performed. And in the hours of early morning the last head would be placed upon a pole in front of the big chief.

It was the big chief's privilege to carry the bloody trophy into the fire's light. The tribes people pressed around him in excitement.

Suddenly a great hush fell upon the throng. The singing, the shouting ended abruptly. Faces froze in shock and horror. For the light from the great fire cast its glow upon the face of their beloved Magistrate Wu, calm and smiling in death.

Many years have passed, and now any man, white or yellow, may walk the wild mountain trails of Formosa without fear. The memory of a man who gave his life that others might learn and live more happily is kept alive and ever before the mountain people by the tiny shrines perched upon the mountain peaks, built in his memory.

Chapter 2

THE heart of Asia, the story of its struggle, cannot be understood only in terms of its leaders. The lives and statements of the Chiangs and Rhees, the Maos and the Ho Chih Mins tell but a part of the story. It is in the dreams and heartaches, the victories and defeats of little men and women that much of the story lies.

Mr. Hsu Ping Wu, better known as Tommy, is one of those whose story is important. This is the same Tommy Hsu who first told me the later oft-heard story of Magistrate Wu. It was he who introduced me to the wonders of sterile night-soil.

We should at once understand that Tommy is not important. He is a very minor Chinese official. Although once in the Chinese army, he wears no decorations. Neither as civilian or soldier has he gained fame. He is but one of the several million Chinese who have entered the third act in the drama of life in today's China.

There are those like Dr. C. who stayed behind, who suffer but whose spirits remain unbroken. There are those like Captain Shih and Magistrate Chang Chow who left the mainland, but who have now to play their roles on lonely island outposts. Then there are the Tommy Hsu's who managed to reach Formosa, there to play a role that may determine the fate of those on the islands, those still in mainland bondage.

I first met Tommy Hsu in 1943, at a lonely boat landing near Amoy on the mainland and directly opposite Kinmen, which was then held by the Japanese. The Second World War was not going well for the Chinese, and part of the China Coast was held, or was threatened by Japanese invasion. I had walked thirty miles that day, always close to Japanese positions along the coast. The night before I had slept in a sampan, for I had to rendezvous with one of my agents out of Japanese-held Amoy, and a tossing boat seemed best suited for that purpose.

It was the day following a not-too-restful night on the water, and my destination was an inn, five hard miles away by foot. I was not only tired but homesick and therefore responded quickly when a young Chinese spoke to me.

"My farm is near here," he said in English. "You seem very tired. We would be honored if you would spend the night with us."

My grateful look was all the acceptance needed. So it was that I met Tommy Hsu and his charming wife. It was a meeting much frowned upon by Sing Kie, my secretary and general factotum. As we traveled the few miles to Tommy Hsu's farm Sing Kie reproached me in whispers.

"He may be a spy, in the pay of the Japanese. You should let me handle business like this."

But I was far too exhausted to worry about spies. I thoroughly enjoyed the small talk and relaxation, the quiet peace of the farm so near the battlefront, the excellent dinner cooked by Tommy's wife.

The next day I moved on, up the dynamited coastal highway, to forget Tommy Hsu and his wife.

It was ten years later that our paths crossed again, and then purely by chance. I asked the American officials of the Joint Commission on Rural Reconstruction if they could loan me a guide for a few days, so that I might see something of Nationalist China's land reform program. It was pure coincidence that Tommy Hsu was in Taipei, that he was shortly returning to his post as a JCRR Inspector at Taichung. And so it was that I drove south to Taichung with him, to visit scores of farms, to travel with him for several days, covering hundreds of miles of central and southern Formosa.

Tommy and I talked to rice farmers and tea planters and I walked over so many fields of this and that, that I lost count. In between our stops, we talked of old times, and I heard the story of what had happened to Tommy and his wife during the ten years since we first met near Tungan in south Fukien. It is a story no more dramatic, indeed less so, than thousands of others. Yet it is a story which gave me an understanding of the tremendous change that has taken place in Free China since the days of bitter defeat. Unlike the stories of so many others, it can be told. Tommy's father has escaped to Hong Kong; his mother crossed to Formosa during the last days of Shanghai. He has no close relatives who can be tortured and persecuted.

Tommy Hsu belongs to that class of society which is in some degree responsible for China's present sorrow: the educated families of means which could have done so much more than they did do to give the people of China good government. His father is a general of the old school. The family land holdings in Fukien were extensive. The Hsus were landlords and warlords. And it is upon the shoulders of both landlords and warlords that responsibility for the success of Communism must in part fall.

"Things got worse and worse after we saw you in Fukien," Tommy began his story. "You remember it was not long afterwards that the Japanese landed all along the coast. We evacuated again—the fifth time during the war years. I joined the army and went south to Kwangtung province.

"We did little fighting. In fact, I never saw any action myself. And at the end of the war we went back to the farm in Fukien. I suppose that is when I really got interested in farm-

92

ing and agriculture. The farm was run down and needed much attention. We worked hard, and we were just getting things in order when the Communists swept across the Yangtse.

"There was never any question but that Fukien would fall. Everywhere the traitors and Red agents were at work. The only question was whether or not we should take the chance and stay on.

"I had two very black marks against me. I was a 'landlord' and I had been an officer in the Nationalist Army. It seemed the wise thing to do to get out.

"We sold the things we could: pigs, water buffaloes and the cattle. It was a forced sale, and we got only $300. We simply abandoned the farm to the tenants, and my wife and baby and I went to Amoy. There were many ships there taking army people to Formosa. For $270 we bought passage for the three of us.

"When we landed in Formosa in 1949 we had $30 left. The first months were difficult. We very nearly starved. A college education did not do me much good because there were thousands like me. The government was demoralized. We expected the Communists to invade all through that first year. Had it not been for the Korean war I believe they would have invaded.

"One day in the newspaper I read that there would be examinations for persons to work with American authorities. I took the exams and passed, and that is how I ended up working for JCRR."

We were traveling through the lush jungles surrounding Sun-Moon Lake and Tommy paused to point out one of the many shrines built to the memory of Magistrate Wu. Being a philosopher as well as agriculturalist, Tommy started telling of the dreams he had once had when he lived on the mainland. In the evolution of these dreams, his story is not unlike that of the Chinese magistrate who gave his life for the aborigines.

"During those years on the mainland I had three dreams," Tommy explained. "First, soon after I graduated from college I wanted to be a merchant prince. And I knew exactly what field I would make my fortune in—perfume. Just think, China was becoming modern. Our women were dressing differently. I could make a fortune selling perfume to beautiful women!

"I'd go to Paris and learn all the tricks. Eventually I would have offices in Paris, in Hong Kong, Shanghai and perhaps Peking. I'd not only make a fortune, but I would be dealing every day, all day, with the most beautiful women of China!

"But somehow that dream didn't work out. So I got another one quickly. You know my father is a general. I decided that I would join the army. With my father's name to help, I would rise fast. Many men would be under my command. I might control a whole province, perhaps even a whole section of China!

"I tried the army,—several times. First, it was by choice and then during the war by force. But it wasn't what I wanted after all. I don't like bloodshed, and perhaps I am really a coward at heart. So that dream, too, faded away.

"My last dream was pretty practical, maybe. I had read many American cowboy stories when I was young. I was fascinated by your West, by buffalo hunts, fires on the plains —all that stuff.

"So I decided that I would go to our wild west, to Singkiang or Kansu, and with the family money I'd buy up thousands of acres. I'd have a palatial ranch house somewhere, and I would soon be a cattle baron."

Tommy smiled, as he continued: "I can't really remember what happened to that dream. Perhaps war changed it. You know I can't even remember a time in my life when there wasn't a war in China. Maybe my father put his foot down. Perhaps when faced with the difficulty of life in west China, I gave it up myself. Anyway, it's gone. And here I am in a little city in Formosa, teaching farmers how to use better

seeds, setting up projects to make night-soil safe for mankind!"

But there was no bitterness in Tommy Hsu's acceptance of
his fate. There was no bitterness that three beautiful dreams
had evaporated, that a great and valuable ancestral farm was
gone, that he and his family were now exiles, only 120 miles
from home in the manner in which men measure distances,
but for all practical purposes, ten thousand times ten thousand li away.

All of us have dreams that we must give up. I, too, have
had my share. But at least I have been able to live in peace,
the wars I have seen have been seen at my own choosing. I
know that in all probability (although there are times when
I am not so sure) no enemy will ever confiscate my home,
that I will never have to make the choice to flee or stay on.

I felt that I was prying, but I felt also that I must know if
Tommy still was able to dream.

"Yes," he answered. "I still have a dream, and this one will
materialize, I'm sure. When we go back to the mainland I
want to become a rural sociologist. There won't be as much
money in it as in the perfume business! But here on Formosa
I have learned much about my people that I never knew before. I have learned to respect the farmer, to understand his
problems.

"When we go back home we must make good. To make
good we must have a program for the people. There will be
some of us who will slip back into old ways, who will seek
only to get rich quickly, who will forget all the lessons of
these past years. To counterbalance these, there must be many
among us who have not forgotten, who will be trained to
make our government what it has become here.

"We will have only a short time to make good, and all the
world will be watching us. I will go to school for a little while,
to pick up some of the theory that I have never learned. Then
I will become a rural sociologist, perhaps in Fukien near our

95

old estates. I might even become an official in the land reform program."

Then Tommy Hsu's face brightened, his voice became eager as he continued. "Think of the tremendous problems we will have to face: reconstruction, getting a whole new educational program started, setting up agricultural experiment stations, starting an honest land reform program all over China! We have done it all here, but this is a small island. On the mainland our problems will be multiplied a thousand times!"

I have seen Tommy Hsu twice since that day we traveled together over the twisting highways in the Formosan mountains. He is no longer an agricultural inspector at Taichung. Perhaps he would not even realize it himself, but he has taken a tremendous step towards realization of his final dream.

Tommy Hsu volunteered for special duty in the guerrilla islands a few weeks after I left him at Taichung. For the Chinese government wisely decided that the rural reforms of Formosa must be transplanted quickly to the islands, making of them a show case fronting directly upon the enslaved mainland.

Tommy Hsu made the first surveys of Kinmen, Liehyu, the Ta-chen Islands. I have read his reports; they influenced me to visit guerrilla-land. For Tommy Hsu reports more than statistics, he is able to capture the drama of Kinmen, the dreams of farmers and fishermen, can make the successful demonstration of a new seed variety as thrilling as a battle. It is unfortunate that the representatives of the American press who began suddenly to take notice of Kinmen in the fall of 1954 did not read Tommy's reports before making their own inaccurate estimates of the island's area, defenses and significance.

Tommy has never had time to get the "theory" he feels he needs. He has been too busy to go back to school again. But he has been able to capture the feeling, the hopes and the fears of the people who live on the guerrilla islands. He has won the respect of farmers and generals alike. Already there are scores of JCRR projects under way, and a trickle of American money is going into guerrilla-land.

During the late summer of 1954, four American destroyers visited Ta-chen. This was a significant visit indeed. For it was the first indication the people of the islands had that the mighty United States might, just might, extend its interest to their tiny outposts.

And it is not too far-fetched to believe that Tommy Hsu had a little to do with the visit, with the fact that an American admiral stopped briefly at a guerrilla stronghold. His report, as much as anything else, began to focus attention on the island in 1953 and 1954.

But of course again we must admit that Tommy Hsu is not an important person, that he is but one of many, and that a few men with dreams will not be enough. Perhaps so. But the program of which Tommy Hsu is a part is of tremendous importance. It is a program that has never been given attention in the press of America. Yet the successful activities of the Joint Commission on Rural Reconstruction on Formosa and now extended to the guerrilla islands point the way to what can be accomplished in Asia. JCRR may well become a blueprint for Asia's oppressed, might and can be the ultimate defeat of Communism in that part of Asia which has the will to remain free.

The story of JCRR, its accomplishments on Formosa, its methods of operation, is tremendously heartening. Not only has JCRR breathed new life into vast segments of Free China's officialdom, it has proved that Americans and Chinese can work together at little cost to America, yet can with little money spent, accomplish miracles.

And miracles there must be if China is to be freed. It was enslaved as much by the force of ideas as by the force of arms. If it be free again, indeed if the rest of Asia is to remain free, ideas and dreams must play their part. The intelligence experts of CIA, measuring and balancing the fate of Asia in

97

terms of divisions and air squadrons, seem not to understand
that Communism cannot be prevailed over by force of arms
alone.

The JCRR idea, of practical aid at the rice-roots, has worked
wonders on Formosa. *If* it can be transplanted to the mainland, *if* it can also work there, it will have the power of a
hundred divisions. That is why I traveled five hundred miles
on Formosa, seeing what JCRR has done. That is why I spent
as much time studying JCRR operations on the guerrilla islands as I did visiting military installations.

Chapter 3

"You know we are able to do things even the Japanese could never do!" Mr. Yeh exclaimed.

We were sitting in the testing room of a tea factory high in the mountains above Taichung, Tommy Hsu, the manager of the tea factory, and myself. Then Mr. Yeh Won Sui proudly ticked off the accomplishments: tea production in the district increased from 33,000 catties (a cattie is one and a third pounds) under the Japanese to 250,000 catties; a better grade tea than ever before; quicker growth; disease resistant plants.

Mr. Yeh fumbled in his desk drawer when I asked him the reason for the great increase in production.

"This is what did it," he told me as he brought out a dog-eared copy of a booklet on tea production. "This book teaches us how to fertilize, how to cultivate, how to pick the leaves."

The little booklet showed the familiar imprint of the Joint Commission on Rural Reconstruction. It had been jointly written by an American and a Chinese. It was a simply written manual, filled with line drawings and illustrations. It began the story of tea in these words: "Mother China has many children. But unless the children are properly fed and cared for they will not be healthy. Tea plants too must be properly

99

cared for, must be properly nourished if the leaves are to be healthy and of good quality."

"But, Mr. Yeh, the Japanese were among the world's best in tea culture, were they not? How is it that a little book can make so much difference?"

Mr. Yeh replied quickly. "There is one great difference now. The Japanese ordered us. Now we are taught."

Yeh is thirty-five years old, a native Formosan, which means that his family came over from the Fukien mainland two or three hundred years ago. He has spent his life in the tea fields, is now the manager of a big plantation. As we sipped and tested the various brands packaged from his neat rows, we talked of other things that have a bearing on how many leaves can be harvested from the bushes.

"Tell me honestly, Mr. Yeh, as one 'Lao' Fukien to another, how is life in general now as compared to life under the Japanese?"

We spoke in the Foochow dialect so that it was unnecessary for Tommy Hsu to interpret the reply.

"I can answer your question quickly and honestly," Mr. Yeh replied. "As I mentioned before about tea culture, so in all aspects of life under the Japanese we were told what to do, what to study. We had absolutely no freedom. Even up here in the mountains we were always afraid, never knew when our remarks would be overheard, or even when our thoughts might be read. Now we have more freedom than I can ever remember. I can travel to Taichung any day I wish, without special passes. I can manage my tea plants as I wish. I can send my children to school if I wish. I can read many things."

And then because he was an honest man, speaking honestly, Mr. Yeh added, "And I can speak out freely on *almost* all things."

Therein lies the secret of the great success of the rural program of which Tommy Hsu is a part. Men have been lead and taught, rather than ordered. And along with the teaching has come basic freedoms never before enjoyed by the Taiwanese. In its successes and in its methods, JCRR points the way to a program that can be freedom's defense against Communism among the rural people of Asia. While the polished and brilliant Mr. Nehru has *talked* of what must be done for the peasants, the government on Formosa has acted. To date the actions have touched the lives of nearly every farmer on the island.

Consider the problems facing those who work on Formosa. Ten miles west of Mr. Yeh's tea fields the vast aborigine reserve begins. In a wild and tangled mass of Formosan mountains live the nearly quarter of a million aborigines, people of Indonesian stock who came to the island centuries ago. These are the "Indians" of Formosa, with their own language and customs, the people who once upon a time were headhunters. Few of them speak Mandarin, the official language of China. Many of them do speak Japanese, for that language was forced upon them. So the Chinese JCRR inspector who works with the aborigines must speak Japanese.

Within a few miles after one leaves the borders of the aboriginal reserve, one enters the farming lands where the Amoy dialect of China is spoken. These are the people whose ancestors came to Formosa in the seventeenth and eighteenth centuries. Few of these Taiwanese speak Mandarin, so that the Chinese officials who work with them must also know their language.

On the borders of Tommy Hsu's district one finds several of the many Hakka settlements. The Hakkas (Guest Peoples) have come a long way in their torturous migrations. From somewhere in Northern China at the dawn of civilization, they migrated into the mountains along the Fukien-Kwangtung border near the coast of China. Thence many of them joined the migration to Formosa three hundred years ago. Tommy Hsu and the others who work with the Hakkas must speak the distinctive Hakka language.

Further South are the extensive settlements of those who crossed from Kwangtung province. They still speak their native Cantonese.

And so the work on Formosa is a gigantic task of working with minority groups. Tommy Hsu must use Amoy, Hakka, Cantonese and Mandarin in his daily work. The inspectors of JCRR must know English so that they can work with their American advisors. The men who work in the high mountains must know Japanese, in order to reach the aborigine chiefs.

What has the Joint Commission on Rural Reconstruction accomplished and how does it operate? Statistics tell a little of the story. More of the story is seen merely by traveling the highways and the byways. For still more, one must talk to the farmers who have benefited most from the first program in Asia's history that has actually resulted in a better deal for the tiller of the soil.

Farmers can be driven to produce more. That is the method used in Communist countries, and it works up to a point. Farmers can also be led to produce more. Statistics clearly show that Formosa's farmers have produced more, far more even than when managed and driven by the efficient Japanese.

From the 1938 peak production of 1,402,000 tons, rice farmers on Formosa produced over 1,600,000 tons in 1952, and each year the production goes higher. Once forced to import rice, Free China now has several hundred thousand tons to export. From a peak production of 1,770,000 tons, under the Japanese, sweet potato production has increased to over 2,000,000 tons. The production of wheat has tripled over the best year under the Japanese.

In some less important categories production has not as yet reached the peak set by the Japanese in the years before

World War II. But significance lies in the fact that since "take over," when Nationalist China regained Formosa from the Japanese, production of everything has been increasing. This means that the people of Formosa not only have more to eat. They have more than enough to eat, and the surplus can be exported to help in the developing of a balanced economy.

How has this vast increase been accomplished? Could it have been accomplished if the farmers were dissatisfied, if they hated the Nationalist government? Has there been any case in Formosa where farmers, in an act of defiance against their government, have dumped their produce into the river rather than sell it to *their* peoples' government?

Formosa's progress in agriculture has come because of many things: more fertilizer, an excellent pest control program, better and more irrigation, use of new seed varieties. But above all it has come about because of the manner in which these changes have been sold to the Formosan peasant by the men of JCRR, by the manner in which JCRR operates.

The Joint Commission on Rural Reconstruction was created in 1948 during China's darkest hours. The act which established JCRR as far as the U.S. is concerned stated that the Joint Commission "shall be composed of two citizens of the United States to be appointed by the President of the United States and three citizens of China to be appointed by the President of China." JCRR was a last ditch effort to give the peasant of China a break, and as far as the mainland was concerned, it came too late.

The United States contributed to JCRR's failure to get into operation quickly enough to help on the mainland. Many months were required by the Department of State and President Truman before the two American commissioners were even appointed. For this was the beginning of the "wait and see" period during which the Department of State was torn by conflicting advice and, not being able to declare itself on the issues, clambered onto the fence to watch the Communist victory.

On Formosa where JCRR has proved itself successful, its strength lies in its "jointness," in the fact that it is not a program in which Americans tell Chinese what to do but rather one where Chinese and Americans together decide what is best.

In simplest terms, the objectives of JCRR are to increase agricultural production, promote rural welfare and encourage good government. Projects calling for JCRR aid may be submitted by any governmental or private organization on any level. Thus a farmers' association, a city government, all may request that which they believe is needed to better the lot of the people who live in their area.

When a request for a JCRR project is received, American and Chinese experts are sent to see if a problem exists and if the proposed project will solve the problem. Sometimes the experts do not approve the project; sometimes they do, in which case a project proposal is then drafted. Since JCRR moved to Formosa, over three thousand projects have been submitted. The selectiveness of operations is indicated by the fact that only about twenty per cent are approved.

Sponsorship of the approved projects has been in the hands of over 150 organizations. There are Hsien (county governments), city governments, farmers' associations, cooperatives and church groups.

Another aspect of its strength is in its methods of financing. I visited a rural health center, built by JCRR in the city of Tai-yuan. The total cost of the project was $873,000 (Taiwan) of which the city Government of Tai-yuan had provided $800,000 and JCRR the balance. The people who benefit from JCRR help pay for the help they get. The proportion of JCRR money per project becomes progressively less and less as people become more willing, even anxious to help themselves.

JCRR projects are often simple, sometimes peculiar. I have already written of the night-soil disposal project at Taichung. I have mentioned one rural health center, of which there are many. All through the land one sees new compost houses, built from JCRR blueprints; concrete drying areas for rice, taking the place of the old patch of hardened earth outside each farmhouse. In scores of farm homes I saw JCRR posters on the walls; posters telling how to use fertilizer, or which insecticides to use for which pests. I saw new water supplies, new irrigation projects, locally sponsored, locally financed and locally managed and built.

JCRR has literally worked itself into the very fabric of rural life in Formosa. But it must have cost a lot of money, it must require much personnel, the reader may say.

During its five years' operation on Formosa JCRR has cost the American taxpayer less than *one million dollars* in aid funds appropriated by the Congress. The total staff of JCRR includes 260 persons. Of these only thirteen are Americans, including the two presidentially-appointed American Commissioners.

Measured in dollars alone, this investment has paid for itself hundreds of times over each year. With few dollars and fewer men, through JCRR, America has had a part in a miracle of progress on Formosa.

But that miracle would never have occured had not JCRR sponsored, with the whole-hearted support of the Nationalist Government, a far-reaching land reform program on Formosa that won the support of the peasants.

The land reform program was not accomplished overnight, nor without opposition. But the opposition was not ruthlessly liquidated; it is even now still vocal. No man, or few men are public spirited enough to give up the family holdings of generations without a struggle.

The first step in the land reform program was the reduction of rentals charged by Formosa's landlords from an aver-

age of 55 per cent of the annual yield of the principal crop
to a maximum of 37.5 per cent of that crop. All over Formosa
I saw abuilding what the farmers call "37.5 houses"—the better homes made possible by that great reduction in rent. The
reduction of rent has also made it possible to feed families
better, to buy more consumer goods and thus to strengthen
the whole economy.

I talked to farmer Li Tai Ho who lives off the coastal highway north of Taichung. Farmer Li is now building a new
"37.5 house." What, in terms of dollars and bushels did the
reduction of rental mean to him? Li Tai Ho farms one hectare of rice paddy, producing about 2700 pounds of rice from
his two annual harvests. Before rent reduction, he paid 1500
pounds of rice in rental. Now he pays slightly over one thousand pounds a year. He has an extra five hundred pounds to
sell to whomever he pleases, for the best price he can get.
With that extra income he can build his new home, buy fertilizer and food, can visit the nearest JCRR Public Health
center and buy at cut rates the treatment and drugs he or a
member of his family might need in time of illness.

The next step in land reform was the sale of public land,
making up over 20 per cent of all the arable land on the island. To date, 50,000 hectares of this land has been sold to
96,900 former tenants and farm laborers. The price of the
land is fixed at 2.5 times the value of its annual main crop,
and the buyer pays in ten years.

The third step was most difficult of all, for it involved
150,000 hectares (one hectare equals 2.47 acres) of land held
by landlords. JCRR financed the program of re-surveying
and classifying that was necessary before the program could
be fairly and impartially implemented. To date 240,000 former tenants have taken advantage of this third step in Formosa's land reform program, and are now buying land on
long terms. These successive steps have reduced farm tenancy on the island to about twenty per cent.

I visited many men who were buying their lands, men like Mr. Li Jen Chen (and I noticed that the Chinese officials with me addressed him as *Mister.*)

"My family came here from Fukien 200 years ago," he told me. "In all that time no member of the family ever owned land. Now for the first time we are buying our own land."

And then he proudly informed me that he was paying twice the required amount each year because he wanted to own the land in five years, instead of ten. Li Jen Chen also has a fine old Chinese farmhouse of his own. It was not necessary for him to do so, but the landlord for whom Li was once a tenant *gave* him the house.

Like many Americans I am buying a home "on time." Mine is a twenty year mortgage, and it still has many years to run. I can imagine how glorious will be the day when the mortgage is paid, when the house is mine, when no more will hundreds of dollars go into interest. How much more thrilling it must be for the Li's of Formosa, whose ancestors never knew the pride of ownership, to at last own a farm, to have the privilege of using the land as they wish it used and not in the way a landlord orders it used!

As I stated earlier, there are difficulties in connection with land reform. The Nationalist Government admitted that during 1951 alone there were 13,303 cases of dispute and litigation. Some landlords object strenuously to selling their ancient holdings. Some tenants argue about price and details.

How great a difference there is in Formosa and mainland China in the manner of settling these disputes! How many of the 13,303 disputants on Formosa were led through the streets for execution? None. How many peoples' courts conducted trials of landlords? None.

In the foothills east of Taichung I noticed a fine new factory. Tommy Hsu informed me that it had been recently built by a dispossessed landlord. He had owned considerable land in the area and had been forced to sell all but a couple of acres. He put the money from his land into building a small factory to process tung oil.

Just 120 miles across the straits of Formosa I know of another landlord who lost his land. He was not much of a landlord at that. He owned nine acres of land near Futsing. Some of it was good rice land, some of it was waste land. But he was definitely classified as a landlord. It was not too difficult for the Communists to find someone to prefer charges against him. If no injustice has been committed by a landlord, it is a simple matter to force someone to invent some. Or if that fails, it is possible to go back one or more generations. Perhaps the father or grandfather committed a sin against the people.

And so the Futsing landlord was arrested, was hauled through the streets, was tried in a peoples' court. Men and women he did not even know came forward to bear witness against him. He was harangued and beaten, his family shamed and at last he was mercifully dragged through the streets to the Futsing hillside where he and his fellow "criminals" were executed.

It is a strange commentary upon the American press that so much has been written about the wonderful land reform of Communist China and so little about what has taken place on Formosa. In Fukien Province, just across the straits from Formosa, 400,000 landlords have been dispossessed. None has been paid for the land taken. Approximately 52,000 have been executed, thousands more are in prison, other thousands have fled to the hills.

On the island of Formosa not one landlord has been executed. No person has ever been imprisoned because he was unfortunate enough to have owned land.

The thousands of ex-Communist prisoners of war who renounced Red China at the tents of Panmunjom and who now have returned to Formosa marvel at what they have seen.

Over and over they say, "Why if the people on the mainland knew how you handled land reform there would be a revolution!" Unfortunately the people there do not know. They do not even know about it here in America.

I have seen every phase of the land reform program on Formosa. At Tai-yuan I visited the land office where the immense job of classifying land holdings, of checking the records of each plot is handled. I have watched surveyors of the land office in the field checking the lines of plots so that the records may be correct. I stopped once in south Formosa to talk to a farmer who worked his fields while nearby a surveying crew was checking his lines.

"In the old days," he remarked, "if any well dressed person stopped near my farm I would be afraid. More than likely it would be a tax collector, forcing me to pay more taxes or taxes I had already paid." And then pointing to the surveyors he continued, "now things are different. If a car or truck stops along the highway I am no longer afraid. It may be men from the land office, or it may be some agricultural people from JCRR to help me."

Yes, JCRR must be given a great deal of credit for the success of Formosa's land reform. It was JCRR money which financed the tremendous job of resurveying and classifying hundreds of thousands of acres. JCRR experts helped establish the land offices, guided the program from beginning to end.

Although it is only one hundred miles across to the mainland, it is difficult for the news of Formosa's new deal to get across. The news can spread in small measure through leaflets dropped by Nationalist planes. But there are few who dare to read, fewer still who dare to listen to Radio Free China.

If JCRR's program is to be known, it must move closer to the mainland, and that is just what it is doing.

I spent three days on Kinmen traveling with Bill Fippen, one of JCRR's two American commissioners. Bill is a presidential appointee, remember. There is no need for him to endanger himself, to take the chance that one always takes in visiting the offshore islands. But Bill Fippen is typical of most of the JCRR staff, American and Chinese. They go where they are needed, regardless of discomfort and danger.

JCRR's program on the offshore islands only began in 1953, after help had been requested by the commanding general on Kinmen, after Tommy Hsu had gone over and made a survey of needs and possibilities. And of those possibilities Tommy Hsu wrote in his report: "The sea is the meeting ground of fishermen from these islands and those from the Communist mainland. The fishermen from the mainland will hear of what we are doing on Kinmen, will take the news home with them. From Kinmen, soon the news of JCRR will spread up and down the coast."

So I traveled over Kinmen's dusty roads with Commissioner Bill Fippen and two American-educated agricultural specialists. With them I attended farmers' meetings, visited experimental plots and the Berkshire boar who has become a citizen of great importance on the island.

At the farmers' meetings the farmers were slow to speak up. Most could not speak Mandarin, nearly all were puzzled and a little bit frightened. Never before had anyone taken an interest in their problems. Somewhere there must be a catch. Like the mountaineer of Tennessee, the farmer of China is extremely suspicious of government in any form.

But slowly I saw the attitude relax, change from suspicion to interest and finally to enthusiasm. On Kinmen even more than on Formosa, JCRR must *lead* men to a better life.

Suspicions and superstitions must be overcome. Before farmers of a whole area will plant a new seed variety or use a new fertilizer, some one or two must be found who will agree to allow their farms to be used as experimental plots. Before all the farmers will use the Berkshire boar, one or two must be found to take the first step.

Bill Fippen and his crew were on Kinmen for over a week, and by week's end I could sense and see the change. The last two days the people started coming to JCRR. All through the days and until late at night there were delegations calling upon Bill at our guest house headquarters. Representatives from a fishing village came, asking if JCRR could assist in building a cold storage plant. From the northern end of the island came a deputation asking for help with their peanut crop; assistance was requested a score of times in getting more water.

But the most exciting caller for me was one who came a few hours before the JCRR men were to leave for Formosa. A young man came hesitantly into the Guest House, asking for the "men who help the farmers." Having learned during my days on Kinmen to spot guerrillas from my home section of Fukien by the numbers on their insignia, I saw at once that this man belonged to the Foochow-speaking guerrilla units in training on the island. Quickly we established our identities. He was from Lungtien and had attended a school my father had established. Later in life, he had belonged to a church my father built.

It was a thrilling experience for me to act as interpreter on that occasion. Captain Song had walked ten miles over the rugged Kinmen mountains to meet the JCRR people. He had an unusual problem, and I was able to see JCRR go into operation to solve that problem.

Captain Song is the leader of a group of guerrillas from the Lungtien Peninsula and Haitang Island. Two hundred dependents had been moved out of Communist territory and had arrived on Kinmen. Seventy-five families in all, they had left everything behind. There were no tools, no seeds, nothing. The guerrilla command had settled the refugees on barren land; had helped with simple housing; but unless the families could begin to farm again, they would be living on handouts.

One by one Captain Song detailed the simple needs: a certain number of hoes and rakes and spades; only a few ploughs, for these would be used as community tools. Two yoke of oxen only, for these too must serve the whole colony; cabbage seed, enough for each family to begin a garden plot; rice, sweet potatoes to be communally cultivated until the colony was established.

Slowly I saw the shape of new life being formed for people who had nothing but the will and courage to escape from enslavement. In the case of Captain Song's guerrillas, JCRR will make an exception. It will pay all the costs, will provide all the tools and seed, the oxen, a few chickens and ducks, until the colony has established itself.

JCRR's help to Song's guerrillas is simple as are all JCRR projects in guerrilla-land. For all the Ta-chen islands, the most northerly Nationalist holdings, JCRR had appropriated just 370,000 Formosan dollars. This is the equivalent of less than $15,000. The money is little, the projects simple. Most costly, and taking a third of the total budget, is a project to train technical personnel from among the civilians and the guerrillas. For JCRR never forgets that people must be trained to help themselves. There will be agricultural and health trainees, new school teachers. A tiny hospital for civilians will be built. All the houses will be sprayed with DDT, handled by specially trained guerrilla spraying teams; $1500 worth of drugs will be supplied; $275 will be spent on seeds and new farm implements.

And Tommy Hsu will shuttle from Ta-chen to Kinmen to Matsu and back to the security of Formosa, planning, coordinating, helping the people of the guerrilla islands to help themselves.

Tommy's original task was to survey problems and possibilities on Kinmen, a natural assignment since his native place lay less than fifty miles distant on the coast. He knew the local dialect and local problems well. But after JCRR realized the potential on the islands, it decided that a full-time man was needed. The job was offered Hsu, and he immediately accepted, even though it meant separation from his family. Mrs. Hsu accepted the new arrangements gracefully and is now also doing her part by working in a chemical factory on Formosa.

Each day scores of fishermen put out from all the islands, to meet and visit in that only contact that is allowed the people of divided China. For it is difficult to divide the sea into Communist and Nationalist fishing grounds. As Tommy Hsu said, "The sea is the meeting ground." And from the meeting ground the news of China's new deal is spreading out up and down the coast of China from Shanghai to Hong Kong.

Brief engagements these be, between a fisherman out of Amoy, Foochow or Wenchow and fishermen out of Matsu, Ta-chen or Kinmen. But brief as the engagements may be, they are far more important in affecting the future than is a raid on Kinmen by forty Communists. The raiders kill a few Nationalists, take one prisoner, and their feat is headlined in American newspapers. "Communists strike at Chiang Islands. Nationalist Positions Imperiled," the headlines shout. But not yet has everyone understood that in the war between Free and Enslaved China there are weapons equal in importance to guns. There are engagements between fishermen of more importance than engagements between ships and planes.

Free China's new deal for its peasants is a tremendously important part of the total war which I have attempted to describe. As far as Kinmen and the rest of guerrilla-land are concerned, it may yet fail as an effective weapon, brought into action too late, its effectiveness lessened because the Free World has had insufficient interest to make available also the military weapons in conjunction with which it must be used.

The total JCRR budget for all guerrilla-land totals the equivalent of $125,000 U.S. to date. The projects are simple, just as the JCRR projects for Formosa are simple: $14,000 (New Taiwan) for the purchase of Kankrej bulls and Berkshire boar for Kinmen; $51,200 (NT) for the repair of hog shelters; $226,188 (NT) for the ground work necessary for the beginning of land reform on Kinmen; $13,325 (NT) for the training of midwives on Kinmen; $48,350 (NT) for DDT spraying of all households on the Ta-chen Islands; $134,500 (NT) for building a hospital ward for the Ta-chen Islands.

The U.S. dollar cost of these JCRR projects can be approximated by dividing each project figure by twenty-five. The cost to the United States taxpayer is from twenty-five to ninety per cent less than the total dollar figure. For remember that, over-all, Free China's government, national and local, pays the major cost of JCRR.

When I consider the tiny amount JCRR has allocated for guerrilla-land, I think inevitably of Magistrate Chang Chow's remark about Kinmen's being the West Berlin of Asia. When the chips were down, the United States spent hundreds of millions of dollars in an airlift to keep the people of West Berlin alive. And even though the forces of the Free World within Berlin could not have held out for more than an hour or so had they been attacked, we made it plain that an attack would be resisted to the limit of our vast strength. Of course no attack came, and, confronted with strength, the Communists lifted the blockade.

Guerrilla-land's American "lift" has included no fighting men, no strong policy statement, only the $125,000 in JCRR assistance. It may be, probably will be, too little. But I believe JCRR has been enough to make Formosa very difficult to conquer. The men who boast proudly that "we can do things even the Japanese could not do" have a determination and strength that will stand firm against everything but over-whelming attack. For JCRR is not the only great accomplishment on Formosa. Free China's strength lies also in the accomplishments of its engineers, its soldiers and generals on Formosa, in its painful but demonstrable growth in constitutional government.

Chapter 4

SOUTH of Taichung a wide river flows westward from the towering jungle mountain mass of Formosa, emptying into the South China Sea. Called the Cho Shiu, it has been a troublesome river, overflowing vast areas, creating down through the years a broad expanse of gravel beds. The Japanese tried hard to throw a bridge across the river. From an economic standpoint the project was important, for in wet weather nothing could cross. In order to move goods and people from north to south, a long detour through the mountains was used many months of the year. Militarily, too, the necessity of a bridge across the river was obvious.

Yet, try as they would, the Japanese during their time on Formosa could not bridge the river. The remarkable thing is that what they could not accomplish, David Hung, a Chinese engineer, graduate of an American university and before that of the Anglo-Chinese college in Foochow where my father and my sister once taught, was able to do.

David Hung and the Silo bridge are almost synonymous on Formosa. The bridge is an engineering feat, the longest highway bridge in Asia. It has been of tremendous value in linking North and South Formosa, enabling more complete economic development of the fertile south, making it possible to move military convoys quickly to points of attack. It is a toll bridge, and on the basis of use during its first year of operation David Hung's bridge will be paid for in thirty-seven years.

But the real significance of David Hung's bridge lies not in the fact that it provides all-weather connection between north Formosa and the south, nor in the fact that it will be paid for even before schedule. The bridge is a tremendous psychological victory for the Chinese.

For here was a project the efficient Japanese could not complete! What the Japanese could not do, Chinese did, and with a minimum of outside help. The completion of the Silo Bridge gave confidence to people who have had to feel inferior to much of the rest of the world. It gave them faith in themselves, made it possible to say, as I heard over and over again, "Why we can do things, we have done things, even the Japanese could never do." It is said, not entirely as a boast but also in a childlike wonderment.

But man cannot live by bread alone. It is not enough to build bridges that others failed to build, or to raise more tea, or rice, or pineapples per hectare. Without freedom and democracy, land for the landless, food for empty stomachs even, is not enough. Chiang Kai Shek can bridge the Straits of Formosa but if he rules with tyranny, without basic democracy, it will not make his government great, nor will his people fight for that government.

Or at least these are things we Americans believe. We measure other countries by the degree of "democracy" achieved by their governments, by the amount of freedom allowed the people. There is cause for debate on this criterion for judging those who are to benefit from our largesse. Too much democracy and "freedom," taken by systems not fully prepared to digest it, may generate considerable painful gas. Peoples so afflicted may respond to the medications offered by Communism just as quickly and with just as serious results as in the case of those who buy the cure in order to fill their stomachs and better clothe their bodies. Too much democracy there can be, too much freedom for unprepared peoples can cause devastating results.

But still even the most enthusiastic supporter of the Generalissimo must admit there were strange goings on during the Nationalists' last days on the mainland. There was corruption in high places, there was no representative government, there was still much government by war-lord fiat. If Free China is to combat Communism on equal footing, it must have fair and efficient government, must provide more freedom and democratic government than it ever did on the mainland.

How does Nationalist China rate today? Has its government developed efficiency? Is there any degree of representative or constitutional government? Or putting it in more vital rice-root terms, are the people living under the rule of Nationalist China getting a fair deal?

At the outset let us admit that there is inefficiency and evil, there is even some corruption. But for those who are willing to seek, to compare, to study Free China in the light of past history and the inexorable demands of the present, there is progress and hope, a stability and goodness of purpose in government which China has never seen before.

I have seen China at her worst and at her best. As a child, I lived in the China of the war lords; then I saw Chiang's revolution, his sweep northward to power. I saw the Japanese strike and the first months of gallant defense. I saw China, free and Japanese-occupied, during the darkest days of World War II when the land had already suffered from six years of struggle, when the very warp and woof of Chinese family life had begun to crack through separation of hundreds of thousands of families.

I saw good men turn to the enemy because they could see no other path to take. I saw fence sitters jump from side to side as the war news changed. And I also saw a hard core of China's best who never considered disloyalty.

I was in Shanghai at various times during 1946, 1947 and 1948. These were China's saddest days; millions of people who had expected peace found only more war, more insecurity, more heart breaking separations ahead. Many were those who went to the other side, some because of idealism and conviction, more because they were too tired to run any further and had no place to hide.

As I look back over my own lifetime in China and remember the different Chinas I saw, I set up certain criteria for measuring reasonable progress in democracy. The first is the behavior of soldiers. As a child and as an adult thieving and misbehaving soldiers were a common sight. The second is the behavior of public servants. Brutality and corruption were the rule rather than the exception. The third is in the election of officials. I never saw an election on the mainland.

To my mind the progress of Free China can be plotted along these three points. For therein lies the oppression of people, without recourse, without the right to speak out freely, to take matters to higher authorities, to fight back if they value their heads. I do not mean to indict all Chinese officials and generals. Rather I set these down as a general pattern of government in China over decades and centuries.

To return to our first criterion, how are the soldiers of Nationalist China behaving today? During the fall of 1953 I drove south from Taipei to Taichung. The main highway of Formosa connects these cities, then going on south across the Silo bridge, it extends to the island's southernmost tip. All along the main road, even on the miles of byroads I traveled in visiting farmers and JCRR projects, I saw soldiers. Sometimes there would be three or four, sometimes a company, occasionally major elements of a complete division on one of the ceaseless training maneuvers. One fact struck me with tremendous impact: not once in five days of traveling did I see a Nationalist soldier attempting to hitch a ride. Not once did I see a truck, or bus, or private car stopped by soldiers. Next I realized something else: all the soldiers I saw were doing something. Sometimes a small crew would be stringing new phone lines; others were working on new barracks; those I saw in the villages and cities were not lounging about. I watched men stop briefly to buy some little article in a village store—and they paid for their purchases. At a tiny seaside restaurant Tommy Hsu and I stopped to enjoy fresh shrimps. Three officers entered, scanned the menu carefully, grumbled about high prices, ordered and paid like any other citizens.

"Do you ever have any trouble with the soldiers?" I asked the proprietor.

He was surprised at my question and seemed unable to come up with a ready answer. I amplified my question, "Do they pay for their food; are they well behaved?"

"Why of course," he answered. "They are just like any other people. Some complain about my food; some like it; most of them think I charge too much. You know they do not make much money."

My host's answer interested me. I had just read parts of a new book, had read a number of rave reviews about the book. Written by Vern Sneider and called *A Pail of Oysters,* the book took some pretty terrific swipes at Free China's government and particularly at the military. Mr. Sneider had, I knew, spent several weeks on Formosa before completing his book. It was fiction, to be sure, but surely no American writer would completely falsify, even in a novel!

And so I began everywhere to ask about the conduct of Chinese soldiers. I watched them, officers and enlisted men. Later on Kinmen and the other guerrilla islands I had opportunity to talk to the soldiers themselves, literally hundreds of them.

At a village south of Taichung, near the northern end of the Silo Bridge, I attended a farmers' association meeting.

Afterwards Tommy Hsu and I walked to the house of farmer Lin Jen Ching (a fair share of all the people on Formosa are named Lin!). We enjoyed fresh watermelon and we talked of many things.

"Tell me Mr. Lin," I said, "about the soldiers. I saw a good many in the village putting up new telephone lines."

Tommy Hsu thought it necessary to add his bit. "You can tell Mr. Caldwell anything without fear," he told Mr. Lin.

Mr. Lin went into quite a harangue about soldiers. It seems there had been a bad accident that morning. A military truck had run into a bus full of girls bound for work in a factory. A number of the village girls had been injured. Tommy and I had passed the place of the accident earlier in the day, had seen the bus overturned in a rice field.

"These soldiers drive much too fast," Mr. Lin complained. "Our highways here are narrow. We have too many accidents."

Then he added a significant observation. "Later today a committee from the village is going to call on the general. We are going to tell him that this fast driving must stop."

In my years on the mainland of China it was rare indeed that a committee of citizens called upon a general. And certainly they did not call to criticize or demand. Or if they did so, it was at considerable personal risk.

Having disposed of the problem of fast-driving soldiers, Mr. Lin continued.

"Actually the soldiers are our friends now," he said. "They are well behaved; if they need things, they buy. Why they will not even take a watermelon from the field without paying for it. But it was not always so. Three or four years ago the soldiers were pretty bad. They stole from us; we had trouble all the time."

Everywhere I went I found that common people noted a

significant change in the actions of soldiers beginning about 1951. Everywhere I heard the statement, "Now they are our friends." Everywhere I found that the incidence of rape, of arguments between soldiers and civilians resulting in fighting, was extremely rare.

The Chinese GI is kept very busy. When not working or maneuvering, he studies. Literacy among the rank and file is now 94 per cent. He has no time off, has no chance to go to towns and cities and get in trouble. He is well fed, well clothed, and the temptation to steal has been removed. Above all he has a self-respect he never had before. He knows that he will be paid what little he is due regularly. He knows he will have reasonable medical attention when ill. Certainly his life is hard, but he knows that he is as well off as most of the civilian population. He has learned to work with the civilian population, to respect its rights.

On this score Nationalist China has gone a long, long way indeed, Mr. Vern Sneider and his *A Pail of Oysters* to the contrary notwithstanding.

As Tommy Hsu and I drove away from Mr. Lin's house, I expressed considerable interest in the fact that Lin and his fellow villagers dared to complain to the general. Tommy told me that this is quite a common occurrence now, that it extends also to relations between the civilian population and the police.

Each month there is a people's police meeting, where the local citizens have opportunity to complain to the police about actions of members of the force. And at this point let me note a significant fact: under Japanese rule the police had vast powers, arresting thousands of people, trying and punishing in police courts without benefit of counsel, without any chance of review by higher court or authority. In 1938 for instance, Japanese Police handled 174,026 cases, levying fines, prison terms and brutal corporal punishment as they saw fit.

The Nationalist government has gradually diminished the control of the police, has removed literally scores of police regulations. During the past six years cases handled directly by the police have been as low as 15,000 and never higher than 59,000. Among these cases, it may be added, there were many transferred to regular courts.

It must be remembered that Formosa is not at peace. The Nationalist government lives always under the threat of military action, must always be alert to fifth column action. There have been arrests, executions, too. According to law any person endangering the safety of the nation may be sentenced to death or imprisonment for not less than ten years. The government has not been lenient on this score.

But there is absolutely no evidence of any reign of terror on Formosa. Four years ago the government ruled that "in making arrests, security officials must show their identification certificates together with the warrant issued by a responsible security organ." In 1951 it was further decreed that "all suspects must be provided with counsel."

As Formosa's military strength has increased, security regulations have been relaxed. There is still some spot censoring of mail, entirely confined to persons who are suspected of leftist leanings, who are known to be in communication with persons on the mainland. Travel is free and unrestricted all over the island. Persons must have identity cards and when visiting in another city, must make known to police where they are staying, where they are from. Yet, are these unreasonable regulations for a nation at war? And surely now we must understand that Nationalist China is at war with Communist China just one hundred miles away.

The Nationalist Government does not run a police state. The very fact that the people to whom I talked were willing freely and openly to answer my questions should be an indication that people *feel* free. There is more and more freedom of the press, even vigorous criticism of government actions. For instance when a Communist plane flew over Formosa in September of 1954, the press vigorously criticized the government and the Chinese air force for not shooting it down.

But it must be admitted that there is still far too much unnecessary red tape, for Chinese and foreigner alike. Partly the red tape is indicative of lingering bureaucratic inefficiency; partly it is because minor officials still operate and think in terms of 1949 and 1950 when security was so important, when a Communist invasion was expected at any moment.

Unnecessary red tape is especially noticeable in connection with the aborigine country. The Nationalists have not wanted to have the trouble with tribes people that the Japanese had. They have been careful to see that smart Chinese operators did not get into the mountain reservations to exploit the tribesmen. They have feared that dissident elements, underground radio stations, sabotage teams might hide out in the vast central mountain system. Accordingly they made it difficult indeed for any person to enter aborigine country. Special passes of a dozen varieties were necessary. But the tribes people have proved themselves loyal; general conditions are such that it would be difficult for enemy agents to operate in the mountains undetected. Yet the passes are still necessary, the special check-points are still in operation.

For Americans who want to hunt, or to get into the magnificent mountain country on camping and hiking trips, the regulations are a cause of friction and continual complaint.

One Sunday I went into the aborigine preserve at Ulai, just a couple of hours drive from Taipei. This is the nearest concentration of tribes people, rather civilized to be sure. There is magnificent mountain scenery, places for picnics, and the tribes girls give regular dances for the tourists. But even at Ulai there are check-points; one must stop, haul out his passport, have all the information taken down. It is stupid and unnecessary, a lingering bit of inefficiency that should, for the sake of good public relations, be removed.

But do the people have any voice in their government, I have been asked over and over. Is it not true that Nationalist China is a dictatorship, ruling by order and fiat? It will come as quite a surprise to know that Free China is governed under a Constitution drafted by a celebrated American lawyer. Dean Pound of the Harvard Law School is responsible for China's Constitution. It was adopted in 1948 before Chiang's collapse. It has been implemented, step by step, on Formosa.

Representative, constitutional government in Free China begins at the rice-roots. Each township elects a township assembly and a township chief. All actions of the township assembly are binding. Everyone, male and female, Taiwanese, mainlander and aborigine has the right to vote. Nearly always there are multiple choices for the voters. In a check of 76 townships, with a total of 579 assemblymen, it was found that there were never less than two candidates and in several cases as many as five standing for election. Who wins out in the elections? Do the rich classes and the Kuomintang control all offices?

A check of the same 579 assemblymen reveal these figures: 206 (36%) were non-farmers, business and professional people; 42 (7%) were landlords; 222 were land-operators; and 109 (19%) were tenants.

Party politics play little part in rice-roots government. In fact there is almost a complete absence of party thinking. Candidates normally offer themselves as individuals, are elected on the basis of personal popularity and appeal. The typical voter unfortunately still does not vote on issues but rather on the basis of popularity. But vote he does, averaging about 80 per cent for every election, regardless whether it be for village assemblyman or for the mayor of a large city.

Constitutional government has been implemented slowly,

and it has a considerable distance to go. The citizens of Hualien and Taitung on Formosa's east coast elected county councils in the summer of 1950. Mayors and magistrates were elected in the fall of the same year. County and city elections have been gradually extended to all parts of the island.

A provincial assembly of fifty-five members is elected by the county and city councils. Of course this is not democracy as we know it where senators and electors are selected by the people directly. But for those who wish to criticize it might be wise to look back at the time when United States senators were not elected by direct vote either.

Certainly democracy has a long way to go yet. There is still but one important party, the Kuomintang. But KMT candidates sometimes have hard sledding. In mayoralty elections for two of Formosa's largest cities, Taipei and Taichung, KMT candidates were decisively defeated. The Taichung case was especially interesting to me. The KMT candidate was much the better qualified man. But unfortunately some of his election workers became a little too enthusiastic. They enlisted the help of the police. There were no strong arm methods whatsoever. Policemen just "suggested" that the KMT man would make a mighty good mayor. But the people were not interested in receiving suggestions! They decisively defeated the KMT candidate.

The growth of constitutional government has had an interesting effect upon the racial animosities that have been a part of Formosan life. The aborigine tribes have never gotten along any better with each other than with outsiders. But during recent elections in aborigine areas strange things have happened. An Atayal tribesman was elected to a seat on the Nanton County People's Council by the overwhelming vote of the Bunan tribe. Also a large proportion of Atayal tribesmen supported a Bunan tribesman in an unsuccessful bid for township chief of Jenai. Thus old tribal jealousies are slowly disappearing—an unexpected by-product of free elections.

Certainly representative government has been established in Free China. It has weaknesses which are still to be corrected. The absence of a true party system is regrettable. But no nation can have party government until the electorate is educated to vote on issues rather than personalities. It can also be argued that the KMT sometimes negates the results of elections by appointing civil servants to "assist" an elected official. Sometimes the assistance turns into control of the activities of the office.

Leadership still too often centers in prominent families, although more and more tenants and poor people are being elected. There are more women candidates for office in each election. In many areas the decrease of landlords in leading positions is more apparent than real. For although fewer landlords hold positions they still exercise indirect control simply because they are by tradition the leaders, and tradition dies hard in China.

Free China's progress on Formosa whether it be in agriculture or government, must always be judged in contrast with conditions under the efficient Japanese government. Under the Japs there were elections too, but only *Japanese citizens* could vote. On the rice-roots level, in the township councils, one half of the membership was *appointed* by the Japanese government. The township chief was also appointed. The assembly had only advisory powers while now it actually operates the township; its actions are binding.

But it is among the aborigines that the difference between Japanese and Nationalist Chinese methods is most noticeable. The Japanese controlled the tribes people entirely through the police. There was no civil government. The Japanese would not allow tribes people to leave their reservations. The Nationalists encourage them to do so. The hard kernel of tribal isolation and rivalry has been cracked by the opportunity of self-government. The aborigines not only have political rights at the rice-roots; they take part in provincial and county governments.

I saw the difference dramatically highlighted one day. An aborigine woman, dressed in tribal clothes, unconcernedly boarded an airplane on the east coast for a shopping trip to Taipei. Certainly, she had her identity card, picture and all. But she had the right to leave the reservation, the right to buy a ticket for Taipei, the right to spend her money there.

The treatment of the aborigines is indeed a far cry from that accorded them by the Japanese. They are governed now more truly in the spirit of Magistrate Wu Feng than at any time in the memory of the mountain peoples.

It might be interesting to compare the Nationalist treatment of this minority group with our treatment of the American Indian. As I visited the tribes people in the mountains near Sun-Moon Lake, I thought particularly of my own state of Tennessee, of the activities of Andrew Jackson, of the "Trail of Tears" over which thousands of Cherokee Indians were driven, taken forcefully and in violation of solemn treaty and deported to a far away land.

But are the people happy? Are they content? Will they support their government? Over and over again I asked people how they felt, tried to ascertain if psychological factors complement what one sees on Formosa. For there is an appearance of stability everywhere. I saw one beggar during all my days on Formosa where I saw hundreds in Korea and scores in Japan. There is little evidence of starvation anywhere. There are many poor—average annual individual income after taxes is about sixty-five dollars a year. But there are no rich either. Everyone lives simply, because there must be austerity in a nation that is at war and which may be at war for years ahead.

It would be foolish to say that all the people on Formosa are happy. There are many Taiwanese who still remember the misgovernment of early liberation days. There is resentment sometimes even over the good things that have come to the people. Schools are better than ever before, with greater opportunity for an education. But I heard people complain because their children must study an "outside" language. Mandarin, the official language of China, is just as much an outside language to many Formosans as was the Japanese language they were forced to study for fifty years.

City and village people sometimes complain because they do not get as much attention as country people. Country people too have their complaints. I sat in a small apothecary shop in a central Formosan village and listened to the vigorously voiced complaints of the proprietor. He was upset about land reform. Because of some technicality he could not buy the plot of land he wanted. He did not like it at all. But his greatest complaint was about the village water supply.

"The authorities have not done right," he almost shouted. "They have been talking about new wells, new this-and-that for a year, and yet they have done nothing." And then pointing at a sluggish stream nearby he said, "That's where we have to get our water and its full of all kinds of germs!"

Two Chinese soldiers, an enlisted man and an officer were resting in the shade of a banana tree nearby. They were listening to our conversation. As nearly all Chinese will, they had even entered in. They laughed at the vehemence of the old medicine man.

But they laughed, the soldier who receives a salary of eighty cents a month, the captain whose salary is six dollars a month. And when they resumed their tasks it would not be to report an old Chinaman because of criticisms of the government.

The millenium has not been reached in Free China, has

not even been approached. But there is bright promise in what has been accomplished. There is justifiable pride on the part of men and women who have risen from defeat and retreat, to work and build again. Nowhere in Asia does the rice grow greener.

Chapter 5

GRANTED that the soldiers are well behaved, the people have rights they never before enjoyed, what of Free China's top leadership? It too, must be good, if there is to be any chance for the mainland to become free. The mainland was lost in part because there were so many generals who were corrupt, so many other high officials with greedy hands. In my home province of Fukien I saw the Nationalist government at its worst, saw Governor Chen Yi and his henchmen milk the province dry.

Was Chen Yi dismissed? No, as was so often the case, he was promoted! Generalissimo Chiang Kai Shek made him Formosa's first governor at the end of World War II. And the exploitation of the island that took place under Chen Yi has left scars among the native Taiwanese that will require a generation to erase.

If Free China is to remain strong there must be no more Chen Yi's. Too often in the past Chiang Kai Shek has trusted old friends too much, has been so blinded by personal loyalty that he could not see their incompetence and corruption. But most of these old cronies are gone. Some, like Chen Yi, have been executed. Others stayed on under the Communists. Some have been kicked "upstairs" and are not in positions of influence and power.

131

One night I talked of these past failures, of future hopes, with a group of Chinese on Kinmen. Chang Chow, a retired major general, his deputy magistrate, Mr. Fang, a colonel invalided out of the army with a bad wound, talked freely of past incompetence and failures. Dr. Ma, an agricultural expert, graduate of Iowa State College, was reciting the criteria on which promotion to general officer ranks in the Chinese army is now based. Chang Chow and Fang agreed with Ma's statement that a general in Free China's armies must have definite qualifications now if he is to rise to a command position. The qualifications necessary are stringent indeed, a far cry from the old mainland days when there were almost as many generals as privates. If a man is to attain a command position in Chiang's armies of today, he must have these qualifications:

1. He must be a graduate of a regular military academy— no more courtesy generals.
2. He must have had actual combat command experience, either against the Japanese or the Communists.
3. He should have studied and traveled abroad, either to the United States or at least to Japan.
4. He must have had teaching experience in a military academy.
5. He must have graduated from Free China's Staff and Command School on Formosa.
6. His record at the Staff and Command School must be excellent.

Admiral Tang, deputy commander of Kinmen, who also sat with us that night, added, that as far as the Chinese navy was concerned, a commanding officer must have had at least three years of sea duty (it might be noted here that it was not too many years ago that the admiral of the Chinese navy was a general).

If Free China is to give a good account of itself, its top military and civil leaders must be better qualified than in the past. I would not dare say that all China's leaders are well qualified today. I do know that the qualifications listed above seem to be followed rather closely. The commanding general in the lonely and exposed Ta-chen Islands is a graduate of Fort Leavenworth. I have talked to men like Chen Yi Ming, chief of all continental operations; Hu Lien on Kinmen; Li Yeoung Seoung, my old friend from World War II days in Fukien, now a lieutenant general. I have met and traveled with division commanders all through the guerrilla islands. All of the men I have met are alert, well educated, experienced, with a full knowledge of the enemy and the difficulties of defeating him.

But I have two favorite generals, and I think that in their stories, in their viewpoints, lies the secret of Free China's top echelon strength today.

Last year I was in New York just prior to a trip to Formosa.

"When you get to Formosa look up General Chow Mai Yü. She is quite a person." Isabel Stewart, for years Dean of Nursing at Columbia Teachers' College, world known author in the field of nursing, was speaking.

"You said 'she,' didn't you?" I asked, somewhat amazed; for I had never heard of a lady general in the Chinese Army.

Miss Stewart then told me something about the Lady General of Chiang's army, a woman well known in American and European nursing circles.

But when I arrived in Taipei and requested the Government Spokesman's Office to arrange an appointment with General Chow, I found that she was unknown to the personnel. As I was to find out, this is a part of the modest General's personality. At home in Formosa, she prefers to stay out of the limelight, devoting all her energies to the job of training nurses, technicians and aid men for Free China's armies.

I was finally able to locate General Chow in her "afternoon" office in the sprawling combined services hospital in downtown Taipei.

133

Chow Mai Yü is a small, vigorous woman in her early forties, wearing her uniform and stars with dignity, speaking colloquial English perfectly. During the mornings she teaches in the national defense center where she is director of nursing and where her students intern before becoming lieutenants in Chiang's army.

The Lady General is so modest it is difficult to draw her out. Slowly, as we talked in her office, as she showed me through wards and spick-and-span operating rooms, I learned a little of her story.

"Nursing has always been considered a very low profession in China," she told me. "Until a few months ago our girls received a salary of three dollars a month when they graduated as lieutenants. Their food was poor, they lived in crowded quarters. When you add all that to our natural aversion to the nursing profession, you can see that we might have a hard time getting qualified girls to enter training."

And then Chow Mai Yü grinned as she told me how she had appeared personally before China's cabinet and had argued until she got a better deal for her girls.

"They told me I didn't know anything about budgets and government finances," she snorted. "They claimed we could not afford more food and better pay. But I won!"

Now General Chow's nurses get a better salary. Their food has improved to the point where they are guaranteed 3,000 calories a day; living conditions during and after training have been improved. But she admits that there is still a long way to go before nursing is considered an honorable profession, one that will attract really talented girls as a lifetime career.

General Chow has a master's degree in public health from MIT, another master's in nursing from Columbia, has traveled all through Europe and the Americas as Asia's leading authority on nutrition. These things I had learned from Isabel Stewart. The reticent general did not mention her accomplishments, and I was hard pressed to learn the story of her amazing career on the China mainland.

"I got my start under Jimmy Yen, the mass-education man," she told me. "I established the first rural health center in China. But all that work blew up when the Japanese invaded North China."

When the war began, General Chow went into the army. She established the nursing services of the Chinese Red Cross and the first school of nursing in the Chinese army. These were hectic days for Chow Mai Yü and her nurses. As the Japanese advanced, they retreated. She did not say much about these days except that on three occasions she lost all her belongings and ended up in a mountain retreat in the wilds of West China.

General Chow's work caught the attention of Lady Stafford Cripps who helped her get to Europe for a four months' tour of rural health work. From Europe she went to America, as an ambassador seeking the support of overseas Chinese in the States. She is a brilliant speaker, in Chinese and English, and she was so persuasive that she raised enough money to purchase twenty-four ambulances for the Chinese army.

Chow Mai Yü's great challenge is her fight for the welfare of her "girls." But she has spearheaded many other medical advances in Formosa.

"Chinese have emotional problems just like Americans," she told me. "And that is particularly true now with so many of us separated from our relatives." Then she described one of her pet projects, a new 100-bed psychiatric ward for Chinese soldiers—the largest such service in Asia.

Chow Mai Yü has spent a good deal of time moving during the past fifteen years. Or as she puts it herself, she has spent about half her time "running." She has narrowly escaped Japanese capture a half dozen times, has refugeed all over mainland China, moved out of Shanghai just in time to escape Communist capture in 1949.

STILL THE RICE GROWS GREEN

"But there is still one more big move I expect to make before I die," she said. "I am going home again, to the mainland."

"Tell me General Chow," I asked, "do you honestly think that will ever be possible?" For the first time in our two hours together the little general showed emotion.

"It has to be, it has to be," she said as she pounded her desk.

General Chow Mai Yü's cash salary is $10 U.S. a month. She did not tell me that the United Nations had just offered her, and that she had declined a $12,000-a-year position in the safety and luxury of New York.

My other favorite general is far better known. I had met him very briefly in China during the war, when he operated the "model" city of Kanhsien in southeast China. His name is Chiang Ching Kuo, and he is the eldest son of Generalissimo Chiang Kai Shek.

But my interest in General Chiang Ching Kuo was also enlivened by something I heard in America. I was lecturing in Louisville after a trip to the Far East in 1953. It was not long after Adlai Stevenson's tour of the world. A Louisville newspaperman had accompanied Mr. Stevenson and had brought back dark reports of the activities of the Generalissimo's eldest son.

"Why he heads the secret police," I was told. "He is a menace. Certainly, some good things have been done on Formosa. But Chiang's son is building a machine to take over, to become a dictator."

Later *Look* magazine featured a story about Chiang Ching Kuo. A disgruntled, ousted Chinese politician reported that it was widely suspected that young Chiang would, if he had opportunity, sell out to Mao, would turn Formosa into a province of Communist China.

And so it was that I made immediate effort to gain an appointment with the general, also to question Chinese in every walk of life about him and his activities.

Chiang Ching Kuo is not difficult to see. The Government Spokesman's Office arranged an appointment in short order. At four o'clock one afternoon I took a taxi to the modest house which serves as his office. I had forgotten the exact street address but surely that would not matter. Would not every taxi driver know exactly where the Head of the dreaded Secret Police held court? Unfortunately the driver did not know the address, and it was necessary for me to return to the Spokesman's Office to get it, to be late to my engagement with one of Free China's most controversial figures.

Chiang Ching Kuo is a small man, only slightly disposed towards middle-aged fleshiness. He is soft spoken, smiles frequently. We sparred a bit, I apologizing that my Foochow dialect was not understandable, he apologizing for his own atrocious Chekiang *patois*. Then we got down to business, speaking through an air force captain who acted as interpreter.

Chiang Ching Kuo is chief of the Political Department of the Chinese army. In that sense he is chief of the Secret Police. The United States Army has a similar "political department" although it is not called that. In our army we have a CID with many secret agents whose duty it is to ferret out crime within the army. We also have a CIC, a hush hush outfit, responsible for counterespionage.

"There are things about my work I do not like," the young general said frankly. "I am responsible for seeing that security measures are maintained here. We have had to arrest people, we have had to execute some people too. It is not a pleasant job, but it is a necessary job."

The necessity of the job can be understood if we realize that one of Chiang Ching Kuo's projects was the arrest of General Wu Shih, vice-chief of the general staff. Wu Shih, it turned out, was a top Communist agent, with a radio communications set in his home, in constant touch with the Red government on the mainland. Chiang's men secretly arrested the traitor general, and for nearly two months operated the radio station themselves. As a result, it was possible to pick up a total of just under 1000 Communist agents on Formosa. It was a tremendously important haul, occurring at a time when the Government was still weak with defeat and retreat.

Perhaps—quite probably—some of those arrested were mistreated. Many were executed; many more were sent to re-education camps; a few are now respected, if watched, members of Free Chinese society again.

But the general is much more interested in talking of his other jobs. (The Louisville newspaper man did not take the trouble to find out about the rest of his responsibilities.) He detailed his assignments, one by one. The Political Department of the Chinese army has five major functions.

1. It is responsible for the education and morale training of the Chinese soldiers. In this respect it is the exact equivalent of the T. I. & E. units of the American army.
2. It is responsible for all psychological warfare activities against the enemy.
3. Within the department it is the Inspector General Corps of the army.
4. The department is the Secret Police of the government. However, General Chiang told me he preferred to call it the CIC of the army, operating much as does our American army CIC.
5. The department is in charge of civil affairs, or military government, where such is needed. It is also responsible for developing good relations between the army and the civilian populations.

As a part of these many duties, Chiang Ching Kuo was in charge of planning for the reception, the re-education, the future lives of the 16,000 POW's from Korea. His eyes fairly sparkled as he told me of his plans. The first "pilot" group had already arrived, had been taken on a tour of the island, had even gone to Kinmen to broadcast to the Communists, with the startling results I have already described. Did I want to meet with any of the POW's, the general asked? I could have complete freedom, could talk privately if I wished, to any and all the men who had renounced Communism for Free China.

We talked of many things, the general and I. One of his biggest jobs lies in the never-ending psychological warfare against the Communists. His men plan the leaflets that are dropped by plane, train the agents who move in and out, plan and write the radio programs that are directed to the mainland. He utilizes captives for broadcasts, he often releases captured Communists back on the mainland (much to the chagrin of the prisoners who have no desire whatsoever to go back to their Peoples' Paradise).

Sensing my surprise at this part of the program, Chiang Ching Kuo said, apologetically, "Yes, I know some of the men we release have a difficult time. They are tortured and sometimes executed. But this is war. The release of such prisoners makes the Communist army and the people feel uneasy."

Then he continued: "We have developed a lot of tricks. We are trying propaganda balloons now with our message written all over the balloon. We drop rice, too, in areas where there is starvation. And always we have a message that goes with the rice.

"Our rice drops have worried the enemy," he went on with a grin. "Now they have tried to discourage the people from taking the rice by proclaiming that it has been discovered that every bag of rice also contains guns. Since it is a crime punishable by death to possess a gun, they hope to frighten the ignorant people."

Chiang's rice drops are potent propaganda, for much of Communist China has been suffering from starvation the past two years. Yet the fumbling U. S. Department of State has rapped Free China's knuckles for dropping food to starving people. During 1954's disastrous floods, Generalissimo Chiang Kai Shek ordered his son to drop tons of rice on villages and cities hardest hit, announcing with the order that in time of suffering Christians should help others, regardless of ideological differences. Not only was Chiang Kai Shek being a good Christian, his move was smart politically and psychologically. But the Department of State criticized Free China for giving aid to the enemy! During the same week our government also announced that certain trade restrictions were being lifted. Henceforth certain non-strategic goods could be sold to Red China. The "non-strategic" goods included tractors, diesel fuel, generators, locomotives and welding equipment. While rapping Chiang's knuckles for a powerful Christian action, Uncle Sam blindly announces that tractors and locomotives can now be sold to the enemy, for what earthly military use can be made of these things anyway?

The Communists seem worried also over Chiang Ching Kuo's leaflet drops. He told me something I had also heard from people on the mainland, that the Communists tell the peasants the leaflets are coated with a poison. If anyone even touches a leaflet the poison begins to work and eventually the fingers drop off, one by one!

But of the things Chiang does, he is proudest of his program of education and recreation for the Chinese GI. He told me with pride that literacy in the Chinese army is now 94 per cent. It was perhaps ten per cent five years ago.

"Our men must be educated, must be able to read and write," he exclaimed. "We have made it clear that in the new army of Free China, captains will become sergeants unless they are educated."

I have seen Chiang Ching Kuo's education and recreational program at work among the regulars and guerrillas on the islands. Every village has its simple recreation and reading room, its basketball court. Mobile units tour the major islands, showing motion pictures to soldiers and civilians.

Time after time I have seen whole companies, sitting in rows, taking literacy, history or economics examinations. To be sure the training is "political" in the sense that it is thoroughly anti-Communist and pro-Free China. Would the newspaper editor in Louisville believe that freedom of information should be applied to the extent that Chinese soldiers on Kinmen island, bombarded with ten thousand artillery shells on September last, should study the benefits of Communism?

Chiang Ching Kuo is also criticized, declared a menace, not only because he directs Free China's political police, but because he has studied in Moscow, speaks Russian. *Per se,* he must be dangerous, is apt to go over to the enemy. This of course is a prime example of guilt by association. The young Chiang's father studied in Japan and on the basis of such reasoning he should have collaborated with the Japanese!

Lieutenant General Chiang Ching Kuo's critics not only fail to consider the many responsibilities of his office, they fail to give him credit for considerable personal bravery. He is not content to sit at a desk in Taipei and order others to risk their lives. He has himself gone ashore on mainland raids, is often on hand to guide and direct the defense of a guerrilla island when the Communists show signs of attack.

Just as I was to leave Chiang Ching Kuo, I said something I had been wanting to say for some time.

"General, there are people in America who say you aspire to be a dictator, that you are a menace."

Quick as a flash came the answer. "I think that people like the Adlai Stevenson party who came here, stayed 48 hours, and then told the world about our mistakes, are a far greater menace!"

Perhaps Chiang Ching Kuo does have a pretty good secret service at that!

Chapter 6

W HEN I was a small boy, living in the province of Fukien on the China Coast I learned there were two kinds of Chinese, those who had all their roots deep in the soil of China and those who had relatives "overseas."

The latter had better homes, for the sons and cousins and uncles who lived in the *Nan Yang*—the "southern seas area" always sent money back to Fukien. Nearly always they themselves came home at last, to be buried in ancestral soil.

Ninety per cent of the Chinese who have emigrated to other lands, whether they live in New York's Chinatown, in Burma or in Bangkok, come from China's Fukien and Kwangtung provinces. In Borneo there are whole cities of Foochow-speaking Chinese; in the Philippines the bulk of the 150,000 Chinese are from Amoy, also in Fukien province. Nine-tenths of all the Chinese in America hail from one county in Kwangtung province.

In part, economic conditions have caused Chinese from the south China Coast to seek their fortunes elsewhere; partly it has been because the south Chinese are more adventurous, more willing to explore, more apt either to fight against oppression, or simply to move out.

When Sir Thomas Raffles claimed Singapore for the British Crown in 1819 he found it a jungle-covered, deserted island.

He let it be known that settlers would be welcomed—workers, merchants, just plain coolies—and within four months five thousand Chinese had arrived from Fukien.

And so it has been for centuries. In the second century before Christ, Chinese ships from the China Coast touched at all the ports of Southeast Asia. Normally they went south in the summer because the prevailing winds were to the south. They traded and fished, then northed homeward as the wind shifted to the north. But as the years passed, more and more of the Chinese stayed over between winds, to settle and to build the prosperous society that has existed now for several centuries.

The development of Southeast Asia would never have occurred, or would be centuries behind, had it not been for the ubiquitous Chinese. They have controlled all fisheries, either through operation of the fishing fleets or through middlemen. They monopolized the production of tin in Malaya for generations. In Thailand Chinese artisans even built the magnificent wats and monasteries of glittering Bangkok. It will be remembered too, that Formosa was settled by coastal Chinese, men and women from Amoy in Fukien, or Hakkas from northern Kwangtung.

And it should also be remembered that it has been the Chinese Communist guerrillas who have cost Britain millions of dollars and thousands of lives in the eight years of jungle warfare in Malaya.

Thus China and the Chinese have woven themselves into the fabric of life in all of Southeast Asia: 260,000 in the Portuguese colony of Macao; 150,000 in the Philippines; 1,000,000 in Vietnam; 217,000 in Cambodia; 360,000 in Burma; 807,000 in the city of Singapore and 2,000,000 more in Malaya; 220,-000 in north Borneo, 1,600,000 in the other islands of the Indies.

They number over 10,000,000, these sons and daughters of China who live elsewhere in Asia. They come from Fukien across the straits from Formosa, from Kwangtung further south. There is a never-ending struggle for their allegiance, and whoever wins that allegiance may well win Southeast Asia.

In a valley on Kinmen Island, surrounded by great black rock mountains, there is a mammoth statue of Chiang Kai Shek. Symbolically, the statue faces westward toward the enslaved mainland. But the importance of this pile of concrete and bronze lies in this fact: it was paid for by overseas Chinese, was even built by artisans who came from a half dozen Southeast Asia countries.

For even little Kinmen is a part of life in Thailand and the Philippines and north Borneo: 100,000 of its sons and daughters live abroad. What happens to Kinmen will have repercussions in every country in Asia. This we must understand if we are to understand the struggle for that vast continent.

There are many ways in which we can measure the ebb and flow of the battle for Asia's overseas Chinese. The statue on Kinmen is an indication of Free China victory; the number of young Chinese students who go from any country to Communist China each year is a measure of Communist success. The flags that appear, Nationalist and Chinese Communist, on each Chinese New Year's Day are a further indication of how the battle goes. The story of Allen Yeh, who forsook the security of Singapore to run a wine factory on Kinmen is a part of the struggle.

The few Americans who have observed and written about Asia's overseas Chinese find it very easy to dismiss the battle. "When the Communists are getting ahead, the Chinese swing to them; if the Nationalists had a victory it would be the other way."

But how else can men act when they have relatives in the homeland, dependent upon them? Who are we to judge the decisions of men, when letters come, demanding money in return for the life of an aged mother? Who can blame a father who sends his son to college in Red China when Nationalist China has nothing to offer? And for those who criticize I suggest another careful reading of American Civil War history. For then there were thousands of Americans whose allegiance depended upon who won the last battle, who could offer the best business deal.

The truth is that until Geneva, Free China was winning the battle, even though it has little to offer as compared to the largesse of the enemy, even though the enemy is recognized as ruler by a good share of Southeast Asia.

Statistics tell part of the story.

In 1950, the year after Chiang's defeat, only 215 Chinese returned to Free China from overseas homes. In 1951 the figure had increased, but only to 300. But by 1952 nearly 1500 came "home" to Formosa. And in late 1952 there was convincing proof that Free China had a hold upon the allegiance of Chinese everywhere, when over 300 delegates came to Taipei to attend a conference of overseas Chinese. These men and women were influential members of their adopted countries. There were newspaper editors and publishers, teachers and doctors, prominent businessmen and representatives of organized labor.

The overseas delegates visited army, navy and air force installation; they watched troops at maneuvers; they saw Free China's rural reform program in action. Groups of delegates visited Kinmen Island and the Ta-chen guerrilla islands further north.

But of course one meeting, attended by a few hundred Chinese does not mean too much. Again statistics will reveal a little of the change that has taken place in Chinese overseas thinking since the collapse in 1949. In that year, overseas remittances, always an important item in China's foreign exchange picture, dropped to a low of six hundred thousand U.S. dollars and less than five million Malayan dollars.

145

By 1952 over a million and a half U.S. dollars had flowed back into Free China. And the remittances from Malayan Chinese increased from less than five million Straits dollars to over thirty-five million. In 1950 slightly over two thousand pounds sterling came into Free China; two years later the amount had increased to 121,000 pounds.

This increase in remittances to Free China has been paralleled by increasing pressure by the Communists attempting to squeeze money out of overseas Chinese. It has occurred all over Asia, even in the U.S. Every effort has been made to force Chinese to send money back to Red China. There have been threats against relatives, actual arrests and executions—and yet there have been thousands of Chinese who have refused to bend under the pressure.

But it has been on Chinese New Year's Day when the most dramatic evidence of sympathies can be seen. In 1949 Chiang was in full retreat. By New Year's Day, 1950, all China had been lost. In those years Nationalist flags were few and far between, whether it be in Bangkok or north Borneo. But beginning in 1951 the change became apparent. On New Year's Day of 1954, Nationalist flags outnumbered Communist flags in every Asiatic nation which does not recognize Red China, and even in some of those who have recognized the Communist regime.

Even this simple act of flying a flag requires courage. There are Communist agents and spies throughout all of Asia. The relatives of overseas Chinese are carefully catalogued. The merchant who lives in Sarawak, who has a mother back in Foochow, knows that Big Brother will watch, will report on the flag he flies, the newspaper he reads, the amount of money he may send to Formosa. The daily lives of rich and poor alike are haunted by the knowledge of the danger each act may create for the family in China.

Yet today the tide is ebbing. In the aftermath of Geneva, men who have held on and hoped for a democratic China for five years are beginning to give up hope, are realizing that their futures may inevitably be tied with that of a Red Motherland.

Free China is not even recognized in populous Indonesia. So many thousands of Chinese young people are going from that land to Communist China to study that in a matter of years Indonesia will have hundreds of thousands of Communist Chinese amongst its population. The blindly neutral government of Indonesia allows Red propagandists full reign. Communist book stores, magazines, and newspapers flourish. Ties with Free China are made difficult, are frowned upon. The lives of Chinese who are still loyal are made difficult.

For the Indonesian government has ruled that the Chinese have but two choices if they remain in Indonesia. They may elect to become citizens of the United States of Indonesia. Or they must become citizens of Red China. For the Chinese who have lived in Java or Sumatra for generations it is not difficult to choose the former. But for the intensely anti-Communist refugees, those who have gone to Indonesia in recent years, the choice is tragic. If they are to remain Chinese, there is no place to go but to the Reds.

I had hoped to visit old Foochow friends in Jakarta. The friends wrote welcoming me, but they made it clear that my visit might cause trouble. A special pass would even be necessary to leave the city, to meet me at the port.

The Communists have been particularly active in luring young Chinese to China for college and technical education, in infiltrating the hundreds of overseas Chinese schools. In Hong Kong more than a dozen private schools fly the Communist flag, and the British authorities have not felt it expedient to take any action. (Would they allow such a situation in London?) Of the nearly one thousand primary and high schools in Hong Kong, six hundred are private schools, providing education for two thirds of the population. There are hundreds of private Chinese schools in Malaya. The Communists have been successful in infiltrating a vast majority of these schools and thus have a potent weapon in their battle for the overseas Chinese.

Dr. Walter Eells in his book *Communism in Education in Asia, Africa and the Far Pacific* (American Council on Education, 1954) cites conditions among the Chinese schools, tells of the Communist literature filled with virulent attacks against Free China and the British. He writes that one Chinese inspector of schools in Malaya, a loyal Chinese, finds it necessary to go about armed on his visits. He quotes from literature found in various schools. One document, widely distributed in the Chinese schools, was an attack upon the British and was signed "Fourth Mobile Platoon of the Eighth Regiment of the National Liberation Army." As Dr. Eells points out, this would indicate a definite organization among the students, one tying them in with the forces which the British have been trying to wipe out for years.

The tragedy of the situation is that Free China has too few weapons it can use. Nationalist literature is banned in many places. While the Communists can offer 10,000 college scholarships, the total yearly quota for overseas students at Taipei's National Taiwan University has been one hundred! And it has been difficult to fill this quota since a number of our "allies" in Southeast Asia make it difficult for a Chinese student to get out of the country, or impossible for the student to receive funds once he has left.

The Chinese Communists have been alert to the tremendous possibilities of capturing the overseas youth. They have also been alert to capitalize upon the frequent raw deals the overseas Chinese gets in whatever part of *Nan Yang* he may dwell. The Chinese have been accused of many things in their adopted homelands: of entering lands illegally, of running opium shops, of being loan sharks, of sending all the money they make home to China.

148

In the Philippines, until President Magsaysay took over, the Chinese residents were regularly blackmailed by the Philippine government authorities. Hundreds of Chinese business men were threatened with deportation unless they paid the blackmail. Millions of dollars were actually collected in tribute until Magsaysay put an end to the racket.

Elsewhere the *Nan Yang* Chinese have fared no better. In Thailand, the Chinese have been kept under unrelenting pressure. One Siamese king characterized them as "The Jews of the Orient." Naturally the overseas Chinese have become bitter over their treatment, and the Communists have capitalized on the bitterness.

It must be quite a temptation for a Chinese businessman in Bangkok, pushed around by Thai authorities, squeezed and threatened, to think rather longingly of the power of Red China, of the possibility that Red China may take over the very land which has treated him poorly. The song of Red China is an inviting song: "Join us, and you will no longer be discriminated against!"

One of the great tragedies of American policy in Asia is that the importance of the overseas Chinese has never been understood. We have done little to combat Communist infiltration of Southeast Asia's schools. We have not exerted our influence on the Governments of Southeast Asia so that the overseas Chinese might have a better deal.

Fortunately there are leaders like Magsaysay who realize the importance of the Chinese population. Even in Thailand, long among the worst oppressors of the Chinese, there has been a turn for the better. And the overseas leaders are now, more than ever, alert to the fact that the Chinese must be exemplary citizens of their adopted lands as well as good Chinese.

James Michener summed up the importance of the overseas Chinese in a *Life* story in 1951. He stated: "For the startling fact is that the *Nan Yang* Chinese, if they so desired or were so instructed, could cripple the most strategic cities of Southeast Asia. . . ."

In spite of all this, our Department of State has taken little interest in the problems of Asia's expatriate Chinese. Individually, lower echelon foreign service men have expressed deep concern to me.

Of the scores of high ranking official Americans who have journeyed to Formosa, only Vice President Nixon expressed awareness of the problem. He took time to go to Taichung, where the cornerstone of a new Christian University was being laid. He did so specifically because that university will provide opportunities for scores of young Chinese from *Nan Yang* to get a college education in Free China.

The United Board of Christian Colleges has also begun to help by providing scholarships for refugee and expatriate Chinese students in colleges in Hong Kong and in Singapore. In the latter city, a new university is being founded, an institution which may in time provide educational opportunities for hundreds of overseas youth. Dr. Lin Yutang, most famous of contemporary Chinese authors, has gone to Singapore to become the university's first chancellor. Dr. Lin's action is the type of forthright counter measure that is so desperately needed in this unheralded battle over 10,000,000 people.

But will it be in time? So much may depend upon occurrences we hardly notice. Kinmen Island, off the harbor of Amoy, may by its successful defense or its capture by the Communists, be one of those little things that will tip the scales. For remember that I have pointed out that Kinmen's one export has been its people—100,000 strong today are those who live in the South Seas. There were not many who had the conviction or the courage of Allen Yeh, who dared actually to go back and help the motherland.

However most of Kinmen's sons abroad would rather live

under democracy than under the star of Communism. The statue of Chiang Kai Shek on Kinmen—was it built merely as insurance in case the Nationalists would somehow win? Partly so, perhaps. But even more it was a gesture of hope. And if the United States of America, pledged to defend Formosa, refuses to provide the little extra help Kinmen's defenders need, how can we blame the overseas Chinese for losing that hope, for making the quickest and best deal possible with the other side?

Thus little things and places sometime loom large in Asia. Upon the fate of a little island off the China coast, an island with an "unpronounceable" name and considered too unimportant to defend, Asia's future may hinge!

Chapter 7

A s CHILDREN we Americans are impressed always with the basic democracy, the industry, the sobriety, the religious zeal of our pioneer forebears. Our grade school history books emphasize these sterling qualities. We are told how, when a group of pioneers settled a region they immediately organized a school, a church, and how soon thereafter, the urge for democratic government being so deeply instilled, some kind of constitution was written and a representative government, even if it be only a town meeting, was established.

The little bands of American pioneers who, in increasing numbers since World War II, go forth to bring the benefits of American civilization to the backward nations of the world are in some ways no different from our forebears who crossed the Appalachians to settle in Indian territory. The modern American pioneers have no Indians to fight, but they do move into alien surroundings, oftimes into areas of great danger.

They too organize their schools, or, if it be impossible, mothers immediately write off to the Calvert School in Baltimore, world famous for educating American children abroad, and begin to educate their children in the American way through remote control.

But instead of first organizing a church and a school and

a democratic manner of self-government, the modern American pioneer overseas establishes a source of supply for hard liquor. Oftimes it is called a "locker fund," and it is truly a democratic institution, a pooling of resources and know-how so that the benefits of tax-free whisky can be equally shared by one and all. For what is more pitiful than a thirsty American a long way from his sources of supply?

In past writings I have been critical of this propensity of Americans to spend so much time on cocktails. But in their defense I might add this time that I suspect our history books, in deference to young and impressionable minds, did not tell us another thing about our forebears: along with the church and the school and the Articles of Confederation there probably was a tavern established. Or if that were not the case I suspect that someone of the pioneers set himself up in the woods producing something alcoholic, to be sold surreptitiously from under the canvas of a covered wagon.

It is not my purpose to berate my fellow Americans for the American way of life they take overseas. I do not like cocktail parties myself and would be more than happy never to see another bottle of whisky. Furthermore I suspect that many an American who gives his tithe to support the locker fund in a far away capital would not be caught in the local package store at home. I have been impressed and surprised these past years to find that the American diplomat who threw some of the biggest parties in those lush prewar days in Korea is a deacon in his hometown church; that the young couple who were right in the middle of the gayest society in Seoul say grace over their meals. I do not know what this means. Perhaps those of us who saw the rape of Korea had the fear of the Lord thrown into us. Perhaps we are, down deep, so insecure in our overseas relations, so basically provincial, that we have to compensate with liquor in Seoul or Bangkok or Timbuktu.

What I do know is that there has been a great deal of foolishness written about Americans—official Americans—overseas. Theodore White, famed author of *Fire in the Ashes* and coauthor of *Thunder Out of China* mourns for the poor American diplomat. According to Mr. White, the foreign service officer is poorly paid, unappreciated by his country and so driven by the fear of congressional investigations that he is afraid to report the truth. Of course Mr. White is talking through his hat, or is exhibiting the same wondrous judgment he showed ten years ago when he extolled the merits of Chinese Communism.

What Mr. White and many others do not understand is that today's diplomats are numbered by the thousand, that there are Americans in each country who are more important than the American ambassador.

American policy is a combination of military, diplomatic and economic factors. An aggressive agricultural advisor can have more effect upon a nation's willingness and ability to resist than a weak ambassador; the American who advises on banking and currency stabilization can sabotage millions of dollars worth of military aid. In the truest sense all these Americans are members of the foreign service, with foreign service titles. Many have been "in" since World War II and know no other career.

These Americans are not, as Mr. White would have his readers believe, poorly paid. I have met hundreds of them and I have never known one whose soul has been scarred by Senator McCarthy. There are good ones, bad ones, mediocre ones. There are too many to be sure.

There are many who drink too much, a few who drink nothing at all. There are bright ones and stupid ones. Taken as a whole, they represent a cross section of any American city or town.

Some have been used by the Communists, with disastrous effects. It is one of the tragedies of our times that Communism has been able to make use of the very size of our foreign service, and when I use that term I do so in its truest sense, including the thousands of Americans of all ranks and occupations who make up the American team overseas.

In the old days when there was an ambassador or a minister and a few secretaries and consuls it was well nigh impossible to infiltrate an American diplomatic establishment. Now with hundreds where there were a few tens, it is always possible to find a handful of weak men and women, or to plant that one man who may be all that is needed to pervert American policy in a foreign land.

I mention these things as preamble to this fact: I have never heard a Chinese official or non-official blame the fall of China on America alone. Perhaps this in part is because Chinese are courteous people; perhaps it is part of the soul-searching that has gone on on Formosa, where men speak frankly now of past mistakes on the mainland. Perhaps it is just good public relations not to criticize the country whose fleet is protecting your shores.

During the past decade it has become fashionable to blame Americans for the loss of China and equally fashionable to defend those same Americans. I was in China much of the time of disintegration. I know there were fellow travelers and probably party members on our embassy staff. I saw General Marshall in action and was not impressed. But I would never dream of calling him a traitor. Perhaps George Marshall was an outstanding military leader. Of that, I have no knowledge. But he was a second-rate diplomat whose greatest failure was that a huge ego blinded him to his second-rateness. He was a pushover for the few who infiltrated because his judgment of people was poor and easily swayed by flattery.

I know also that every effort was made to use men like myself, who were born in China, who could speak Chinese and who *per se*, might be considered China experts. Every effort was made to use me and I was even propositioned to join the other side. Some of us fell by the wayside and have been disgraced. Others somehow had a combination of luck and good sense and so were not entrapped. That is just what it was: a combination of luck and good sense. I knew nothing about Communism when I was drawn into the maelstrom of China politics. I thank God for the little good sense and the large share of good luck—whatever proportion it was— that made it possible for me to turn down propositions, to understand, even if dimly ten years ago, that Chinese Communism was not what China needed and that no kind of Communism was desirable in America.

Through arrogance and stupidity, a handful of top Americans contributed to the fall of China. Perhaps another score of lesser Americans were traitors and through their efforts used the stupidity of their peers to create a situation in Asia that has already cost many American lives and will, before it is all over, take many more lives.

The point of all this is that we should begin to take our attention from the past and focus more on the present and the future. The mainland of China is, as of now, lost. Americans were involved, yes, but Americans did not do it all. More important, it is time to quit raking over the smelly dung fires of the Marshall period and see if we are doing any better today.

Even though Free China is a small island with a population less than that of New York State, there are many Americans there. There is an Embassy, and by and large it is staffed with excellent people. There is a U. S. Information Service. There is Mr. Stassen's Foreign Operations Administration and the American members of the Joint Commission on Rural Reconstruction, administratively connected with it. There is a Military Assistance Advisory group of five hundred or more American officers and men, many with their families. There are members of Central Intelligence Agency and a half dozen special advisors of one kind or other.

It is inevitable that among these hundreds of men and women there are good and bad Americans, just as there are in any American city or town. We do not get the best out of them because we still have not discovered the value and necessity of giving real training to those who represent us overseas. We do not get rid of the bad ones quickly enough because of the red tape which so securely binds most Americans into their jobs. There are still too many who drink too much, too many who not only have too many mistresses but also flaunt their conquests.

But it is only fair to say that it is better now than it was two or three years ago. What America does is done more efficiently. There have been more deserved firings than occurred in years previous. It is my opinion that we still have too many Americans; we still spend too much money; we live too well. But there is progress and hope in the way that Americans in Formosa are working, the manner in which they share the uncertain destiny of the exiled Chinese.

When I am in Formosa my home is with Gene and Roberta Auburn. Gene and I used to hunt together in Korea. We sat out many a freezing hour in duck blind, walked together over hundreds of miles of Korean hills in search of pheasant and deer. The Caldwells and the Auburns were in Seoul on that fateful day in June, 1950 when the Communists struck. We all got safely out via various routes and carriers.

Gene and Roberta do not agree with me on many things. But ours are healthy disagreements, not hidden resentfully within, but argued over with spirit. I think there are far too many parties in Taipei, too much drinking. I suspect that Gene may agree with me. The Auburns feel that I have been too critical of American conduct abroad. And perhaps I have. For there is much good being done by many people, and perhaps it would be better to write of the good.

Gene is requirements chief of the Foreign Operations Mission on Formosa. That means that with his American colleagues and with Chinese officials, he must decide what the actual aid requirements of Free China are. That is no easy task.

The two million exiled Chinese, the men and women who chose freedom to slavery under the Communists, think only in terms of going home. It is not "if we go back to the mainland." It is always "when we go back." Surely there can be no one except Mr. Attlee and his friends in England who would not agree that this is good and noble and patriotic.

But that same noble desire can cause conflict between American and Chinese. For instance, the Chinese needed a new fertilizer plant. What more natural than that they should think in terms of a plant that could be, would be, someday moved back to the mainland? The American experts who plan and advise on such things wanted a fertilizer plant specifically for the people of Formosa, a plant to meet the needs of that island alone. Of course both sides are right. American official policy is to build up the island of Formosa. American economic aid is given for that purpose. And so Gene Auburn and his colleagues are quite right when they argue about the type of plant that is to be built.

The Chinese officials are equally right. Theirs is the recognized government of China. Their homeland, one hundred miles away, was wrested from them by conspiracy, murder and the help of a foreign power. If we refuse to allow them to hope for the day of return, we have no business giving them anything. Better that we should close up shop completely and quietly retire to some other defense line.

As long as American policy is ambiguous and unrealistic, there will be friction on Formosa, and with that friction there will be frustration. It is to the credit of the Americans and Chinese alike that there has been as little friction and frustration as there has been.

The way of life in China and the way of life in America

are still so different that further friction is inevitable. Our military advisors want to give China a jet air force. That is well and good. The island cannot be defended against Migs with ancient World War II propeller planes. If there are to be jet planes there must be bigger and longer runways, even new airfields. To the American expert that of course means that another step must be taken before the planes are delivered. Bulldozers and other behemoth prime movers are obviously necessary to build jet airfields.

But the Chinese argue that point. "You go ahead and get those planes in the supply line," they say. "We'll build the fields. Don't worry about bulldozers."

And so they argue, the American who knows he is right, that there is a certain logical order in the manner of building a defensive pattern for a nation. And the Chinese knows that he is right, that bulldozers are not needed for the building of an airfield in China.

In this case the Chinese turned out to be more right than the Americans. Five thousand Chinese coolies can do wonders, whether it be building roads or airfields. After all, the Chinese were able to build great airfields from whence the B-29's flew on their first bombing missions against Japan. And they built those fields without benefit of prime movers.

The Chinese are doubly right because Americans though magnificently efficient as individuals are surprisingly inefficient as a government. We read from time to time that such and such a nation has been granted such and such millions of dollars in military aid. There was a time when I thought these announcements meant just what they said, that planes, tanks, guns immediately started flowing forth. But of course it doesn't work out that way. It takes months before "hardware" is delivered. And so it was on Formosa. The coolies had the airfields ready long before American red tape had been unwound sufficiently to deliver the goods.

And so it goes on almost every project. Difference of view-

159

point and objective, even difference of tradition can generate friction. Gene Auburn told me of one of his problems a few months ago. There were a number of coal mines on Formosa, which viewed from the American standpoint were unproductive. The mines produced very little coal and that of poor quality. Within the total economic plan for Formosa those mines should be shut down and the money spent on their operation should be diverted to something else in the plan. (We Americans always develop a *Plan* for each country in which we operate. It is a very important document, generally highly classified, not entirely understood by the Americans and viewed with a combination of awe and resentment by the foreigner.)

In the case of the coal mines, the Americans were of course right. When you have a certain number of dollars available to develop a balanced economy for a country you can't waste those dollars on unproductive activities.

But the Chinese argued that when the mines closed down there would be several thousand miners out of work. It would be some time before the ex-miners could be absorbed into the already tight labor market. For two reasons, one ancient and one modern, the closing of the mines was wrong from the Chinese viewpoint.

In old China one of the greatest sins is to "break your neighbor's rice bowl." You might cheat him, yes; but to take away his livelihood was unthinkable. Only real tyrants would do that, and in China's history there have been remarkably few real tyrants.

Then too, the Chinese officials said, "Think of what good Communist propaganda it will make if we throw those miners out. They can tell the world all about unemployment on Formosa. They can say that the 'corrupt, imperialistic Chiang Kai Shek government' doesn't care enough about the people to give them jobs."

And of course the Chinese were right, just as they are

right in not firing the hundreds of ex-generals, ex-war lords, ex-Kuomintang leaders who sit about doing nothing in Taipei. After all, these men once were important; they did think enough of their country to flee, even if it was fear for their necks that caused them to leave the mainland. But fire them, dump them out jobless? Unthinkable! It is equally unthinkable to the Americans who are attempting to set up a civil service system that these parasites should be kept on the public rolls.

Again, the Americans and the Chinese are both right. The Chinese solution is to kick them upstairs, to give them high sounding titles, and to keep them out of mischief. Uneconomical and inefficient? Yes, of course. But when people come out of China to join their fellow exiles on Formosa they must be taken care of. It would be unthinkable to break their rice bowls. Thus it is that China's civil service must be inflated and inefficient. Both the Chinese and the Americans are right.

Added to difference of viewpoint and tradition is the frustration caused by American policy. The intelligent American on Formosa knows that it is foolish to waste millions of dollars on the island for its own sake. There must be a real purpose behind it all, not just a stop-gap, face-saving spending of tax payers' money. But as yet there is no real purpose to the program. The Chinese know it, realize it full well. They have but one purpose, and that is to go home. One hears it expressed everywhere, by officials and private citizens. American officials are in the frustrating position of knowing that that purpose must be maintained if there be any hope; yet they also know the programs they administer do not in any way take that hope into consideration.

It is vastly to the credit of Americans on Formosa that so much is accomplished with so little friction and frustration. As an American I am proud of the work done by Gene Auburn, his superiors and his associates. Some of them should be fired, and from time to time one is. But considering our

161

ineptitude in foreign affairs, considering our lack of policy, I think America is doing a good job. It is that good job and its implications that we should look at henceforth rather than to the past and the mistakes of the past.

There are many good things happening on Formosa between American and Chinese. There is a healthy participation in the affairs of the island, a cooperation between Chinese and Americans that is good to see.

Every time I visit Formosa I leave amazed and exhausted just watching the things that Roberta Auburn does, not because she has to, but because she wants to. And there are a good many other American wives who do just as much. I single Roberta out only because I know her program and her activities, have listened with amazement while she sat at her phone and arranged a score of activities in a single morning.

There is the Women's Club of Taipei, a truly international organization but one sparked by American wives like Roberta. Its program of activity would put, or should put most American women's clubs to shame. There are meetings and projects of some kind going on all the time: sponsorship of a craft shop so that the skills of the aborigines may be advertised, will bring in money for those who dwell in the hills. Cigarettes and reading materials are provided for the lonely soldiers in the Chinese army hospitals. An orphanage receives part of its support; dependents of guerrillas on the Ta-chen islands get help; reading material is sent forth to lonely outposts on Kinmen; bedraggled Nationalist guerrillas and their families, flown in from Burma, are met with a little gift of clothing, with milk for the frightened kids.

These little projects are carried on by the American wives on Formosa; and by their activities, relations between Chinese and American are strengthened. Some of the projects engaged in by Roberta Auburn and other wives are far from little, are even spectacular. The story of the truly remarkable Taipei American School is worth telling because the school

162

has become international in character, has become a force binding together a half dozen nationalities.

Surrounded by not-always fragrant rice paddies, within ten minutes by jet plane from Chinese Communist airbases, is without doubt the strangest American school in the world. With an enrollment of over four hundred, the Taipei American School is among the largest American schools overseas. Among its students are Buddhists, Catholics, Protestants, Moslems and just plain heathen. Although the enrollment is predominantly American, other nationalities include mainlander Chinese, native Taiwanese, Thais, Filipinos, Germans, Spanish and English. Among the tongue twisters on the roll is Adiphon Anumen Rajadhon who fortunately is nicknamed "Peppy"; there is Xavier de Larrochoechea, son of the Spanish ambassador. There are typically American names such as Davis, Auburn and Bennett. There are scores of Chinese students, including the two sons and the daughter of Generalissimo Chiang Kai Shek's aide. All this heterogeneous group have their education planned and directed by the Calvert School in far away Baltimore, Maryland. My wife and I, all our brothers and sisters, are "graduates" of this correspondence school that has educated thousands of American children on every continent.

The Taipei American School has no legal basis for existence and came into being only after a hard struggle. It is not incorporated or registered in Free China or America. The school was established five years ago with an enrollment of nine students who met in the basement of a church and used ancient textbooks flown out in the retreat from the mainland. As more Americans arrived on Formosa, the need for a real school became acute. There were many Chinese, too, who desired that their children receive an American education. The story of the school's growth is one of international community effort, of disappointments and problems.

Efforts to get financial aid from the U.S. government failed, and so the parents borrowed money for their first building.

Madame Chiang Kai Shek went security on the loan. The U.S. air force flew textbooks in from America; a Chinese business firm donated desks; a U.S. army bulldozer appeared to level the school playground. The Taipei American School began its 1953 school year in a brand new $600,000 (New Taiwan) building. Another loan was necessary, this time guaranteed by the Joint Commission on Rural Rehabilitation. The school is in business now and expects to be around for some time. There are still problems: the teaching staff must be recruited from among island wives, for the school fees are not sufficient to bring teachers from America requiring the payment of transportation both ways. Lesser problems include the matter of whose flag shall be saluted, the nature of the oath of allegiance, the question of whether or not Christian religious devotions should be required of Buddhist, Moslem and heathen. The flag and oath of allegiance problem have been solved rather neatly. Since Chinese and American students are in the majority, since it is an American school on Chinese soil, both flags fly. The oath of allegiance is given just as it is in any American school, with the understanding that each child is pledging allegiance to *his* or *her* native land. Religious services have been dropped from the week day school program. A special Saturday morning Sunday school is conducted for all those who wish to attend.

The vexing problems of running an international school are handled by a seven member board of directors, elected by the parents. The present board consists of an American businessman, the wife of an American economic aid official, a Chinese businessman named "Gorilla" Cheng, a Taiwanese housewife and an American agricultural expert from South Carolina.

The Taipei American School is a parent-operated private school. Enrollment fees are high, for it costs a great deal to operate the school. The grade school textbooks shipped by Calvert School in 1954 cost over $10,000, and the shipment weighed 8,000 pounds. There is still a big loan to repay.

There is a nightmarish problem that is never out of parents' minds: what to do if and when the Communist air attacks begin? A direct hit upon the school would snuff out between 400 and 500 lives. The board had solved the legal problem by requiring all parents to sign a waiver, releasing the school from all responsibility in case of enemy attack. The children and teachers do their part by holding frequent air-raid drills.

With two big years of operation under its belt, the Taipei American School knows that it is succeeding in teaching. American girls and boys who return to the States find themselves far ahead of their schoolmates at home.

And as Roberta Auburn, who has two children in the school, said to me, "I wouldn't have my children miss this experience for anything. Where else in the world could they learn so much about other peoples, where else could they have Chinese, Thai, Filipino playmates?"

K. T. Hu, MIT engineering graduate, builder of the new school, is looking far into the future. He proudly informed me that he had built the school in sections so that it can be quickly taken down and moved to the mainland when, as he put it, "We Chinese go home and will still be needing the help of many Americans."

The spirit of cooperation which has made the Taipei American School a going institution is part of the story of Formosa's strength. That same cooperation is evident in the operations of the Joint Commission on Rural Reconstruction. Chinese and Americans alike have learned from the mainland debacle; given a clear and positive policy they could do wonders together.

Yes, the Americans live well in Taipei, just as they live well wherever they may be stationed. In Taipei even a single girl has a whole house to herself. She does pay for it, and she pays for her servants. She and her sisters have a gay time of it, and there are some Chinese who probably resent the house and the gaiety.

But it is one of the good things one sees on Formosa that

there is real appreciation for what America does in its sometimes bungling way.

On New Year's Eve last I was invited to many parties in Taipei, not because of me or my name but because there are many parties and everyone is invited. They begin at five o'clock and go on until dawn. It is quite a job to figure out how many of the "musts" can be worked in, even if only for a token show in the "line up." But I did not go to any of the many American parties. Instead I was the guest at the home of a Chinese cabinet minister. The gathering was in strange contrast to the many American parties I had attended during the holiday season.

There was no whisky, only beer which a fraction of the guests took. For the others there were cokes and tea, a simple buffet dinner, much quiet and serious talk.

"Tell me," I asked my host, "do you Chinese resent all the money we Americans spend, the big parties we give?"

He was an honest man. First he told me what his party cost. It wasn't much. It couldn't be much if he were to remain honest, for his salary is low, and even though he sits each day in the councils of the great, his wife must work also, as a simple stenographer.

"Some Chinese are critical of the way you live," he began. "But most of us realize several things. First you are away from home; you live in a degree of danger. We know that most of you get things tax-free here. We understand that at home in America you live quite differently. We don't begrudge you your fun here."

Perhaps the minister was being polite, but I think not. And he was pointing his finger at a glaring defect in our national make-up. We don't act the same abroad as we do at home!

We Americans are improving in our foreign relations. But we still have a long way to go. The things that are wrong cannot be blamed on Senator McCarthy or any congressional committee. They cannot be blamed on poor pay, for American men and women abroad are very well paid. Perhaps our deficiencies can be traced to our education. We do not really study languages; we still study foreign lands in terms of this country being green on the map, the next one being red. We are extremely provincial, ill at ease among strange peoples and strange customs. Many of us are not very adaptable.

As a matter of fact, we have never been very good ambassadors. The only complete journal of an early American diplomat I have ever read is that of John G. A. Williamson, first American ambassador to Venezuela. Williamson served from 1835 to 1840 and kept a complete diary during those years.

He had then the same biases that Americans have today. He had the same troubles in his post as Americans still have abroad: trouble with his cook whom he characterized as a "scamp"; (how many times have I heard similar appelations in Taipei, in Shanghai or Seoul!); he had trouble with the local authorities who put red tape where he felt no red tape should be; he had trouble with his wife, who wanted, and eventually did go home. He characterized the people of Venezuela as without intelligence and commented that the leaders were interested only in personal ambition.

Like many of his modern counterparts, he was caught short on his political reporting. When a revolution blew up in his face, he frankly admitted in his diary that "It came like a thunderbolt on me never suspecting such a thing, not dreaming of disaffection of any kind. . . ."

Actually the only difference between John Williamson of 1835 and Ambassador Jones of 1954 is that relations with superiors was informal in those days. Any time he wished Williamson could drop a note to the Secretary of State or even to the President. The informality is illustrated by the fact that once he was a year away from his job and received nothing more than a mild reprimand.

No, there has been no great change in American human nature since the days of John Williamson in Venezuela. We have been thrust too abruptly into the center of the world's activities and our failures cannot be blamed upon Congress, or poor pay. Our foreign service is a cross section of America today, with all of America's weaknesses and strengths and with the added weaknesses brought on by a basic provincialism. But we do improve surely if slowly.

My wish is that, as the American pioneer brought schools and the church house into the wilderness, we might put more emphasis today on things other than the PX, the commissary and the locker fund. That is our greatest failure, the placing of so much emphasis upon the material.

The great strength of Free China today is that the spirit of the people at the top has changed. Certainly there is inefficiency—there are still too many remnants of mainland bureaucracy. There are still a few crooks and thieves in high places. But underneath it all is a spiritual awakening, a willingness to admit past faults, a brightness that extends from lonely Tungting Island to the hideous government headquarters building in Taipei. The light is there to see for those who are willing to search for it.

If we Americans are to fulfill our announced purpose of helping those who want freedom, we too will have to get a bit more spiritual light showing. It will not be treaties or military pacts, economic assistance and military buildups that will win out in the struggle ahead. The final battle will be won by the side which has the most complete spiritual dedication. As of now the Communists are clearly ahead of us on that score.

But light there is on Formosa, and progress too. The question now is what is to be done with the progress achieved at such a cost? The question is asked in many forms: Can China be saved? What can Chiang do? Can the Communists be driven from power on the mainland? On the answer to these questions rests the fate of Asia.

Chapter 8

M R. JOSEPH ALSOP is considered an expert on the Far East. He has spent much time there, traveled through Formosa in late 1953, a few weeks before I journeyed to that island en route to Kinmen and the China Coast islands. The major results of Joseph Alsop's most recent travels was a feature story in the *Saturday Evening Post* entitled "The Shocking New Strength of Red China." "This army," writes Alsop, "is so powerful it is able to upset the balance of world power."

This new, unbeatable army developed because of the Korean war. It so frightened U.S. army officers in Korea that a report on its strength, in Mr. Alsop's words, "has shaken the Pentagon and caused deep tremors in the State Department." The Chinese army and its massive air force are so strong, and here Mr. Alsop quotes unnamed admirals and generals, that it can if it wishes drive the Seventh Fleet from the Straits of Formosa and drive our best generals into their cups. Throughout his dark prophecy Mr. Alsop uses such phrases as "There is convincing intelligence," "A secret report to the Pentagon."

In the light of Mr. Alsop's findings and predictions it seems presumptuous for me to attempt to answer other than in the negative that question which has been asked me, over and over again, in every section of America. That question is usually put: "Does Chiang Kai Shek have a chance?" It is unfortunate that the question is so worded, for the future of China should no longer be considered in terms of one man, one leader.

The question of whether or not China can be saved must be answered too, not merely in terms of the vast Red armies and air forces. Tommy Hsu and the Lady General on Formosa, Allen Yeh and Chang Chow on Kinmen Island, Chiang Kai Shek and his son, Chiang Ching Kuo—all of these men and women and thousands of others on Formosa, on the mainland of China, on the guerrilla islands and in Korea will shape the final answer.

On the basis of military facts, of numbers of men in uniform, of jet planes that can take to the skies, Mr. Alsop is probably correct when he writes of the shocking strength of Communist China. But it is strange that Mr. Alsop, who worries much about the psychological effect of Joe McCarthy on America and our allies, ignores entirely the psychological factors that also play a part in the future of China, of all Asia.

Mr. Alsop totally ignores the meaning of mass Chinese surrenders in Korea. Can an army which suffered such defections be shockingly strong? Mr. Alsop totally ignores the reports of the Communists themselves, reports of such widespread disaffection on the mainland of China that hundreds of thousands of men and women have taken to the hills, to fight as guerrillas. Can any army, in any land, be shockingly strong, if it has a half million armed guerrillas in its midst?

Mr. Alsop totally ignores the "convincing intelligence" that has come out of China, tales from Chinese and American observers, of a hatred of the regime that extends to seventy-five per cent of the population. Can any army in any land be shockingly strong when the people—its people—are against it?

170

One night I had dinner with a young Chinese army colonel in Taipei. He is American trained and educated, one of the youngest full colonels in Free China's army. We talked, as one eventually does with all Chinese on Formosa, of the return to the mainland. I played devil's advocate. I pointed out to the colonel that from a military standpoint Nationalist China did not have a chance.

"How in the world," I asked the Colonel, "can your half million men land in China and conquer the country as long as the Communists have five million men? How can you tell me that you can fight odds ten to one, and have a chance of winning?"

Colonel Wong is an honest man. He admitted that Free China's best bet would be a general war in which the U.S. would be forced to help. But then he began to talk about history, about American history at that.

"How many men did George Washington have as compared to the armies of Great Britain?" he asked. "How large was the American Navy compared to the British Navy? How was it possible for the Confederate armies, representing a small proportion of the American population, to fight for four years before being defeated?"

Of course the Colonel was talking about something that happened a long time ago, before there were such things as jet planes and massed fire power and fifty-mile-an-hour tanks. Presumably these advances in the techniques and implements of warfare have submerged the spirit of man so that it now makes no difference whether or not that spirit burns brightly.

Being realistic, I would say that the young Chinese colonel is wrong and Joseph Alsop is right. Chiang can probably do nothing; China will probably not be saved from Communism, and in not being cleansed of the infection, its illness in turn will lead to the loss of all of Asia.

But I do say that it need not be so, that China can be

cleansed and freed and in the process all of Asia made safe, if only the world's leaders would listen more to the Colonel Wongs and less to the prophets of doom.

No thinking man in Free China believes that the Nationalist armies can land on the coast of China and free her. No thinking Chinese official thinks that any offensive action can be successfully initiated without help far beyond what is presently being given. It should be admitted that there are those, too, who hope for World War III because they believe that to be China's only chance.

Writers of the Alsop school have made much of the fact that Chiang was "unleashed" two years ago but as yet has not freed the mainland. They fail to report that the unleashing was verbal, not accompanied by any commitment of increased logistic support. Chiang has been put in the position of a man deputized as a sheriff but given no gun. The term "unleashing" originated in America and was a hollow American gesture not even requested by Free China.

But Free China can, with proper assistance, take and hold a bridgehead. That bridgehead can, if properly exploited *politically*, be extended. And in the end China can be saved even though it might require five or ten years. For there are factors at work in China and on Formosa which are far more important than the "shocking strength" of Joseph Alsop's Red Chinese armies.

Red China can be defeated. It can be defeated because the people of China are sick of brutality and torture, of mass executions and fraudulent land reform. It can be defeated because the experience in Korea and that along the China Coast has proved that vast numbers of the Red Army will surrender, will desert, if given any opportunity at all. Red China can be defeated because American prestige among the old people is still high; the century of American missionary and other good works has not been forgotten. Red China can be defeated because even geography favors the Nationalists in the type of operation they will execute.

The "invasion" coast of China is that portion south of the Yangtse River. It is along that coast, stretching from Shanghai south to Hong Kong and Canton where a Nationalist landing must take place. Pin-pointing, it probably should be somewhere in the provinces of Fukien or Chekiang.

If Free China is provided with adequate air power, more landing craft and small naval vessels, more antiaircraft protection for its rear and staging area, a landing on the Fukien or Chekiang coast can be made, a bridgehead can be gained and in time extended.

Let us consider the purely military factors for a moment. If Kinmen Island can be held (but because of vacillating American policy and the new policy of co-existence, the island may be lost before these words appear in print), if the other Nationalist islands along the Fukien and Chekiang coasts can be held, the armies of Free China have from five to twenty miles of water to cross to the mainland.

Once upon the mainland, the Nationalist armies will be in wild and mountainous terrain. There is no through highway all along the China Coast. From the coast of Fukien there are only two highways into the interior. The coastal highway extending from Amoy to Foochow has never been completed through to the north. If one is to travel by highway from the Fukien coast to central China or Shanghai, it is necessary to strike far inland to the highway that winds through the mountains of central Fukien, connecting with Shanghai eventually by way of Hangchow.

In order to reinforce its armies, Nationalist China has five to twenty-five miles of protected coastal waters to cross. In order to reinforce their armies, the Communists must move troops over seven hundred miles of highways if reinforcements come from the Shanghai area, over three hundred miles of highways if the reinforcements come from Kiangsi province.

I have traveled those highways by bus, by jeep and on foot. The road from Fukien into Kiangsi crosses two five-thousand-foot mountain ranges. It is wild country, reminding one of the Great Smoky Mountains except that there are vast bamboo forests instead of forests of pine and hemlock and spruce.

It was in Kiangsi province, on the borders of Fukien, that Mao's Chinese Communist army held out for years against everything that Nationalist China could throw at them. It was from these same mountains that Mao and Chu Teh and the other leaders of Communist China began their long march to the wilds of northwest China and on to the shocking strength they have achieved today.

The mountains of the China Coast provide some of the world's finest big game hunting. It is perhaps a measure of their wildness and remoteness that in Fukien and Chekiang is the home of the tiger (probably the greatest concentration of tigers in the world), of wild boars, leopards, the rare serows, and the magnificent Takins, or wild cows. I have walked for a day in these mountains without seeing a village. I have stumbled into villages so remote that the people had never before seen a white man. I have seen tens of thousands of acres of virgin timber, of uncut bamboo forests that ripple over the mountain ranges as far as the eye can see.

As school children we learn that China is one of the most densely populated lands in the world. But we fail to learn that this population is concentrated in fertile valleys, that China has vast areas of unpopulated and sparsely populated land. We learn that China is a land of rice paddies and do not understand that beyond and above the paddies are mountains and forests. The city of Futsing, where I was born, is on the "invasion" coast just north of Kinmen. It is a county seat, a city of 25,000 population, on the highway between

Foochow and Amoy. Yet three times within my memory tigers have been seen within the city limits. I have shot deer within a mile of the city's South Gate; excellent wild boar hunting can be found three miles distant.

Of what use will Mr. Alsop's massed fire power, his regiments of tanks, be in such country? One bomb can block any highway in Fukien at a thousand different spots. True, the highway can be repaired, the bridges can be rebuilt—but they can be again destroyed the next day, and the next day.

The rivers of coastal China offer no better transportation. The Min River, connecting with the inland highway at Nanping, 150 miles from the sea, is a wild and turbulent stream that has never been tamed. Specially constructed motor launches can navigate the river for a hundred-odd miles, at an average speed of four miles an hour upstream and ten miles an hour down river.

Further south near Amoy the Dragon River offers even less possibility. Certainly troops can be moved by sampan and junks, but no junk has ever been able to shoot the gorges and rapids of the coastal rivers at night. With an adequate air force, river traffic can be slowed to a standstill, highways can be blocked and kept blocked. The Communists are clever people; they were able to move complete divisions and complete armies at night in Korea. But in North Korea they had an excellent highway *and* railway system; in South China they have neither.

Also in North Korea the Communist army had a small civilian population with which to contend, and even then it required the equivalent of nearly ten Communist and North Korean divisions to keep guerrillas, saboteurs and other dissident elements under control.

The population of Fukien province is 12,000,000, compared to North Korea's population of 8,000,000. The Communists themselves admit that this population is against them, lament the fact that in 1953 it was necessary for their troops to fight

over 5,000 engagements in the province. There are more guerrillas in this one province of China than there were in all
North Korea. The number could be doubled and tripled, if
the people were given leadership, arms—hope.

The coast of China provides no terrain for fleets of Russian-
built tanks; its roads are not suitable for mass movement of
artillery in division strength. And while troops and guns and
tanks are moving in, what of the twenty-five million people
who live in the coastal provinces? If these people know that
a full scale Nationalist landing is under way, will they sit
idly by? These are the people who dumped their cabbage
crop into the rivers last fall rather than let the People's Government have it, or tell them how to sell it. These are the
people who already control three mountainous areas in Fukien and Chekiang.

These are the people whose hatred is so great that there
are vast areas where Communist troops dare not go unless in
full company strength. These are the people who dislike the
Russian advisors so much that the "big heads" find it unsafe
even to travel the cities during daylight hours.

And what of the Communist troops? In Korea they surrendered to Americans, to Koreans, to British, to French, even
to the blood-thirsty Turks. One of the first POW's to be returned to Formosa made this statement: "Had there been
even a token Nationalist force in Korea, had there been even
a few token Nationalist flags, our men would have surrendered by the tens of thousands."

Another young lad from the far west of China said: "I surrendered to an American unit even though I half believed
the Communist stories that I would be tortured and killed.
But I was sick of brutality, sick of the needless executions I
saw in my home village in Szechwan. And so I took the
chance."

Mr. Alsop forgets entirely the men who did surrender in

Korea; he can see no significance in the fact that these men were willing to venture into the unknown by the thousands. On the China Coast, faced with a real landing, there will be thousands of desertions. Particularly will that be true among the security forces, the second-string divisions made up of local men who have not been thoroughly indoctrinated, brain washed and paralyzed by fear of their political commissars.

A landing on the China Coast will be a massive guerrilla type operation. It will not require vast fleets of tanks and divisions of artillery. Indeed such would be a handicap. It can succeed because every non-military factor and some military factors are against the Communists.

It can succeed because the people of the China Coast hate their masters, because this area is deeply imbued with the century's work of a thousand American missionaries. It can succeed because reinforcing Communist armies have ten times and fifty times the distance to move, compared to attacking armies. It can succeed because Mr. Alsop's frightening fleets of tanks will not be able to move over the unmapped jungles of the Bohia Hills, the tiger-infested wilderness of the coastal ranges which rise, tier upon tier, from the mud flats and the beaches to the farthest horizons.

But still two questions remain. Can Nationalist China take a bridgehead without American aid? And once taken, what happens next? Of what good will a small piece of land around Foochow, or Amoy, or Putien be to Free China?

The generals with whom I talked, on Kinmen, on Matsu, on Formosa, are honest. They admit they need help from America. They have needed help even to hold Kinmen, and it is probable that the help for that will not have been given in time. They need antiaircraft artillery to defend their island bases, their staging areas, their actual landing. It must be reasonably good hardware, not the ancient, third-hand stuff America has seen fit to give. They need more small artillery, not of the variety that was used in World War I but modern equipment that can be quickly moved from place to place.

In a thousand miles of travel along the China Coast, I saw but two landing craft. Can men safely and effectively clamber down the prows of ancient steamers and great-eyed junks? Can they be expected to do so, under enemy fire, and quickly take their objectives? Free China needs ships—not aircraft carriers or even cruisers. She needs landing-craft, and small supporting craft of which the United States has thousands in shipyards. She needs something besides the Nationalist patrol ship P-6 on which I went raiding south of Amoy. For her speed was ten knots maximum, her armament consisted of ancient 13 mm Japanese machine guns. She had once been a trawler in the Japanese fishing fleet—and that is where she belongs today.

Finally, Free China needs planes to cover her landing. She has received a few. In 1953 we first began to see jets over Taipei, but precious few. Her bombers are ancient craft, many of them once belonging to General Chennault's 14th Air Force.

But above all Free China needs something besides a statement "unleashing" her. She needs a positive American policy, one that makes it clear that the United States is interested in the future, not merely the holding of the island of Formosa. As I write these words, it still has not even been decided if Kinmen is to be considered a part of Formosa. After five years, that island, the only logical staging area for the landing that must take place if China is to be freed, has not been considered within the Formosa defense area. The officers and men of the American military advisory assistance group on Formosa have not been allowed to train its defenders, to help plan for its defense. The two American officers killed on Kinmen in the late summer of 1954 were merely observers. The

178

statement of American press agencies that the men were on rotation duty on Kinmen is false.

Americans have been on Kinmen, yes. The men of Western Enterprises, Inc., the hush-hush CIA agency whose activities are known to friend and enemy alike, have been training guerrillas for harassment tactics—nothing else.

At this point it is necessary to begin to agree with Joseph Alsop. It may well be too late, perhaps Red China's armies have become frightenly strong. For with the Geneva settlement, Communist China gained a breathing spell in the push to the south and she gained rice that may well begin to balance out the bad effects of flood, famine and peasants who will not cooperate with the People's Government. Already 15,000,000 mainland Chinese have been executed and more millions will meet the same fate.

If Kinmen, the symbol of Free China's hopes to return, its "Golden Gate," is allowed to fall, it will be a shattering blow for those on the mainland who have fought on. Mr. Alsop has, of course, called the turn on this one too: he announced himself as opposed to American assistance to the coastal islands. Such assistance would of course only further antagonize the frightening military machine that has already set Mr. Alsop to having nightmares.

But let us suppose we gave, or had given, Nationalist China that military and moral support I have advocated. Let us suppose that a bridgehead was carved out of the Fukien or Chekiang coast. Of what value would a few hundred square miles be in the struggle for several million square miles?

It is at this point that psychological factors, so often not understood by American military experts, again enter into the picture. And also the Nationalists would reach the most dangerous part of their return journey, far more dangerous than the actual landing of troops.

If Free China instituted immediately the rural reforms she

has developed on Formosa, if she placed men like little Mr. Chen Shi Ho, who directs the army agricultural experiment station on Kinmen, in charge of agricultural programs in the liberated areas, there would begin a crumbling process that would undoubtedly end in final victory.

Every Chinese in authority, military and civilian, understands how important immediate demonstration of Nationalist reforms will be. And there are many who also understand the problems that will be faced.

"There will be some among us who will see return to the mainland as opportunity to get rich," an agricultural expert admitted, as a group of us sat at one of the long discussions that went on each night that I spent on Kinmen.

Magistrate Chang Chow added his voice.

"There will be people who will not be able to withstand the temptation," he said. "There will be people like those who went to Taiwan in the early days of the Restoration. They went only to exploit, to get rich."

The fact that the men of Free China realize their problem is encouraging. The fact that skeleton civil administration teams are already being trained, on Formosa, on Kinmen, and on the Ta-chen Islands, is also very encouraging.

Already the Fukien provincial government-in-exile is functioning on Kinmen, the Chekiang provincial government-in-exile on the Ta-chens. Two *hsien* (county) governments have been established on Matsu Island, ready to move into the adjacent mainland counties. Already several score guerrilla islanders have gone to Formosa to undergo extensive training in civil government. Already over 200,000 Taiwan dollars have been appropriated to begin a land reform program on Kinmen.

If Free China goes into a bridgehead with rural experts, agricultural specialists, with a land reform program drawn up and ready to apply, with men like Tommy Hsu and Chen

180

and Chang Chow in positions of authority, all of Red China's millions of troops will not be able to stop the advance.

Even the many apologists for Red China, those who once proclaimed the agrarian reformers, keep silent now about Mao's land reform. It has been a fraud and a failure, and when the farmers of China see real land reform there can be no question as to the final results. Here again the importance of tiny Kinmen enters the picture. The thousands of troops on that island will be among the first to go ashore, to fan out into mainland China. Every man, whether he be from the plains of Manchuria or the Yangtse Valley will go out with a new knowledge of farming, with the lessons learned in the agricultural classes he has attended, from the visits to Mr. Chen's experiment station. Sixty thousand strong, these men, whether or not even Free China's leaders realize it yet, will become more potent than an equal number of tanks. In time they will spread to the far corners of the land. Some will fall by the wayside, some will go back to farming and living by superstition. But most of the men will carry on what they have learned. They will bring into battle a powerful weapon.

One of the most exciting stories to come out of the Far East appeared in an August 1954 issue of the *Saturday Evening Post*. Entitled "They Hit Red China Where It Hurt," and written by Allen Whiting, a Ford Foundation Scholar in Formosa, it is the story of the Red soldiers who surrendered, who chose to return to Free China. Mr. Whiting interviewed scores of the men and on the basis of these interviews writes: "No other policy of the Nationalist Government excites these former Communists so much as its *bloodless* [italics mine] land reform and reduction of rents. As one man put it, 'We never knew on the mainland that this government is no longer just a friend of the landlord.'"

Writing of the friendship for America, upon which I have

already commented, Mr. Whiting states: "Time after time I heard outpourings of friendship and admiration for America . . . my sudden, unanticipated appearance [at the camp for repatriates] always brought a crowd of smiling, chattering men."

And finally, Whiting writes: "Most of the former Communists we interviewed had no illusions about defeating Red China. Although all thought it could be done, a significant number attacked the half-way measures now being used!" The tremendous importance of the psychological factors completely ignored by Joseph Alsop is stressed by a frequent comment reported by Whiting: "The people on the mainland don't know about Formosa; they are losing hope."

As the Communists succeeded once because of the ideas they expounded, the bright promises they flashed, the dedication with which they worked, so can the men of Free China succeed. Yes, there will be some crooks and exploiters. There will be some corrupt officials and generals who will still be willing to make deals.

But there will also be scores and hundreds and thousands of Tommy Hsus and Allen Yehs. And with the dreadful lessons of the past well learned, it is they who should prevail. But of course it is necessary to amend that statement: it is they who could have prevailed.

How long would it take? Five years, perhaps even ten. For Communist China is strong, even though her feet are of clay. There would be thousands of the young who have been brain washed and who may never surrender. But in those years Red China would no longer be a menace to the rest of Asia. Her armies would be tied down. As the news of Free China's New Deal spread, there would be uprisings from the Coast to the borders of Tibet. Propaganda warfare would turn millions away from Communism; partisan warriors would keep Red China's best troops engaged. There would be suffering for millions of people, insecurity for more millions, but would not the stakes make it worth while?

One of America's top diplomats in Asia stated the situation clearly and unequivocally when he told me: "If there is to be a free and friendly Asia, there must be a free and friendly China. It may take five years, ten years or a generation. But Americans must understand that fact, must make the decision as to whether we want a free and friendly Asia."

To date, the decision has been in the negative. My diplomat friend might have added that all the treaties, all the SEATO's in the world will not change the validity of his statement. If Asia is to be friendly and free, China must first be free.

And in the final answer, it will probably require more than Free China on Formosa to win the decision. For to the north of Free China there is another land, once a vassal of the Chinese emperors, but now Formosa's only true ally in the fight against Communism in Asia.

The Republic of Korea is a tragic and devastated land. But nothing has so stirred the people of Free China as Syngman Rhee's visit to Formosa in 1953. For Korea has 600,000 men under arms and could have many more. Its fighting men have proved themselves. Of course Rhee's visit to Formosa was frowned upon by American authorities. No American dignitaries were at Taipei's airport to greet him. Neither is Korea included in SEATO, the tragic jumble of meaningless words which seeks to keep Asia free.

But the armchair strategists of Free China can still hope and dream. What would happen, they say, if before Red China recovers from her economic ills, while the people are still fighting back, while men and women still live who are willing to fight—what would happen if simultaneously with a Nationalist landing on the coast of China, Rhee's armies were allowed to strike north? Could the Communists prevail if confronted with a two-front war, with massive partisan and guerrilla operations all the way from the borders of Indo-China to the mouth of the Yalu?

The armchair strategists have a right to hope, even if their hopes may never be realized. For in spite of the greatest devastation known in modern times, the rice grows green in Korea. There, too, men work on and hope—men like the Hsus, the Chens, the Yehs of China. If their hopes and dedication and dreams could be somehow welded together, Asia could indeed be free. There indeed would be a frightening force, one that could achieve, in the words of Joseph Alsop, "the balance of power in Asia."

Korea and China have been linked through centuries. Invaders from the Mongolian plains conquered Korea nearly eight hundred years ago. For centuries it was a vassal of China, paying yearly tribute to China's emperors. There was a time when the Korean kings, like Free China's rulers today, refugeed to an island, there to hold out against the invaders for decades. The future history of Asia may now depend upon an alliance of Free Korean and Free Chinese, fighting together against a common enemy.

BOOK THREE

THEY WILL NOT FIGHT,
NOR HELP THEMSELVES

Chapter 1

JUNE 17th, 1953 was not a spectacular day along the Korean front. There were the usual light forays; the usual number of Americans, British, Chinese, Koreans and Turks were killed or maimed on night patrol. At Panmunjom, in Washington and in London there was talk, not of more fighting, but of possible peace.

Suddenly far behind the fighting front, on barren Koje Island, at POW camps near Pusan at Inchon, thousands of North Korean prisoners of war suddenly broke out of their stockades and rapidly melted into the white-clad stream of Korean life.

After a few hours of stunned silence enraged cries came forth from the capitals of the Western World. A few hours later Radio Peiping added its shrill voice in denunciation of the "puppet" Syngman Rhee and his American warmonger supporters. The name of Syngman Rhee, already well known, suddenly became a nasty word in most of the newspapers of the world. Throughout America, in Great Britain, in France the actions of this frail old man were denounced.

The *Nashville Tennessean*, morning newspaper in the capital city of Tennessee, is a typical liberal newspaper. On the morning after Syngman Rhee released anti-Communist prisoners, the *Tennessean* began a series of editorials which continued through June and July. On July 1st, the newspaper headed its almost daily anti-Rhee editorial: "Blackmail Doesn't Pay, Mr. Rhee."

The editorial then continued: "Blackmail is dirty business, wherever you find it, and those who succumb to it are only asking for more trouble.

"On this basis the United States is wise in turning down President Syngman Rhee's demands in South Korea. The aged marplot is fully capable of violating any agreement he might sign. . . . More and more, Mr. Rhee's position approaches that of open enmity toward the democratic saviors of his country . . . he is now almost as dangerous to American forces as is the Red Army."

Other newspapers were no less bitter. Soon the American radio added its voice. Martin Agronsky, winner of the Peabody Award, pointed out that on the head of Korea's dictator president lay the blame for the blood being let in the vicious Chinese attack that followed soon upon Rhee's action.

A British MP made it plain how Britain would handle such a case! There were demands that General Mark Clark should arrest the dictator, that he should be deposed and a Korean more amenable to United Nations policies be installed in his place. A famous British general opined that *he* would have had the matter under control within ten minutes and left no doubt as to the ineptitude of American handling of such situations.

Here and there in America there were calmer voices, pointing out a certain logic in the old man's position. Other voices began to join in, particularly after the strange spectacle of an American general apologizing to an enemy general for the acts of an allied chief of state. The *New Leader* magazine summed up the growing feeling of many Americans in its editorial of June 29th. Said the *New Leader*:

"However one regards the action of Korean President Syngman Rhee in releasing upwards of 25,000 prisoners of war from South Korean prison camps, our reaction is not that of an understanding and intelligent friend. Judging by some of our official pronouncements, in fact, one would have every right to question whether or not we are speaking as a friend of Korea.

"Consider, for example, a letter written on June 18th by the United Nations' Senior Delegate at Panmunjom, Lieutenant-General William K. Harrison, Jr. The letter is addressed to his opposite number, North Korean General Nam II. In it, General Harrison is most apologetic. He confides to General Nam, in fact, that he strongly condemns President Rhee's act as not quite cricket but as 'actual collusion between the Republic of Korea Army guards and the prisoners.' Maintaining his chivalrous stance to the very end, General Harrison assures General Nam that 'efforts are being made to recover the prisoners.' It won't do, you know, to have liberated Communist slaves running around a country that Communists have done so much to improve and beautify."

The *New Leader* ended its editorial with the statement that "Perhaps, instead of condemning Syngman Rhee, we can learn something from him."

As the days passed into weeks, American opinion began gradually to swing to one of grudging admiration of an old man who alone faced up to the whole democratic—and Communist world. The *Nashville Tennessean,* so violent in its first treatment of the incident, began to realize that public opinion did not support its views. By July 7th, the *Tennessean* had come to the point of observing that: "He [Rhee] merits protection if he will play the part of a loyal and trustworthy ally. . . ."

Other *Tennessean* editorials appeared on July 10th, 14th, 16th, 17th and 21st. On July 14th the paper became downright friendly in its statement that "Yet, it can also be observed that if all democracies' friends were as steadfast and courageous as he [Rhee], the outlook of the world might be far better indeed." The open season on Dr. Rhee finally ended when the *Tennessean* began an editorial with the words: "Whether President Syngman Rhee of Korea is a blackmailer or super patriot, and now it seems the latter to be the case. . . ."

Thus, in less than a month, President Syngman Rhee became for one newspaper as he did for many others, not a blackmailer, not a marplot (one who defeats a plan by officious interference) but a patriot.

The happenings of June 17th, 1953, were but a prelude to another series of interesting and unprecedented occurrences in Seoul. There began the greatest number of Very Important Person visits in the history of a small nation. American generals flew in from Japan to talk, to argue, to pound the table. A soft spoken assistant Secretary of State, native of Virginia, came for two days and stayed for two weeks. He was followed by the Secretary of State. For a nation, unknown to most Americans three years ago, this was well beyond the normal quota of State visitors. The wizened old man who had caused all the trouble had already been called upon by our President-Elect nine months earlier. And to complete the list, the Vice President of the United States also traveled the road to Korea.

How wrong was Syngman Rhee of Korea when he stated that the truce was a mistake, would be a prelude to further Communist pressure elsewhere?

The events since Panmunjom partially justify his stand, prove that not only is his batting average in the field of prophecy not bad, but that others before him were not far wrong in their judgments.

The late Senator Robert A. Taft was considered able in many fields but even among his friends there were those who believed the senator was weak on foreign affairs, could not fathom the intricacies of the art of dealing with other nations. Taft's last major speech, delivered by his son because the senator's last days were already upon him, has been called the "Go It Alone" address. It shocked many, was considered so ill advised that the President of the United States saw fit to comment officially upon it.

In his "Go It Alone" address Robert Taft made a prophecy. He stated on that spring day in 1953 that: "Even the best truce under present conditions will be extremely unsatisfactory. It will divide Korea along an unnatural line and will create an unstable condition likely to bring war again at any minute. It will release a million Chinese soldiers, who no doubt will be promptly moved down to Southern China for use against Chiang Kai Shek or against the French in Indo-China. . . . I believe we might as well abandon any idea of working with the United Nations in the East and reserve to ourselves a completely free hand."

Who can say now that Bob Taft—or Syngman Rhee—was wrong?

Far more recently, General James Van Fleet, one of the few American generals who has been able to effectively work with the soldiers of so-called backward peoples, stated in an article carried by U. S. News and World Report (September 17, 1954) that the Korean truce was a profound mistake "which the American people should greet with a sense of shame."

Van Fleet continued: "A truce is indicated only when a political settlement is in sight. And clearly, to me at least, we had no basis for one either in Korea or anywhere else in Asia. . . . Our superb fighting men plus the equally superb divisions of the Korean Republic might have engaged and destroyed the enemy. Instead, they became the pawns of that diplomatic caucus [the UN]."

But my purpose is not to write of the past, but of future possibilities. Let us presume that the free world wakes up in time to escape the catastrophe in Asia. Does devastated Korea have any part to play? Are there still enough Koreans with hope and courage to supplement that displayed by the men and women of Kinmen, or Formosa?

Neither Korea as a nation, nor Koreans as people are very popular these days. It would be nice if we could forget about the Korean business; for the failure to give the Koreans the independence, freedom and unity promised at Cairo and since must weigh heavily on official conscience. It is not fashionable to damn Syngman Rhee now, but neither he nor his people will win any international popularity contest.

"These people will not fight; they won't help themselves. What can you do with them?" I overheard these words one day in September of 1953, the words spoken through the flimsy partitions which separated me from a British war correspondent living next door in the Eighth Army war correspondents' billets in Seoul.

My British colleague was in conversation with a number of fellow correspondents, American and British. His judgment of the Korean people was concluded by a bald statement that four out of every five American dollars poured into Korean relief went into the pockets of Syngman Rhee and his cronies.

If this be a true indictment there is little hope left in Korea, little use in considering it and its peoples a part of Asia's struggle to remain free.

Granted that there is a certain amount of corruption and depravity in Korea, that there is little of the stability that marks Japan, or Formosa, or even embattled Kinmen. But in Korea too there is progress and hope for those willing to look. And the search need not be difficult. I found tall rice growing green in the city limits of Seoul; elsewhere I found thrilling evidence of a people not yet defeated. Even in Korea there are men like Tommy Hsu, dreaming bright dreams.

Chapter 2

IT WAS the day after I overheard my British colleagues denouncing the Korean people that I drove south to Suwon, an ancient Korean city renowned for its city wall and picturesque gates. It had been over three years since I had seen the city, where in better days I had spent much time.

In the prewar days I had been drawn there often by the fine pheasant hunting and by the thousands of ducks and geese pouring into the mud flats and marshes to the west of the city during the winter months. Gene Auburn and I had spent many hours in those marshes, often uncomfortable hours of bitter cold until the discomfort suddenly disappeared in the thrill of seeing and hearing a vast flight of waterfowl approaching.

Nowhere in Asia can the change wrought by war be better seen than in Suwon. Where once there had been one American living, an agricultural expert assigned to the experiment station, there are now 12,000 Americans living in and around the city. A jet air base nearby constantly throbs and rumbles with life. Everywhere in the city are signs that indicate war and the presence of Americans. Suwon changed hands six times between 1950 and 1953, and each battle took its toll. It is no longer a lovely city, but it is a city where I found what I sought—evidence that Korea's spirit is still alive and unbroken. For in the Suwon hills I met the lepers who would not give up.

High on the hillside overlooking a lovely valley I found a colony of forty-seven men, women and children who have the world's most feared disease. Hansen's disease, the doctors call it, and now we are told that it is not as loathsome and infectious as mankind has been led to believe for the past three thousand years.

For three years the Suwon lepers lived under a highway bridge, their only protection from Korea's winter winds and snow a piece of canvas hung from the bridge railing. The lepers were simply forgotten in the ebb and flow of war. The Communist armies ignored the colony as it moved up and down the valley. United Nations forces, too, thought little of the men, women and children huddled under the bridge. For Korea was filled with human flotsam all through the winters of 1950, 1951 and 1952.

During the spring of 1953, even as the men at Panmunjom were nearing the end of the longest truce negotiations in the world's history, the lepers decided to help themselves. Their valley had not been touched by fighting for months. Peace of a sort had come. It was time to look to the future.

And so the lepers organized in democratic fashion; for without organization and leadership, how could they make known their needs? Forty-four-year-old Kim Man Gu was elected president of the colony. It was agreed at once that the lepers must move out from under the bridge, must find land where they could begin to farm and live again, where shelter could be provided for the children of the group.

Kim Man Gu began then the first of many long treks over the dusty highways. For even though the disease had not yet left its devastating and tell-tale marks on his face, even though he could pass as a normal human, Kim refused to subject others to his uncleanness.

194

First Kim Man Gu walked to Seoul, forty-six miles away. "How long did it take you?" I asked.

"Oh, about a day. Really more than a day," he replied. And then he added: "It would not have been so bad had I been able to find shelter that night. I could not go to a hotel, I had no friends, I was afraid to even sleep close to other refugees."

In Seoul, Kim Man Gu made known his condition and the needs of his people. Sympathetic government officials granted the lepers a tract of land on the hillside above their highway bridge home. Then began the task of finding funds with which to build shelter, to buy farming equipment, seed.

The lepers pooled all their resources: a bit of money here, a piece of jewelry carefully saved through the years of war. Those who could still locate relatives wrote and walked for help. It was not much, the money they collected, but it was enough to build one simple house. And Kim Man Gu provided further shelter by walking once again to Seoul, ninety miles round trip. There he secured three surplus tents.

But one mud-and-bamboo house and three tents still does not make a home. There must be crops, above all there must be rice. The first crop was planted in the spring of 1953, and it was a difficult crop to start. The hillside was cleared—by hand; a water supply for the paddies-to-be was provided by digging a ditch far up the mountainside to a stream. The digging was of course done by hand. There were no oxen in the colony that spring, and the plowing too must be done by hand. Slowly the terraced paddies took shape; the bright green of tightly packed rice seedlings filled a tiny seed plot by May. Then came the transplanting, when one by one the rice seedlings must be taken from the seed plot and planted in careful rows in the flooded paddies.

All of this was accomplished that spring of 1953, and the first crop was ripening when I walked and talked with Kim Man Gu in the first September after the truce. There were other crops, too—sweet potatoes and a bumper yield of cabbage which would be ready when Kimchi-making time came in late October, Kimchi being the pickled cabbage that is Korea's national dish.

But the lepers of Suwon's hills still lacked one important thing. Kim Man Gu is an intelligent and educated man. He knew that medical help was needed, especially for the children, several of whom were still free from disease. He knew little of the United Nations, did not understand that the UN had funds and men to help such as he. But he did know that there were Americans, many Americans, near Suwon and he knew that Americans were kindly and big-hearted people, lavishly equipped with medicines.

And so it was that Kim Man Gu took another walk, this time to the jet air base near Suwon. I do not know just what happened at the air base. Kim did not find the help he needed there, but he was directed to another unit of the U.S. army known as the "Civil Assistance Team for the Province of Kyonggi" in which Suwon is located.

At Civil Assistance Command Headquarters Kim Man Gu had an extraordinary piece of luck. There he met Dr. Gulliermo Lopez of Mexico City, public health officer of the Suwon Civil Assistance Team. In little Dr. Lopez, Kim Man Gu found a sympathetic ally. Perhaps Dr. Lopez' interest stems from the fact that he too comes from what we so glibly call an "underdeveloped" country. In the mountains of Mexico he had seen the pathetic aloneness of men and women in need but who knew not where to go for help.

Dr. Lopez immediately visited Kim Man Gu's colony. He was shocked to find most of the lepers still living in drafty tents, to find that they had no sanitary facilities, no source of safe drinking water. He went into action. Not only did he get medicines, but he enlisted the help of other members of the Suwon Civil Assistance Team. Cyril Pires, sanitation officer, a native of India, went out to help plan privies and a well. Jack Purvis, a Canadian and in charge of welfare, found that Kim Man Gu's people could legitimately receive much help from his department.

By the time I visited the leper colony, the Civil Assistance Team had gone into full scale action, and a new and brighter life lay ahead for the forty-seven lepers. Among other things, new houses were being built, a total of five modest dwellings but enough to provide a roof over the head of every leper, to give a little privacy to family groups, to provide a measure of isolation for those children who had not yet shown symptoms of the disease.

The colony lies three miles off the highway and on a hillside far above it. Kim Man Gu and his people had just completed a new project when I visited them. I suspect that it was done primarily because of gratitude for the help of Gulliermo Lopez. They had built, by hand of course, a narrow roadway through the pine trees so that Dr. Lopez could drive to their village, so that it would be no longer necessary for a busy doctor to walk three miles on his calls.

But in accepting all of the assistance that has suddenly come to them, the lepers themselves have attached strings. Kim Man Gu had asked only for medicine. He had gotten help in building as well, some surplus food and the materials to build five new houses.

"We would like to repay the U.S. army for the building materials," Kim told me proudly. "You see with the government rice ration, with our first harvest coming in this fall, our people will be self-sufficient within another year. We will not need help from America."

Then Kim added an afterthought, wistfully saying: "Of course there are many others like us in Korea. We would like to find them and invite them to join us in a life of dignity. We could use help in getting others of our kind here."

The whole village lined up to bow and wave goodbye when Dr. Lopez and I left. There was no shyness, no groveling among these people who had been human derelicts for three

197

years. The move from the drafty shelter of a highway bridge to homes of their own on a lovely hillside had been made possible by their own efforts. Help they were receiving, and will receive; but the assistance had been accepted with dignity, only with the understanding that it is temporary. Kim Man Gu has fought for and earned what he has achieved for his people.

These are the people who "will not help themselves." The existence of people like Kim and his followers is overlooked, just as is the magnificent struggle of the people on Kinmen Island, in the mad rush to criticize and damn, in the desire always to find something wrong. But for me there is an exciting coincidence in the finding of Kim Man Gu and in my findings on Kinmen. Kim is Korea's most frequent surname. It means "gold," is the same character that appears in the name of the important island of Kinmen in Chinese guerrilla-land.

My visit to Kim Man Gu's lepers came as a climax to a long day with the Suwon Civil Assistance Team, an unusual and truly United Nations group of men, charged with relief and rehabilitation of one of Korea's hardest hit provinces. The Suwon Team was then under the command of Lieutenant Colonel John McNiel of Oakland, California. He is of course long since gone. One of the tragedies of U.S. army-directed activities is that a good man may be just started, developing a program with understanding and initiative only to be transferred to a new post and new duty 10,000 miles away.

The Team consisted of Dr. Lopez, Jack Purvis and Cyril Pires who I have already mentioned, Norman Price, an Australian and Gunnar Fries from Denmark. The civilians on the team were all paid by the United Nations Korean Rehabilitation Administration. But they operated as part of an American Military Command for the simple reason that the UN rehabilitation effort had for months been tangled in so much red tape and bickering that its personnel were powerless to act constructively. Here and there all over Korea UN personnel had been "seconded" (a UN term) to the U.S. army where, relieved of paralyzing United Nations red tape and indecision, they could begin to help the Korean people.

Suwon is the Provisional Capital of Kyonggi Province, in which Seoul is located (Asia is filled with "provisional capitals" these days: Taipei is the provisional capital of China; Kinmen is the provisional capital of Fukien province). Consider the task that faced the men of Colonel McNiel's team in 1953 and 1954:

Of a population of 2,000,000 a total of 940,000 on relief.

A total of 120,000 "extreme" cases—people who are completely, utterly destitute.

Twenty thousand families without shelter during the winter of 1953–54.

Sixty thousand contaminated wells, many of them with still unclaimed human bodies.

Four hospitals to serve 2,000,000 people, most of whom are suffering from serious malnutrition.

To solve Kyonggi-do's enormous problems requires the bringing in of nearly all drugs, tons of rice and other grains, clothing for those who are completely destitute. Each fall a tremendous blanket program, costing $2,500,000 must be initiated. Each family of four receives one blanket, a family of five two blankets. Other blanket distribution must go to orphanages, prisons and hospitals.

No one can give an accurate figure as to the value of relief and rehabilitation supplies that must flow into each province. It runs into the millions of dollars. And if my British colleague in Seoul was correct about the general dishonesty of Koreans and the specific dishonesty of Korean officialdom, here indeed would be a good place to verify his judgment.

I talked to each of the team's technical men: Lopez, Pires,

and Purvis; for they are the men who do the actual distribution of grain, drugs, tents, blankets and clothing.

"How much of this stuff you hand out goes into the pockets of Korean officials?" I asked each man.

And each man gave me separately, and later collectively as we talked together, the same answer.

Jack Purvis, as welfare officer, distributes the greatest volume of relief goods, and his answer was quick and unequivocal.

"A maximum of five per cent of all the relief goods we handle gets into illegitimate channels," he told me.

Was that a pretty good figure? Yes, indeed, Purvis thought it was an excellent figure. Then Pires added this thoughtful statement: "The stomach must come first," he said. "After that come morals."

And he told me of some of the problems his Korean counterparts faced in their work. There is one Korean sanitation officer for each *Gun* or county. He has no jeep, no transportation of any type. His salary will run perhaps the equivalent of one and a half dollars each month. When he travels (by foot, or by hitch-hiking) he has no per diem allowance, must even pay for his own lunch.

In each *myun* or township there is one man who handles sanitation, welfare and health. These officials in general had not been paid in three months.

What a temptation it must be under such circumstances to take a few bottles of drugs, a blanket or two or even a bag of rice!

Yet only five per cent, and all agreed that this was a maximum figure, went into what the U.S. army calls "illegal" channels!

What kind of cooperation did the CAC team members get from the Koreans?

"Excellent!" Purvis said. And he added that it was not servile cooperation. Especially since President Rhee released the POW's, the Korean officials had shown more spirit, more inclination to argue their views rather than to quickly accept whatever the foreigner proposed.

The Suwon Civil Assistance Team is, or was, one of Korea's best. The degree of cooperation between team members and Koreans varies from province to province just as does the calibre of Americans and other foreigners. There are places where the program is inefficient, places where corrupt officials siphon off a larger part of incoming relief goods.

But the record, for those who will investigate fairly and honestly, clearly refutes the charge that four out of five, or any large proportion of American aid, goes into official pockets. The record clearly shows too, that the Korean people are helping themselves, that given direction and understanding of the type provided by the Suwon Civil Assistance Team, they will effectively do their part to solve their problems.

Dishonesty there is in Korea, but it is much like dishonesty in America. There is more of it in shockingly crowded cities, in poverty stricken areas, than in the country. And there is a significant relationship between the degree of dishonesty and the number of Americans stationed in an area. Before the Korean government and people are condemned it might be well to ponder the fact that the amount of stealing, the magnitude of the black market operation varies in direct proportion with the American military population. The more Americans, the more dishonesty and corruption.

Seoul and Pusan are among the wickedest cities in the world, the streets teeming with pickpockets and petty thieves of every variety, the black markets bulging with American and United Nations relief goods, with all the miraculous things sold in U.S. army post exchanges. It is said that from one to two hours is required for a new PX item to reach the black market after it is unpacked at the PX. Or perhaps it would be more accurate to state that the new item goes directly from the truck or the railroad car, sometimes hitting the black market before it goes on sale in the PX.

How does an expensive wrist watch travel in its course from shipping crate to the Seoul black market?

Time magazine, usually friendly to Koreans and Chinese, in its June 7th, 1954 issue, described the event which throws most consternation into blackmarketers, whether they be Korean, Japanese or Chinese. In occupied countries, or wherever the U.S. has large military forces, military personnel and official American civilians use MPC's (military payment certificates) in lieu of green-backs. "GI" money, it is called, and although generally considered a little below green-backs in value, it is always considered far more valuable than uncertain local currencies. It is eagerly collected by hundreds of thousands of people who do not have faith in their own currency.

The military script issue has been changed four times since it was first issued in 1946. Each change is accompanied by the most complete security regulations. No one is supposed to know when the changeover occurs. I well remember the changeover of 1948, when all of us in the little Korean city of Chunchon were suddenly ordered to appear at the military government dining hall with all of our money. It was changed, right there on the spot and henceforth we paid for our PX and commissary supplies with MPC's of a different color.

The changeover that occurred in 1954 was the biggest as far as the Far East is concerned. It extended from the front lines in Korea, through every military post in Japan; it blanketed Okinawa and all the other islands where Americans are stationed.

Time colorfully reports the last changeover, ending its story thus: "For one glorious day, GI's had revenge [on the blackmarketers]. But blackmarketers had the last word.

Three days after the switch, they were doing a brisk business in the new script, at the old price—3,500 hwan [Korean currency] for $10 MPC [new issue]."

Time obviously—and rightly—disapproves of the rapidity with which the blackmarketers got back into business, buying and selling currency they had no right to possess, holding up innocent young American soldiers who were in need of a few hwan for a foray into the native market.

But how do the Koreans, the Japanese or the Okinawans get military payment certificates? Do they present themselves at changeover time and make their switches? Do they walk into army finance offices (where signs announce that "indigenous" personnel cannot possess MPC's) and simply ask that the officers in charge change their hwan or their yen into solid American army paper?

Obviously there is but one way in which "indigenous" personnel can possess American money or, except in the case of break-ins and thievery, any PX items. *Americans* must be involved. It is the American, who in violation of regulations, at the constant risk of cheapening the local currency, passes Army paper into the stream of Korean or Japanese life. The soldier pays his girl off in MPC's, pays for native goods with MPC's. The American soldier too pays for services with a vast variety of PX goods. But what is more damning is that Americans are in nearly every case involved in the mass movement of PX goods from PX to black market.

A Korean newspaper man told me that among Korean women the most popular Americans were sergeants, preferably supply sergeants or those attached to a PX or a Commissary. For the noncommissioned officer will most certainly supply his girl friend, probably will supply her whole family. And always there is the possibility that he can be persuaded or will himself suggest that operations be expanded a bit, that a ring be set up whereby he can funnel American goods into the black market.

203

One American officer told me that he estimated that Americans, officers and enlisted men, were involved in ninety per cent of the major thefts of American property in Korea.

I have seen Americans at work in Korea long before our men suffered from the uncertainty of war. During Military Government days at Chunchon it was discovered that large quantities of gasoline and even tires were disappearing from our motor pool. It was natural that every Korean employee was hauled in and grilled, for surely the Koreans were involved.

One Korean was involved. But he was merely the "fence." The goods were being slipped to him by two nice American lads, who incidentally pocketed most of the profits.

It is not my intention to damn American troops. The proportion of dishonest to honest soldiers is not high. But I maintain that a blanket condemnation of the Koreans as a "thieving" race is manifestly unfair and dishonest. Considering economic pressures, the people of Korea are no more dishonest, nor more thieving than Americans.

The peoples of Asia are under terrific pressure, morally and economically. Like any peoples, of any color, there are those who crack. Sometimes it is a man in high position whose salary cannot begin to feed and clothe his family. Sometimes little real pressure is needed, for there are those already weak, who easily slip into corruption. But any indictment of people must always consider the conditions under which the people live, and about that I shall have more comment in succeeding chapters.

Formosa, Japan, Korea, indeed all of Asia is filled with people who have endured unbearable pressure but many of them still retain their integrity and hope for better days. It is not only the adults whose lives have been twisted by war and uncertainty. It is particularly the children who have undergone things no child should experience in an age of civilization.

For those who criticize Korea and the Koreans blindly I tell the story of one of Korea's children just as it was told to me. Her name is Chai Nam Soon. If Nam Soon lived in America she would be in high school, a sub-deb almost certainly popular because even hardship and privation has not erased the simple beauty in her face. Her story has come, temporarily at least, to a happy ending. As for the more distant future, no one can foretell.

Chapter 3

To UNDERSTAND the story of Nam Soon, one should begin sixty-five miles northwest of Seoul where the north branch of the Han River breaks through the rugged mountains south of the Hwachon reservoir to join the Soyang River at Chunchon. The Pukhan, as it is called, is a tumultuous, rapid-filled stream above Chunchon. Steep, forested mountains rise two and three thousand feet from its banks. A narrow ribbon of road skirts the river, winding northward across the neutral zone into Communist Korea.

For nearly ten years the deep valley of the Pukhan and the road that twists through it have funneled a river of humanity into Chunchon. In the days of uneasy peace before 1950, tens of thousands of refugees moved down the valley, openly at first, then secretly when North Korea's masters tried vainly to stem the tide. Even in the dead of winter when the mountain slopes were carpeted under three feet of snow, the white-clad throng slipped through the mountain passes at night, to cross or attempt to cross the 38th Parallel that stretched six miles north of Chunchon.

In June of 1950 the traffic was very heavy, but the travelers did not wear white. On June 25th Communist armies rolled down the Pukhan Valley, and the military traffic never ceased from that day until the last great Communist offensive of

206

1953 when the Red armies crashed through for miles to punish Syngman Rhee for blocking the truce.

The military traffic rolled both ways in the Pukhan Valley. The city of Chunchon changed hands eight times in three years, thereby losing all resemblance to the lovely mountain town where I lived for a year. In time, fighting men of a half dozen nationalities traveled the road north from Chunchon, sometimes retreating, sometimes advancing.

It was the summer of 1951 that Chunchon changed hands for the third time. United Nations armies were in headlong retreat down the valley. Lost in the dust of roaring tanks and trucks Chai Nam Soon, aged ten, and Chai Nam Rin, aged ten months, were also moving down the valley.

The Chai family lived in North Korea, twenty-five miles above the old 38th Parallel. Nam Soon's father died during the spring of 1951. Two days before United Nations lines on the central front broke, Nam Soon's mother also died. Thus suddenly a ten-year-old girl was left alone, responsible for a ten-month-old brother. What slight security a little Korean mountain girl had, suddenly vanished. There were no relatives, no adults to provide guidance and comfort. Fear mounting to hysteria swept the village. The cluster of huts, once vibrant with the simple life of the Korean mountains, became dead, as men, women and children sought safety in retreat to the south. Chai Nam Soon and Chai Nam Rin were suddenly alone in that frightening time of quiet, which like the eye of a hurricane, exists in the center of battle when one army has retreated and the conquering army has not yet arrived. I have experienced that deceptive quiet that goes before defeat, when the mutter of guns seems suddenly muted, when the terror of the unknown clutches at heart and soul. So it must have been with Chai Nam Soon, age ten, and alone except for the burden of a baby, strapped Korean-fashion on her back.

And so a little girl and a baby started down the dust-

207

churned road to the south. There were many jeeps and trucks roaring down the road, and the children walked in the dust of fleeing vehicles for ten miles. Chai Nam Soon is vague now as to how long she walked. Four or perhaps five hours, she thinks. Progress must have been slow, for she had Nam Rin strapped to her back and carried also a little bundle—all the rice she could salvage from the family home and a few other possessions.

Finally one of the jeeps stopped. The traffic had been thinning because Nam Soon was now on the edge of no man's land. The defeated were ahead of her, the victors just behind her. She looked at me with some embarrassment as she told me: "At first I was scared when the jeep stopped. The Communists had told us how cruel and brutal American soldiers killed Korean children. But there was a Korean interpreter in the jeep. He told me it was all right."

Chai Nam Soon has no idea of the rank of the American soldier who hustled her and Nam Rin into the jeep. He took the children to a South Korean police station just north of Chunchon. The police were very busy, fighting guerrillas and fifth columnists, and after a day or so deposited Nam Soon and Nam Rin in a Chunchon inn.

The children stayed at the inn for two weeks, using the rice Nam Soon had salvaged to pay their board. But when the rice gave out the manager of the inn took the children to a crowded Korean government orphanage.

Chunchon was about to change hands again. The enemy had advanced down the Pukhan Valley and was massed just outside the city. American soldiers entered the picture again. An American army civil assistance team was attempting to move all the hundreds of orphaned and lost children out of the city before it fell. Chai Nam Soon and Chai Nam Rin were taken out by truck and deposited in another crowded orphanage, in Seoul.

During all these moves Nam Soon had her problems. Nam Rin had never been weaned.

"All the time he was crying for milk," she told me. Then with a knowledge far beyond her years she explained. "All the wet nurses were without milk because of starvation. So I made soup for Nam Rin with the little rice I could get." Then Nam Rin added the final straw by getting measles!

The city of Seoul was crowded with refugees including hundreds of homeless children. There were few doctors, few attendants to look after lost children; there was little food. Chai Nam Soon bore all her responsibilities, nursed Nam Rin, scrounged bits of food that a sick child might digest, mended and patched his and her clothes.

Finally there came a day when the months of running, of illness, of responsibility no little girl should have to bear, ended. Nam Soon and Nam Rin were transferred from the crowded government orphanage to the Nam Buk Orphanage in Seoul's southern suburbs, just south of the bombed out Han River bridge.

It was in the superintendent's office at Nam Buk that I met and talked with Chai Nam Soon, now a self-possessed and healthy girl of twelve. And little Nam Rin, now three going on four years old, looks none the worse for wear—except for a few pockmarks caused by infected and untreated measles.

I met Chai Nam Soon purely by chance. The *Christian Herald* magazine had asked me to visit and write a story about the new Christian Herald Orphanage in Seoul. The Nam Buk Home was selected for *Christian Herald* sponsorship. Its name plate had just been changed to read Christian Herald Nam Buk Home. And although Nam Soon is still too young to realize it, she and her brother had a rare stroke of luck in being transferred to that home.

When I visited the home there were 194 children there. A map in the superintendent's office shows the original home of each child. They have come from the north and from the south, from nearly all of Korea's provinces. It was for this reason that the home was named "Nam Buk" which means South-North. Most of the children are refugees like Nam Soon, lost in retreats from North Korea.

The story of Nam Buk, of the loving care given the children there, is one of the bright spots in Korea. Children can forget easily. In Nam Buk they have found tender, loving care, a chance to be educated, vocational training, decent shelter and nourishing food. For most of them the horrible memories of war are receding.

Nam Buk began its existence in 1951. Hong Sung Yoo, the superintendent, returned to Seoul after its last recapture. He is a Christian and he was appalled by the hundreds of children roaming the streets. Without financial backing, without help from anyone, he rounded up seventy waifs in Yungdung-po, Seoul's southern industrial suburb. He took in sixty-five more who arrived from Chunchon and could find no place in the government homes. American GI's brought in others from the front. From time to time the over-crowded government homes simply dumped more children on Mr. Hong's doorstep.

Hong got permission to use an abandoned and partly bombed Japanese furniture factory. A man of some means, he put his own money into making the factory livable. He still takes no salary for his services. In this respect he is not exceptional. I met numerous other Koreans who devote their lives, without compensation, to helping Korean children find a new life. Of course the British correspondent who complained that the Koreans will not help themselves knows nothing about Mr. Hong and his Nam Buk home. It is off the beaten track, reached by a rutted road, inconvenient to get to. Why waste time seeking out these bits of light and brightness when there is so much evil in Korea to write about?

Hong Sung Yoo soon began to receive outside help. First Francis Kinsler and Otto DeCamp of the Presbyterian Mission brought money and clothes. The First Marine Division was stationed nearby. The chaplain heard about Nam Buk, and to the First Marine Division must go the credit for keeping Nam Buk going until the *Christian Herald* magazine came along to firmly underwrite its future.

The old Japanese factory that has become Chai Nam Soon's home is on an appropriate spot. Sixty years ago it was selected as the place of public execution for the Christians, condemned to death during the viciously anti-Christian drive of the Li dynasty. After all these years the hillside overlooking Seoul has become a place for Christian work among children.

Nam Buk will not be confined to the factory for long. Already a lovely twelve-acre tract on the hill-top above the factory has been optioned, four acres actually bought and paid for. A two-story brick building, heavily pockmarked with machine-gun fire but otherwise in good condition, stands in the center of the tract. Vegetable gardens have already been planted, workshops started. For *Christian Herald* always includes vocational training and a maximum of self help in its operations.

When the whole twelve-acre tract is acquired, there will be land enough to feed the children. The furniture factory and adjacent buildings will be maintained for vocational training. Already the older boys are hard at work, repairing and repainting war-damaged trucks and buses. Nine of the older girls are sewing for their living, while others are preparing to be practical nurses. Nine older boys are studying agriculture and are now supervising the Nam Buk fields.

Mr. Hong's plans cover the years ahead and include even the small children like Chai Nam Rin. If his dreams come true, more buildings will rise, more fields will go into rice and potatoes. Meanwhile there will be schooling and religious instruction for the small children. When they become old enough they will begin to learn a trade. In time each child will graduate, will join the stream of Korean life in a productive job.

Nam Buk is not the only progressive orphanage in Korea. Twenty miles away, on the outskirts of Anyang, there is a magnificent home managed by Dr. Oh, eighty-year-old dean of Korean doctors. Dr. Oh has developed the first cottage plan orphanage in eastern Asia. The children live in cottages with a cottage mother. They too, work to feed themselves, tilling the extensive fields, gathering chestnuts to sell in Seoul, learning trades.

Dr. Oh's home receives part of its support from one of the finest and most efficient Christian agencies at work in this war-troubled world. The "Christian Children's Fund" of Richmond, Virginia, with work scattered all over the world, is helping Dr. Oh's children and hundreds of other children in scores of homes throughout Korea. The efficiency of CCF is in sharp contrast to the bungling efforts of the United Nations in Korea. CCF experts are continually in the field, guiding, checking, seeing that minimum standards are maintained, seeking money for new homes, locating children that need care. I could not but reflect upon this fact: The American responsible for supervising all the activities of CCF in Korea receives a salary of less than $2400 a year. He travels all through the land, by jeep and truck, on crowded Korean trains, stopping at whatever inn he can find at the end of the day's journey. The typical United Nations expert receives a salary of between $7,000 and $10,000 a year, lives in swank comfort in Seoul or Pusan, and if he travels at all it is by UN train or U.S. army plane.

Chai Nam Soon and her little brother are well taken care of, will enjoy a measure of security. Their ordeal has ended in comparative happiness. But as I talked to her I could not but wonder why we Americans with all our wealth and efficiency could not see that all the waifs left in the wake of our wars were sheltered and fed.

We correspondents who have covered the Far East during the past decade have seen human misery at its worst: the wartime bombing of Chinese cities; the stream of refugees fleeing Seoul in the dark summer of 1950. But nowhere have I seen such concentrated misery as among the lost children of Korea. It is bad in Seoul, but it is even worse in Pusan, in the other cities behind the front. No one has ever taken a census of the waifs caught there in the backwash of war.

Last year in Pusan, in one fifteen-minute walk I counted fourteen children, some as old as my own thirteen-year-old John, Jr., others as young as four-year-old David, lying half naked, desperately ill, uncared for on the sidewalk. There is no one in Pusan to take them in, no hospital with enough beds or big enough budget.

For each of the ill, there are scores and hundreds who have somehow existed, selling newspapers, shining shoes, stealing, crawling into some deserted warehouse to spend the night. The children have to eat. Without help and guidance, they steal and pilfer, for they are human beings, with human stomachs and hunger.

There are scores of orphanages in Korea, including the largest in the world and the worst in the world. In all the land there are perhaps fifty that even approach minimum standards. But there are some 75,000 children for whom as yet there is no place, no home, good or bad.

The story of Chai Nam Soon is one of victory, courage and faith with a happy ending. But again I wonder why cannot the United States or the United Nations, able to spend billions of dollars killing the parents of the waifs, spend the tiny fraction of that amount needed to shelter and clothe and feed the homeless children? What magnificent propaganda it would be if we could say to the world: "See, we fought for and devastated Korea. But we have also taken care of the needy and the homeless that resulted from the fighting. We cannot only stop aggression. We can and will help those who are willing to fight back. As we were willing to spend billions to stop the enemy, we are also willing to spend to rebuild."

Of course the United States has said words to that effect, usually shrouded in diplomatic double talk and combined with a threat: "But you will have to be good and not start any trouble. None of this business of making us keep our promises about uniting your country!" Meanwhile, 75,000 homeless children wander through the land, the maimed and the halt crowd the streets; cities and villages remain devastated.

And what of the real future that lies ahead for Chai Nam Soon? How long can half-a-nation exist? As Nam Soon and the others who now live in happiness and hope grow older, can understand what has happened to their country, will they remain hopeful and happy? Will there always be an enemy army twenty-five miles away, a sterile neutral zone cutting squarely through the land? What dreams of the future can Nam Soon have when she is old enough to understand?

Chapter 4

KOREA is filled with men and women who dream. Many have accepted the conditions that produce heroines like Chai Nam Soon, but in their acceptance see only bitterness and hopelessness. There are some who dream of better days, who have plans for their country just as Tommy Hsu has plans for his land. But there are more whose dreams have become nightmares.

One afternoon I sat in a tea house near Pusan's lovely harbor, talking to an old friend I had not seen since the day in June, 1950, when the Korean world fell apart. He is a well educated man, has studied in America; but he finds no place in Korea where his training can be used. He is able to make a living for himself, his mother and his sister. They have a home of sorts, in a building housing thirty other people.

I call him Mr. Pak, which is not his name. He is young still, but by Korean custom should have married long ago. But he has no dreams to dream, no desire to share his nothingness with another, no desire to bring children into his bitter world. He sees no possible solution to his country's problems, no good in his government, nothing but the worst in Korea's leadership. As we sat in the crowded tea room Mr. Pak spoke his bitterness loudly so that others about us could hear.

"President Rhee is a dictator, just as bad as any Communist dictator," Mr. Pak told me. "It is laughable to talk about democracy here. This is a police state, with no freedom. Why look at the corruption, look at the black market!"

There was a pause after this outburst. Then I asked my young Korean friend a question.

"Mr. Pak, what you say may be true. But how long would you last in a Communist state if you talked as you have here, with such bitterness and so loudly that dozens in this room could hear?"

Mr. Pak look rather startled. He said nothing for a long moment, and then replied with honesty.

"I guess I'd last about three minutes."

I have seen him again, this disillusioned young Korean, in the city of Seoul. And in the past year I have received numerous letters from him. Always the bitterness is there, always the complaint that his talents are wasted, that living is hard. "There is no place for me in Korea," he wrote a few months ago.

Mr. Pak lost one good job because he was declared a security risk. He has not been arrested or bothered in any way. But he lost a job because his bitterness and criticisms were well known.

Young Mr. Pak proudly calls himself a neutralist now. He told me once that the only hope of small countries and people like himself was to stay clear of the struggle between the Free and Communist worlds. There are many like him, men and women who choose to sit out the battle. They are, of course, security risks. Mr. Pak has brought many of his troubles upon himself.

In Seoul one day I visited an old friend, a woman in her forties. She is foreign educated, a member of one of Korea's distinguished revolutionary families that fought the Japanese for decades. I went to her home in the once fashionable Gold

Coast district of Seoul, my visit arranged in advance by telephone.

But when I knocked on the gate there was no answer. I knocked long and loud; I even shouted until finally an upstairs window opened. Someone peeked out and called down that the gate would be opened.

After I had greeted my old friend, I chided her upon her slowness in admitting visitors. This is the story she told me, a story I later verified from other sources.

A few weeks earlier a group of North Korean women spies had crossed the neutral zone. Five had been apprehended, several having moved as far south as Taegu. Each agent carried a list of prominent South Korean women leaders' names. The list was more than a blacklist. It was an assassination list. My friend's name was on that list of twenty women to be liquidated.

She is not a coward. When Seoul was captured in 1950 she stayed on, hiding under the floor of her house for days, living in daily risk of capture, often going without food and water.

Has the truce brought peace to her home? Has Panmunjom meant that she can now begin an orderly, constructive life again?

No, the deadly seriousness of her situation makes it necessary that her gate be locked except to known visitors. She can take no chances. The gate is not opened until she or a servant first looks out an upstairs window to identify callers.

Panmunjom has brought no more peace to my friend than it has to Mr. Pak. But her feelings about dictatorship and police differ from Mr. Pak's bitter denunciation. As an added measure of protection, she has a buzzer system connecting with a Korean police station two blocks away. If unwelcome callers come in the night, she can signal the police from her bedroom; help will be immediately forthcoming.

Here and there in Korea there are also men who have

bright dreams of the future, even as Tommy Hsu dreams of a Free China's future. Consider the story of Walter Jhung, an American citizen of Korean ancestry, willing to give up the security of that precious citizenship and life in Honolulu to return to his ancestral home and work for his people.

Walter Jhung is among the several young men who hold top positions in the Korean government, and he has made some sort of record in that he has held his position for nearly four years. In the ever changing ROK government structure that is unusual. Walter Jhung is special assistant to the prime minister, with offices in the only completely whole building remaining on Seoul's once beautiful capitol grounds.

I was especially interested in Jhung because he is a graduate of Vanderbilt University, my school. He lived in Nashville for several years. I asked him if he planned to return to America.

"No," he answered. "At least not for a long time and then only to visit. There is so much to do here. Every day there is a new crisis, a new problem to solve."

And then Walter Jhung told me of his many duties, of his hopes and dreams for a future Korea. One small project, carried by his initiative, consisted of building up a library of books on Korea, the Far East and foreign affairs. Few such books get to Korea. Strongly anti-Communist books or those favorable to Korea do not even reach the State Department's library in Seoul. Jhung feels that cabinet ministers and other high government officials should read everything they can get their hands on. The books are loaned out to officials. A card index includes notations on books not available and needed. Walter Jhung pays for the books out of his own pocket.

But it was Walter Jhung's dreams that interested me most. He does not plan to stay on in Korean government work. Already he has had many lucrative offers to enter private business, but as long as he is in President Rhee's service he will not even take on advisory posts.

Walter Jhung dreams of a day when there will be American tourists coming to Korea. As an American citizen he is keenly aware of the criticism voiced by many American soldiers, the general dislike expressed by Americans for Korea and Koreans.

"Over a million Americans have been in Korea," he told me, "and most of them left disliking the land and the people. I can't blame them, for the days they spent here were not very pleasant. But I think they will forget their bitterness after a while and many will want to come back, to show their families the hills over which they fought. If they can see us as we really are, in a time of peace, if they can visit us in comfortable circumstances they will become our friends."

And so Walter Jhung is collecting every bit of information possible on the tourist business. He plans to establish a tourist and travel bureau, says that he has already talked at length with President Rhee about building modern hotels near Korea's scenic and historic spots.

There is a practical side to this dream of Walter Jhung, thought it may be years before it can materialize. Korea is a land of real beauty, of magnificent mountains and lovely beaches, of temples, monasteries and ancient capital cities. The tourist dollar can be important in the Korean economy. Tourists might also revive the ancient and lovely Korean handicrafts industry, offering income to people who are better suited to such work than for labor in a great factory.

Walter Jhung is one of the most optimistic men I have met in Korea. His intelligent face fairly flashes as he talks of his plans, his hopes. He has limitless faith in his boss, President Syngman Rhee. Walter Jhung has a vision for the land of his ancestors.

According to a news story in an American magazine, Congressman Charles Brownson, Republican of Indiana, has made a study of Korean reconstruction plans and has heard of Walter Jhung's dreams. The congressman is reported to have been critical of such foolishness, of plans to build hotels, to lure tourists. Perhaps it is not time to build hotels, new highways. But neither is it time to discourage dreamers. Korea needs men like Walter Jhung and his boss, men who have the courage to look beyond the ruins, who can see and plan for bright days ahead.

Mr. Ro Chang Kah is a middle-aged Korean with teen-age children. He is a man of means, loving children and devoting his time and money to the orphans of his country. Mr. Ro is cheerful; with the children he is tender. I watched him in a half dozen orphanages. One evening as we ate Korean kimchi together in an orphanage that sits on the side of Seoul's South Mountain Mr. Ro spoke of his dreams. Behind the cheerfulness, the tenderness and love for children, Mr. Ro kept carefully concealed his own dark dreams.

"For us—for my wife and me—there is no hope," he told me. "My children might be able to carry on because they are going to America and may escape."

I asked Mr. Ro why he felt so hopeless, and his answer was one that I got more and more often as I traveled elsewhere in Asia.

"The only hope against Communism is force, backed by your Atom and H bombs. The bombs must be used the next time the other side makes a move anywhere. But I know you Americans well enough to know this will not be done. So in five years it will be all over here in Korea. My wife and I will die here, probably in a Communist prison."

It was strange to find this quiet, dedicated man, pinning his slender hopes on America's atomic might and sure that that might will never be used to save him. I found many others like him in Korea, even in Japan, in Formosa. What hopes they may have lie in the Atom bomb. Their hopes belie the many American correspondents who write that Asiatics distrust us because we have used the bomb in the past. Robert Sherrod, writing in the *Saturday Evening Post*, in 1953, stated: "But throughout the Far East the atomic bomb was considered immoral, in-humane and un-American; it made us suspect, and a lot of our postwar troubles out here stem from the decision to drop it."

Whenever I read words like those, I know that the man who writes is not a good reporter, that these sentiments are not shared by the great mass of people in Asia. Those who know what Communism is know also that force may be the only answer; the Mr. Ro's of Asia know too that there is nothing more brutal than, let us say, death by napalm bombing. Mr. Sherrod's deep words must be especially interesting to my Mr. Ro with his widespread work among the orphanages of Korea. One of the homes he helps to supervise will be known for many years in Korea because of the fact that 152 of its inmates were killed in one burning moment, not by atom bombs but by napalm bombs, dropped from American planes attacking a Communist position nearby. Mr. Ro is realistic; he knows death is permanent and often painful; he knows too that his hopes and dreams may depend upon the use of the weapon which Mr. Sherrod claims is immoral. Mr. Sherrod and the *Saturday Evening Post* do not speak for the people of Asia; especially do they not speak for those who have experienced the living death of Communism.

I met a Korean girl who had that experience. I do not know her name and never shall. It was a bright September day that I met her as I was driving through the streets with Mrs. Sue Adams, grand old lady of the Presbyterian Mission. We noticed a young Korean woman lying in the gutter on the main street of Seoul just beyond the railroad station. I noticed her especially because beauty could still be seen beneath the dirt, under the rags. We passed her by, our attention diverted by the crowd gathered around the bloody body of a Korean high school boy, just killed by an army truck.

We drove on to the Eighth Army's new headquarters compound, for a tour of the new officers' area at old Camp Sobingo. Mrs. Adams had been quiet for some minutes when she spoke to me.

"John," she said, "I won't be able to sleep tonight unless we go back and help that young woman. She may be a street walker, but she is ill and needs help."

I did not relish the attention we would cause, foreigners in an American station wagon, stopping to talk to a woman in the gutter.

The young woman was where we had seen her, thirty minutes earlier, but now squatted on the curb, head in hands.

Mrs. Adams addressed her, in Korean fashion. "A-gi-moni (Auntie), you seem to be ill. There is a hospital nearby. We can take you there. Or if you are in need, we will take you to the welfare department where you will receive help."

The woman, perhaps twenty-five, perhaps thirty years old, looked up in amazement that she had been noticed, and by foreigners. She spoke dully, almost as hypnotized and pointed to her feet.

"Yes," she said. "I need help. But I have only one shoe. I cannot go to city hall with one shoe!"

"But the welfare people will help you," replied Mrs. Adams, "even if you have no shoes! Come, we will ride in our car, and I will see that you shall receive the help you need."

The young woman got into the back seat of the station wagon, still talking of the impropriety of going to city hall with one shoe off. We had driven by Seoul's ancient South Gate when a strange thing happened. The young woman began to chant; in a kneeling position she chanted in perfect Korean high talk, and even with my limited Korean I caught

the meaning of the words: *Our Father which art in heaven,
Hallowed be thy name . . . Thy will be done . . .*

On and on she went, with the Lord's prayer, her voice rising almost into a scream as we approached city hall. This was
no ordinary street walker we had behind us. She spoke as
educated Koreans speak, with a slight accent from the Cholla
provinces. She was, or had been, a Christian.

I will never know what experience this once beautiful
woman had gone through. For as we climbed the steps to
city hall she became hysterical. As we entered Seoul city welfare offices her mind broke. Now the lost shoe was forgotten,
the words she spoke were not in supplication. She screamed
in terror, she begged not to be beaten again, she implored
Mrs. Adams not to leave her. She could not give her name,
her age. From her lips came only shrill cries and animal
moans, the sounds of a mind that has broken, of a soul tortured by nightmare dreams.

The woman who lost her shoe is a part of the Korean story,
as is that of a ten-year-old girl heroine, of Walter Jhung and
his dreams, Mr. Pak and his bitterness, the woman in Seoul
who is afraid to open her door, yet who still has faith in her
country and its leadership.

And what of the Americans in Korea, of whom there are a
good number, even today? Wherever Americans are gathered
there are dreamers, and most of the dreams are happy ones
like Walter Jhung's. All along the front lines, in the supply
areas far to the rear, American boys dream of going home,
greet each announcement of a new division to be withdrawn
with enthusiasm. I shared some of these American dreams,
sat in on the bull sessions where each man told of his plans
for the future. There were a few who planned to stay in the
army, but most had big plans: college education for some,
jobs and marriage for others. Take Corporal Charles Gar-

diner, handsome 24-year-old from Roanoke, Alabama. Born in the western cattle country, Chuck has big plans for raising white-faced cattle in Alabama. His wife had already made a down payment on a big acreage. Chuck's plans are big and heady. When the Alabama place gets going, he'll buy a big spread out West somewhere.

There is no limit to Corporal Gardiner's plans; yet the chances are that his dreams will come true. For him and for his buddies there is security, a rich and prosperous homeland to which to go home. America has been made great by dreamers, and the field is still wide open. But what a contrast between the future of the Chuck Gardiners and that of the little people of Free China and Korea. For many there is no home to go back to. Devastation and poverty and insecurity are the lot of all. It affects the thinking and the dreaming of young and old. For many like the woman who lost her shoe, life has become a nightmare.

Chapter 5

THERE were one hundred and eighty "war" correspondents accredited to the United Nations Command in Seoul during August, 1953. There were Americans, British, Koreans, Japanese, Belgians, Swiss, Swedes, Chinese and Canadians. There were a few good correspondents, some very bad ones, many inexperienced men. But whether good or bad, for most of the men, the story to be written was found at Freedom Village and at Panmunjom. The road north, Route One, the army calls it, that leads from Seoul to Munsan and on across the Imjin River to Panmunjom was heavily traveled each day. Occasionally correspondents strayed off this beaten path to cover a story elsewhere. But for most writers, Korea was Seoul and Munsan; for the great majority other place names in Korea meant little. For the land has become nameless except in terms of "outpost" numbers, map coordinates and "K" numbers, designating the airfields in South Korea. K-16 is Seoul, K-9 is Pusan and K-2 is Taegu. I flew with pilots and with correspondents who did not know the names of the teeming cities we visited. One day, crossing the railroad bridge that spans the Imjin River on the road to Panmunjom an army colonel, who had served on the United Nations truce team for months, asked in complete seriousness: "This is the Yalu River, isn't it?"

There are men who see that Korea has more than highways and airfields, who are hurt with the hurt that has come to the land. There are men like Dick Erman, young American correspondent for Reuters News Agency, who is supporting an orphanage on his own, who plans now to build a model village near Pusan. There are a few others who have dug deep into the history and the culture of the land, for only by knowing of Korea's past, only by understanding the struggle of today can one judge the actions of President Syngman Rhee.

Statistics tell a little of the story. Six hundred thousand homes destroyed; coal production down 50 per cent; property damage between $1 billion and $3 billion in a nation whose gross national product is $1.4 billions; on September 15th, 1953, in Seoul alone, 356,000 people on relief; in Kyonggi province, with a population of two million, 940,000 on relief, and of these 250,000 considered destitute cases. Statistics determine the nature of a ruler's actions. But even more important than figures, are the faces, the souls that lie behind the figures. Human beings, too, determine policy and procedures, the goodness or the badness of a national administration.

During August and September, of 1953, I took the well traveled road from Seoul to Freedom Village; I flew along the central front; I visited Pusan and came back to Seoul on the blacked-out United Nations express; I traveled twelve hundred miles by plane, train, jeep and boat; and I tried to get the feel of Korea today, to jot in my notebook facts, figures, statements, impressions that would help me understand the problems and the actions of a people and its leaders.

One day I toured the central front in a light army plane. We flew near such historic spots as Old Baldy and T-Bone Ridge; we circled the valley down which the Chinese pushed for five miles just before the truce was signed, down which Chai Nam Soon traveled in 1951. One gains a tremendous respect for the American army after such a tour. The central front is much like our own Great Smokies, except that there are more mountains, and the mountains are more rugged. All along this mountain front there are vast military encampments, trench and bunker systems and roads where no roads have ever been in Korean history. I flew, not in an air force plane, but in one of the many light planes flown by the airmen of the army. These are the men who are spotters for artillery, who act as couriers carrying messages into remote mountain airstrips. These strips cover the land today, and how the pilots get into them is something I cannot understand. We landed on a strip near the Hwachon Reservoir. On one side was a 5,000-foot mountain mass. The strip lay at the bottom of a deep valley, making it necessary to circle corkscrew fashion until the five-seater Beaver plane was low enough to make an approach. In the process it seemed to me that the wing tips would scrape the mountain sides. After many stops along the front, my pilot dropped me in Chunchon so that I could visit the city where my wife Elsie and I had worked for nearly a year back in '48.

This was the city from which Chai Nam Soon and her baby brother had fled. You remember that it had already changed hands eight different times. After each battle a little more of the city was devastated. Ninety per cent of the downtown section is gone now. I walked the streets for an hour visiting places where old and dear friends once lived. I could not find a person I had known before. As I walked through the ruins I felt also the spiritual destruction that has come to these people. There seemed to be few smiles on the faces of those who now live in jerrybuilt shacks, or are camping out among the ruins.

Perhaps I am wrong, but I felt a certain anti-American feeling in the air. These are largely illiterate mountain people, and it must be difficult for many of them to understand why their city had to take so much punishment, why a great airfield with thousands of aliens must be in their town. Worst of all is the little these men and women of the Korean mountains have to hope for in the future. Their homes shattered, life made difficult by the world's highest inflation, they live on one of the main invasion routes to the south. The few who talked to me believe that Chunchon will sometime experience its ninth battle.

Elsie and I supervised the first elections in Chunchon in 1948. We were proud—the Koreans with whom we worked were proud—when we had the highest percentage of votes among all South Korean provinces. Ninety-six per cent of our people registered; 91 per cent voted. The majority of our friends were for the Syngman Rhee candidates back then. I wondered if there was any change after all that has happened in the five years since we left. I got my answer from one of the Christian leaders in the city. When I asked him about Syngman Rhee, he told me: "It is not so much a matter of being loyal to our president as it is a matter of being all united for one common ideal and idea of saving our country from extinction."

The majority of Koreans feel as the man in Chunchon felt; they are behind their president; they understand the tremendous difficulties he faces. They feel that only forthright outspoken leadership will save the land from extinction.

The task of postwar leadership in Korea has been made difficult by the necessity of working with large and cumbersome United Nations organizations. And when we add the realization on the part of Korea's leaders and its educated people that the nation can never really exist as half a nation, we can understand a little of what appears sometimes to be stubbornness and intransigence.

"Never have so many foreigners, connected with so many agencies been involved in rebuilding so small a nation," was the comment of one Korean when we talked of progress in reconstruction.

228

The United States Army is involved in many phases of reconstruction. Harold Stassen's Foreign Operations Administration has millions of dollars to spend. The United Nations Rehabilitation Administration, known as UNKRA entered the field nearly three years ago with its millions. There are men and women of a dozen nationalities running about the land, each with a plan, a panacea. Plans made by other American agencies four or five years ago, and just as useful and valid today as then, are either unknown or scrapped. Robert Nathan Associates, headed by an erstwhile bright young New Deal economist, sent a team of experts to Korea. The cost was $50,000 for an off-the-cuff survey. It was made against the recommendations of Syngman Rhee's government; it covered territory already covered by a dozen other surveys. The bright young men of Robert Nathan Associates had never been to Korea before; doubtless will never return. But being bright and being economists, it was of course not necessary that they know anything about Korea, its past or present.

The money spent on short term "experts," whether they be working for the United Nations or an agency of the United States Government, is a disgrace and a waste of funds. General Mark Clark in his memoirs *From the Danube to the Yalu* comments on those that afflicted him:

". . . and many came from Washington as governmental experts to make quick surveys to determine what economic and financial aid was necessary to rebuild South Korea.

"Most of these men were rushed out from Washington to make their studies and fix things up. I always felt . . . my headquarters included American civilian economists and financial experts who were just as capable as these specialists hurried from home as trouble shooters . . . these 'resident' economists had the advantage of familiarity with the people, issues and the problems. They did not have to make a preliminary survey. . . ."

229

The United Nations hired a man to go to Korea and make a public relations film. Pat Frank is his name, a bright and witty American writer, author of *Mr. Adam,* with no knowledge of the Far East. I do not know Mr. Frank's feelings about Syngman Rhee and Korea, but I do know that he is one of the nastiest and bitterest critics of President Rhee's ally, Chiang Kai Shek. It was not long ago that Mr. Frank penned these lines: "All the American help and all the American money will not put Chiang Kai Shek together again."

It is rumored that Mr. Frank was paid $25,000 to direct the making of a motion picture on Korea. It was UNKRA money, but it was also our money; for the United States puts up most of the funds to operate the United Nation's agencies in Korea. I have never seen Mr. Frank's production, nor have I ever met anyone who has seen it.

Consider these further facts about the United Nation's relief effort in Korea. Two hundred and fifty thousand dollars has been spent on public relations equipment: cameras, film projectors, motion picture cameras. The average salary of a UN expert in Korea is $7,000. In addition, each employee receives free a trip to his homeland each year, with transportation paid both ways. And since Korea is a hardship post, each foreign employee also receives three free "R. and R." (Rest and Relaxation) trips to Japan each year. Altogether, the UN expert is on the job perhaps ten months of the year, for the rest of the time is spent in going to and from the flesh pots of Japan, or to and from home which may be in Denmark, or America or England.

There are good men and women in UNKRA, of course, men like Dr. Lopez, who are doing an excellent job. But among its more than three hundred experts there are also the dregs of other international efforts, the international teatsuckers who will hang on to UNKRA for a while, then shift on to other pastures.

When UNKRA was established it had offices in New York, Tokyo, Pusan and Geneva. It has improved after doing little for two years. Its administration has been tightened, some of the unqualified personnel have been removed. But now UNKRA is faced with a new problem. The members of the United Nations who had pledged aid now refuse to pay their pledges. UNKRA is actually forced to send representatives knocking on the doors of Europe's chancelleries, begging European governments to pay what they pledged two years ago to contribute to Korea's recovery.

Is it surprising that Korea's leaders are difficult, that men and women lose hope completely?

There is supposed to be coordination now, among all the agencies at work in Korea. A planning board has been established; all activities must be approved by it, channeled through it. And under the direction of Mr. Tyler Wood, director of the Foreign Operations Administration in Korea, there has been solid progress.

Yet the reconstruction of a nation over which we bled, where we have a golden opportunity to show that America cannot only destroy but can also efficiently rebuild, is handled in an amazingly off-hand manner.

An American engineering friend of mine who served in Korea before the war went back recently to bid upon a U.S. army contract to rehabilitate Korea's electric power industry. My engineer friend knew Korea's power system, its needs, had visited every power plant in the land.

He was amazed upon reading the army specifications to find that inferior Japanese power equipment was required, that equipment unsuited to certain installations was listed.

"I told the army officer in charge," the engineer related to me, "that the equipment was not right, that most of it would not last two years, that then the whole job would have to be done over again. The army officer told me brusquely that it

231

was not my responsibility to comment on the specifications. I could bid for my firm or I could go home."

My friend filed a report, but it was ignored. The Koreans are having their power system rebuilt. There will be breakdowns soon, of course, and in a couple of years the whole job will have to be done over again. But by that time the officers in charge will be far removed; they will never be held responsible for their part in the business.

It is unfair to blame the army. Officers are assigned, willy-nilly, to reconstruction projects. The men are waiting for that day when they will leave Korea, will be able either to rejoin families or go into civilian life. Can they be expected to have too much interest in reconstructing a benighted land they dislike?

At last report the American army was in charge of one of the most vital phases of agricultural reconstruction in Korea. The U. S. Army distributes fertilizer to Korean farmers. Here is a job where real experts are needed, men like Ralph Gleason of Formosa who fathered the Taichung night-soil disposal plant. But instead, army officers, counting the days until rotation, knowing nothing about the needs of the land, are in the saddle.

Is it indeed any wonder that President Rhee proves difficult at times? Is it any wonder that men like Mr. Pak are calling themselves "neutralists?" In Korea the Free World had, and still has, a magnificent opportunity to show that it can rebuild just as it can devastate. It is an opportunity not yet seized upon, to date hopelessly bungled. It will be a difficult task at best, and Americans might as well realize that it must go on and on for years.

South Korea is but half a nation. It does not have the natural resources with which to compensate for those lost to the Communists in the area north of the truce line. A half billion dollars will be required, year after year, to rebuild and to attempt to compensate for resources and industries lost to North Korea. This is one of the by-products of a foolish truce, a cost saddled upon us because we were not willing to win.

But perhaps it can be done, perhaps South Korea can become a tremendous psychological weapon in Asia, a clear indication that America will help rebuild what has been destroyed in an effort to halt aggression. But if it is to be successfully done, it should be done by the United States alone. It will be far more to American interests to have the United Nations step out, to allow us to do the job and take the credit—if there be credit. For to date the United Nations has not shown much more ability to work efficiently in alleviating human misery and suffering than it has in winning wars or in solving political problems.

It is a tragic situation. The Republic of Korea came into existence under UN supervision. The first elections in 1948 were held under UN sponsorship. Then and through the early days of fighting, the UN flag flew from school houses and public buildings. The United Nations was a respected organization, the only hope for a small and weak nation.

But Koreans understand that their land is still divided because some members of the United Nations would not risk a fight to victory. They know that certain members of the United Nations have refused to live up to their pledges to underwrite Korea's reconstruction. They know that the United Nations truce team is powerless to stop the truce violations. Lieutenant No Kum Sok, the Communist jet pilot who flew his MIG to freedom (thereby receiving Mark Clark's $100,-000 reward) stated: "I saw the Reds break the Korean truce the day after it was signed."

Koreans, educated and uneducated, see their nation becoming a United Nations pawn. It is little wonder that they are unhappy and bewildered, that Korean leadership has become touchy and hard to work with. They fight back against what they consider to be unjust and unwise decisions with the pitifully few weapons they have: hot-headed pronouncements by President Rhee and other high officials, mass demonstrations against withdrawal of American troops, against use of Japanese products in the reconstruction program. The Land of Morning Calm has become a land of misery and chaos, a nation unable to help itself because it has no voice in any major decision affecting its future.

Chapter 6

THE American GI cannot wait until time to go home. Few can be found who have any use for Korea or the Koreans. However, all over the land are monuments to American soldier generosity. The story of the good things done by American soldiers in Korea is a bright story, one that could have great value in the propaganda phase of the Cold War.

Soldiering far from home does not bring out the best in men, whether they be American, British or Chinese. The American soldier abroad is no angel; his conduct is better than that of some other soldiers, sometimes worse than that of other nationalities. In Korea, the American GI has been involved in black markets, just as he has in Japan and in Germany. Some soldiers have become dope addicts—probably more in Korea than in any other country where Americans have been stationed. There is at present a widespread dope smuggling ring in Korea and Japan, a ring designed not only to snare Americans in the habit but also to get dope into America.

In Okinawa Americans are involved in a vicious prostitution business. Young girls barely in their teens are brought into Okinawa from the small outlying islands, there to service the thousands of GI's on that crowded island.

Though I have first-hand information to convince me of the truth of the above-mentioned accusations, I believe that the American soldier in the Far East has been accused unjustly of other things. For instance, two years ago a magazine of national circulation announced that in Japan alone there were 200,000 illegitimate GI babies; yet a recent careful census by the Japanese government reveals that there are only 4,000.

The conduct of the American fighting man, good or bad, is of importance. The Communists fear American prestige and American intervention in Asia more than anything else. Since 1945, the Red propaganda machine has been attempting to turn the Asian people against America by depicting the American soldier as a brutal and corrupt monster. The campaign against the American fighting man began in China in 1946 and has continued unabated since. Its culmination has been in the germ warfare charges of 1953 and 1954.

Obviously then the conduct of Americans is important. Any wrongdoing is grist for the Communist mill. At the same time, if the American soldier leaves good works behind him, these can be invaluable in counteracting the Red barrage against the GI. And with all his faults, the American fighting man does do great good, does make friends by his big-heartedness, has left a trail of decent acts wherever he has been stationed.

Driving through the city of Suwon one day, I noticed a sign reading "Children's Nutritional Center." I investigated and found that the center, established to feed the hundreds of waifs that wander Suwon's streets, was made possible by the gift of $8,000 from the men of a nearby engineering service battalion. On that same day I visited Suwon's hospital, one of the four that exist in the province of Kyonggi. The hospital had been hard hit by artillery but was being rebuilt; most of it was already rehabilitated. Five thousand dollars from the American flyers at the nearby air base had made the rebuilding possible. In the month that I spent in Korea a year ago these American soldier activities came to my attention: during Christmas of 1953 the soldiers of the Eighth Army contributed $596,117 and over 9,000,000 pounds of parcel post packages received from friends and relatives in America. During that same Christmas period, 181,000 Korean children were given Christmas parties by American GI's.

The men of the 45th Division gave one check for $41,000 to establish a trust fund for the maintenance of the orphans' home on Cheju Island. During the three years it was in Korea, this division donated $300,000 to Korean charities.

Soldiers of the 32nd Infantry Regiment contributed $3,500 for the rebuilding of schools in their sector. During one period, men of the First Corps raised $25,000 for similar purposes.

The men of the Fifth Regimental Combat Team collected $18,000 to establish a "Boys' Town" on an island in the Han River near Seoul. Soldiers of the Eighth Army collected $5,000 for the family of Reverend Pang Wha-Ill, who died as a result of a beating by an American officer and three soldiers.

According to Eighth Army officials, known donations of American soldiers through April of 1954, totaled $582,992; from men of the First Corps, $561,000; $436,000 from the Ninth Corps, and $115,071 from the Tenth Corps. And added to this there are thousands of unknown and unrecorded donations and acts of mercy.

Bill Shaw, veteran Methodist missionary, told me that a week never passes that a chaplain or an officer or a soldier does not bring him money.

"Sometimes it may be only ten dollars," Dr. Shaw said. "Sometimes it may be a hundred dollars or even a thousand. Sometimes it is for a specific project; sometimes they tell me to use the money any way I think best."

So it has gone for four years—Boys' Town, new schools and

237

churches, orphanages and hospitals, a tremendous outflowing of money and help from the very men who hate Korea, who cannot wait until the day when they can shake the last of Korea's dirt from their shoes. So it is also in Japan, in Okinawa, in Formosa, in the Philippines, wherever American soldiers are stationed.

There is one example of American generosity in Korea, which if known and properly exploited in propaganda, could erase any and all impact the germ warfare charges might have had upon the people of Asia. It is a story that had its beginning in the compassion of an American general and that has come to full fruition because of the generosity of thousands of American GI's combined with the skill and facilities of American missionaries.

One day a Korean child on the central front stepped upon a mine, losing his arms. General Paul Kendall, commanding general of the First Corps, known more simply as "I" Corps, heard of the child and determined to help him. General Kendall knew that there were hundreds of similar cases, children and adults. He asked his commanders from division down through regiment to raise funds for the development of facilities to care for child amputees. I have not talked to the general and do not know if he thought in terms of that one child or of all the children.

But his request touched off an amazing sequence of events. Within a few days a total of $75,000 had been raised from men of "I" Corps. The generosity of foreign troops touched the hearts of Korean fighting men. The men of the 101st Division of the Korean Service Corps contributed $3,136. Other donations poured in from the Korean First Corps Security Police, from Korean civilian workers at "I" Corps headquarters, even from the workers of the Kangwon bus line which served cities behind the central front.

The money raised by "I" Corps, totaling nearly $100,000, was placed in trust in a New York bank. On December 17,

1952, the "I" Corps Korean Children's Amputee Clinic was established at bomb-scarred Severance Hospital in Seoul.

I visited Severance Hospital to look over the project, and as I drove up to the hospital a little five-year old boy came hopping merrily out on one leg, making the request he makes of all who visit the amputee clinic: "Give me a jeep ride, give me a jeep ride."

Little Kim, he is called, and the story of how he came into Severance and of the care he now receives, can be duplicated a hundred times.

Little Kim was brought into Severance near death from shock and loss of blood, with a simple, brutal explanation of his wounds.

"Some bad men came to my house last night. They killed my daddy and my mother. They shot my leg off."

Now Little Kim is one of over three hundred Koreans who are getting a new start in life through the activities of the Amputee Clinic. The armless and legless are first prepared for artificial limbs, have the limbs (made by fellow amputees) fitted, will learn to walk, ride bicycles, use their hooks; will be taught a trade and will be able to go back, already are going back into the stream of Korean life able to work and make a living.

The "I" Corps project is actually combined with the Korean Amputee Project, sponsored by American missionaries. Even before General Kendall went into action, the Methodist and Presbyterian Missions, operating through Church World Service, were developing a program of medical assistance and rehabilitation for the estimated 22,000 amputees in Korea. The Korean Amputee Project was first centered in Seoul's Severance Hospital but was soon extended to Taejon and Chonju.

The activities of these two related amputee projects, one soldier-initiated, the other missionary-inspired, are a monument to American generosity and a guide post on the road to genuine inter-religious cooperation. The use of the "I" Corps trust fund is determined by an inter-religious board of directors in Korea made up of a Catholic, a Presbyterian, a Methodist and a Seventh Day Adventist missionary, an officer from "I" Corps and another officer selected from the staff of the American embassy military attaché's staff in Seoul.

The Methodist church brought Dr. Reuben Torrey, veteran Methodist missionary from China, to direct medical facilities at Severance. Dr. Torrey is himself an amputee, can understand the morale problems that beset the terribly crippled children, men and women who are brought into Severance. Paul Kingsbury, young Presbyterian lay missionary, took a special course in the making of artificial limbs and was rushed to Seoul. Dr. Paul Crane, medical chief at the Chonju unit, is supported by the Southern Presbyterian church. Down in Taejon, Corporal Neil Stowe, a Catholic enlisted man, attached to 171st Evacuation hospital, and a trained artificial limb-maker, is giving his time to the maintenance of a limb shop. Thelma Maw, Methodist occupational therapist, and Louise Scarin, Presbyterian nurse, complete the staff. Missionary direction of medical facilities, combined with "I" Corps purchased equipment, have produced at Severance a magnificent amputee clinic.

I spent two days in the Severance unit of the project. It was a heart-breaking, yet heart-warming experience. In the orthopedic children's wards were those who still must go through pain and anguish before limbs can be fitted. For some of the amputees this is a long process. Stumps must be prepared—and that means new operations.

I talked to thirteen-year-old Yu Chong Sang who lost both arms when he got in the way of a hand grenade. One hook has already been fitted, and with that hook he can do wonders. But the other stump is not ready, must receive further surgical attention from Dr. Torrey before a hook can be fitted. Then the boy must learn to use the hooks. After completing his course in the Seoul "rehab" ward, he will be sent south to Taejon to learn a trade.

The equipment used in making artificial limbs and to train amputees in the use of the limbs is simple and inexpensive. Six of the eight Koreans working in the limb shop are amputees, and Paul Kingsbury told me he hopes eventually to employ only amputees.

In the room next to Paul Kingsbury's shop, amputees are trained in the use of hooks. On the wall is a board, extending almost from baseboard to ceiling. On the board there are locks of every description, door knobs, light switches, even a dial 'phone. Before the armless can "graduate" they must operate every gadget on the board, must be able to dial a set of numbers—in 90 seconds. I watched Yu Chong Sang "do the board" with his one fitted hook. He did it in the prescribed time but was criticized a bit for fumbling. I asked Dr. Torrey if there is anything the armless cannot learn to do.

"Yes," he told me, "there is one thing, and it makes the children especially a little upset. There is no hook we can devise that can be used to manipulate chopsticks. The boys and girls will have to learn to eat with knife and fork."

While the amputee work is a monument to the generosity of American soldiers, it does no credit to American artificial limb manufacturers. When Church World Service initiated the project, it tried to find just one experienced American manufacturer of artificial limbs willing to go to Korea and train Koreans to help themselves. Not one was willing to take on the job. It was for this reason that Paul Kingsbury, completely without experience, was given eight weeks training and rushed out to Korea to set up the shops.

I asked Dr. Torrey just how inter-religious activities worked out in the project.

"Above all else," he replied, "we try to make the project as Christian as possible. No child is ever turned away. All children receive religious teachings according to their known faith. Last week I was having lunch with Father Carroll in Taejon when a new case was brought in. I was called out to examine the boy and noticed a cross around his neck. We found out that he was from a Catholic family. I informed Father Carroll who informed a local priest. That boy is in a Protestant hospital, but he will receive religious help from a Catholic priest. That's the way we operate."

There is a big job ahead for the combined amputee projects. The three hundred who have received help constitute a tiny fraction of those who need help. Thousands of amputees are scattered through the country, in the cities, in remote villages. This fall a man supported by "I" Corps trust funds will begin beating the bushes, hunting for amputees, especially children. The parents will be told that help is available, their fears will be allayed, their children brought into Seoul, Chonju or Taejon. Dr. Torrey estimates that there are a minimum of 22,000 more who need help.

For the children, the road to complete rehabilitation is long and painful. Little Kim, for instance, may need four or five artificial legs as he grows older. As the size of his legs and stump increases, he will need a bigger, more adult artificial leg. Children and parents must be taught how to keep the stump clean, must learn the importance of wearing a clean stump sock every day.

But already those who are working with the amputees can see the success of their efforts. As I left Severance Hospital one afternoon, a young Korean boy rode up on his bicycle. He dismounted nimbly and walked into the building. I would never have known that he was a legless bi-lateral had not Paul Kingsbury pointed him out to me.

With well deserved pride Paul said, "There is one of our boys. We made his legs, we taught him how to use his legs, we taught him a trade."

Surely the story of the young Korean, without legs, but who can now ride a bicycle because of the generosity of Americans should be told to all of Asia. The operation of the

"I" Corps project and the missionary amputee work with which it is connected should provide excellent counter propaganda directed at the people of Asia who have heard and who even believe the germ warfare charges, the other stories of American soldier brutality.

Yet, as far as I know, neither the amputee project, nor the heart-warming work of the American GI has ever been used by the Voice of America. This is an important and costly failure. Since the end of World War II the Communists have tried desperately to belittle the American soldier, to paint him as black as possible. And the desperation with which this effort has been carried on indicates the fear Communists have of the vast reservoir of friendship and good feeling for America.

Thus the germ warfare charges are really nothing new, are but an extension of Red Chinese charges of 1946 which began in Shanghai where the Americans attached to a military police unit were attacked for their "brutal" conduct. From that slender beginning, the charges spread and were multiplied.

In December of 1946 I was director of the United States Information Service in China. I reported to the Department of State in detail the extent of the campaign directed against American service men. I quoted a conversation I had with an American just returned from Communist-controlled areas in northwest China: "She tells me that the anti-American campaign there has been vigorous, with lurid posters depicting rape, murder and robbery in dozens of ways."

The pattern of Communist propaganda has never changed, is the same whether it be in China or in Korea. While visiting Kinmen, I secured several Communist leaflets, floated over from the mainland in bamboo tubes. The attack against American fighting men was there, their brutality and cowardice, their "defeat" in Korea documented down to the last exaggerated detail.

The cleverness of the Communist technique is indicated

by the fact that, wherever possible, Americans have been used to discredit fellow Americans. Thus it was that a leading American magazine accused American soldiers of fathering 200,000 illegitimate babies in Japan. An American newspaper man (a Communist sympathizer) in Shanghai was used to tell the story of American brutality in Korea, through the pages of his English language magazine.

While I was attached to the U. S. Embassy in China in 1946–47, I saw an excellent example of how the Communist program developed, using Americans to transmit the anti-American propaganda.

During that period U.S. marines were stationed in North China. The presence of the marines was of course vigorously denounced by the Communists. A series of stories began to appear in the leftist press detailing atrocities committed by the marines. Specifically it was reported that marines were using Chinese farmers for target practice. It was inconceivable to me that American marines or soldiers would use human beings for target practice. I made a trip to North China in early 1947 and personally investigated the situation. I found that one Chinese farmer had been wounded by a stray bullet fired from a marine target range. From this slender thread, the story had been woven into a first class scandal, passed on by Communist-inspired Chinese newspapers, by American dupes led by a few Americans who knew exactly what they were doing.

American soldiers do misbehave, and their sins should be criticized and punished. But the good they do far outweighs the evil. I believe strongly that the story of American generosity has never been properly told by our Information Agencies. It is told in fragmentary form by our newspaper and magazine reporters, but that telling is only for American reading. Yet it is a ready-made answer to a decade of Communist vilification against our fighting men. Why do we not use the weapons we possess?

Chapter 7

I T IS ONLY the isolated mountain valleys like the one where Kim Man Gu and his lepers live that do not show the ravages of war. From the truce line, on far to the south are still the actual signs of combat. From Taegu southward cities are unmarked by physical violence, but their limits are horribly swollen by thousands of refugees who still have found no place to really settle, who have no home but the jerry-built shacks that are a part of the Korean scene today.

But there is one spot in Korea, completely untouched by war, where one sees no beggars, few of the armless and legless veterans who crowd the streets of mainland cities. For that spot is an island, just off the mouth of the Han River. It is called Kangwha which means "Flowery River" and it is among the most historic spots in Korea. There are other historic spots, places like Kyongju, seat of the Silla dynasty 1500 years ago. There are temples and monasteries all through the land, but for me there is no place quite like Kangwha. Sentiment enters in, for it was there that Elsie and I spent our short honeymoon. John, Jr., and I have hiked the hills of Kangwha together. Many times during the peaceful years of 1948, 1949 and 1950 I journeyed to Kangwha to hunt, to explore, or just to rest in the peaceful quiet of ancient Chung Dong Monastery.

We Americans, who fought a long war for independence, who were forced to fight again a few years later, who were split by bloody civil war when our nation had still not existed for a century, should be able to appreciate Kangwha Island, for there can be seen physical evidence of Korea's long fight for independence.

Korean history begins on Kangwha. Kim Chong Sop, ancient abbot of Chung Dong Monastery, points out the nearby mountain top where Tan Gun, legendary first king of Korea, landed from heaven nearly three thousand years before Christ. A cairn of stones marks the sacred spot.

But unification and independence did not come easily for the Koreans. There were centuries of war before the land was united during the Koryo dynasty, from which the land has received its foreign name. (The Koreans called their country Hangook or Chosun.) Then, four thousand years after Tan Gun's descent from heaven, began the alien invasions that have been Korea's lot for centuries.

In 1232 the Mongols swept across the Yalu River and spread throughout the land. The Korean kings were unable to fight off the Mongol horde, but they did not give up. They retreated to Kangwha and holed up there for several decades. In 1233, second year of exile from the mainland, they built a wall, not only around the landward side of the island but on the crests of all the mountains guarding the mainland approaches as well. The Korean kings built their refugee capital in Kangwha city, but when it was burned in 1246, they moved into the mountain-encircled valley where the Chong Dong Monastery now stands.

The wall built then around the monastery still stands. For, according to legend, Tan Gun sent help. He ordered his three sons to leave heaven and to build the wall quickly. It was done in a day, and is called the Wall of the Three Sons. Behind that wall the kings of Korea lived in exile until the Mongols retreated.

Again in 1636 Chinese hordes drove south, and again the royal family retreated to Kangwha. The new enemy was able to cross the narrow channel from Kimpo, was able to breach the wall and to destroy Kangwha city.

But Koreans are stubborn folks. The new enemy in time departed, and a new wall, even stronger and higher was built along the shores of the island. The Korean kings had no occasion to again use the island as their "Formosa" until the nineteenth century. The Western World had by then discovered Korea, sought to bring its religion and its trade to a people who wanted only to be left alone.

In 1866 the French attempted to reach Seoul. Kangwha lies at the mouth of the Han River, in those days the only avenue of approach to Korea's capital. The French attempted to storm Kangwha, but the Wall of the Three Sons held them back. The invaders were repulsed, and for a short period Korea was left alone by the outside world.

The next-to-the-last Korean king was born on Kangwha in 1851. He was of the Li dynasty, a family to which President Syngman Rhee is related. There remained for Korea only a few more years of independence after the birth of the king. For when the Japanese invaders came, walls built seven hundred years earlier were of little value. A mile wide channel could no longer serve as a giant moat. There was no retreat to Kangwha because retreat would be useless.

Much of Korea's history was written on Kangwha and still can be seen in its monasteries, walls, its mountain-top cairns. And the face of the future, the nature of the problems facing Korea's present leaders can also be seen from the tops of Kangwha's mountains. The island now is the most northerly United Nations position on Korea's western front.

From the mountains above the Chong Dong Monastery I could watch the new invaders with field glasses. There were thousands of Chinese coolies at work that day in September, 1953, building giant subterranean bunkers, digging new trenches—building their new wall.

While Kangwha is at peace, it lies closer to danger than

at any time in its history. Two and one-half miles away are thousands of Chinese, more ruthless, more determined than were the Manchus or the Mongols. Kangwha's history, all of Korea's history, repeats itself across the mouth of the Han. Chinese invaders again threaten the island and the nation. And these are Chinese whom no wall, no fortress monastery can ever stop.

And for Syngman Rhee, descendant of a king born on Kangwha, there can be no retreat. There is no place to go—except to the north where a new wall of water and mountains could perhaps give the nation security again.

But how can half-a-nation expect to breach the great new wall the Communists have built across Korea? And what about the correspondent who said: "What can you do with these people—they won't help themselves; they will not fight?"

No testimony of mine is needed on the fighting ability of Korea's troops. General James Van Fleet, the man who trained and commanded them, has called them "superb." Other Americans who worked with the ROK's have testified to their ability. Even a majority of American war correspondents, men not generally predisposed to praise anything Korean, have written of their valor. The ROK's have deficiencies, of course. They have not mastered the problems of modern logistics; they are deficient in the operation of some modern equipment.

Even on the day my British colleague damned the people, the leaders and the soldiers of Korea, a dramatic occurrence took place in the heart of Seoul, a few blocks away from the Eighth Army correspondents' billets.

Each day through most of August and September of 1953, a succession of helicopters roared in to land in the heart of Seoul, setting down in a cleared spot where once a government office building stood. Each day crowds of Korean civilians gathered too, to greet the helicopters. For each ship carried ROK soldiers repatriated during Operation Big Switch. These were the ill, for the others were processed near Freedom Village.

The civilians who came each afternoon came sometimes to greet returning heroes, sometimes to look hopefully for a son or for a father. As each helicopter landed, the throng would push forward, silently and anxiously watching as each man was taken out on a litter.

I was there one day in September when a crowd of school girls had come to sing, to welcome the wounded and the ill. As each broken man was brought out he was cheered by the girls. One Korean boy was lying on his stomach on the stretcher as the orderlies lifted him out. He made no movement, did not even acknowledge the girls who were there to greet him. Then one of the orderlies tapped him on the shoulder, spoke to him, asking that at least he show a little appreciation. But still the Korean soldier did not move.

Suddenly the white-clad oldsters, the brightly clothed school girls all understood. It was as if a message simultaneously reached the mind of each person.

The Korean soldier was dead. For him freedom had come too late. Somewhere between Freedom Village and Seoul he had died.

Few American correspondents watched the daily drama that took place in the heart of Seoul. For them—and quite naturally so—the big story was in the American boys who came each day into Freedom Village. But the story of the Korean repatriates is a further indication that the British correspondent who said they would not fight did not know whereof he spoke.

Not only did the Koreans fight, and fight well, even when captured they did not break. And the average Korean POW suffered far more torture, received less food, than did his fellow soldiers from America, or Britain or Turkey.

The Korean soldiers had no long democratic tradition to bolster them in their fight against the brainwashers. Most of them were country boys, never even knowing how to handle a gun until war suddenly burst upon their country. Many had actually gone into battle before firing a practice shot.

Neither did the Korean GI have the incentive of home and loved ones to keep his spirit alive. For in many cases homes, even whole villages had long since been devastated. Loved ones were dead or long lost or themselves prisoners in some North Korean prison camp.

Yet in spite of these facts, less than five per cent of all Koreans captured gave in to the brainwashers. The stories these boys told were stories of unbelievable suffering, of a will to fight back that was never, for most of them, broken.

It might be well to compare the record of Korean repatriates with that of the American men who have returned home from prisoner camps. Of the 3,332 American men returned, over 300 are now facing or have faced charges concerning their activities while prisoners. Nearly ten per cent "broke" in some way. In the fall of 1954 an American army officer was court-martialed for disloyal acts while a prisoner. Never before in American military history has there been a similar case.

The unwillingness of the simple ROK soldier to break under enemy pressure ranks along with the willingness of Chinese Communist soldiers to surrender as a psychological factor of great importance.

Not only will the man of South Korea fight—and superbly, according to General Van Fleet—he is as good a soldier as any in his steadfastness, his moral fibre, when faced with the torture that has caused even Americans to break.

There are 600,000 ROK's today. I watched them in Seoul and in Pusan and Taegu. They are well behaved boys, well thought of by their countrymen. I have visited their new training camps, high in the mountains along the central front, where a division at a time can be given refresher training. I have seen a little of their partisan training. For the northern part of Kangwha Island is now a base for training of Koreans in all the tactics of guerrilla and partisan warfare.

Where there are now 600,000 men under arms in South Korea, there could be many more. An army of a million ROK's with adequate artillery and planes and naval forces, what it might do to complement the men of Free China I saw on the guerrilla islands and on Formosa!

Could Red China with its economic problems, its thousands of guerrillas and dissident peasants, withstand a two-prong attack, one from Korea in the North, one against the China Coast? Could it withstand at the same time the widespread guerrilla activities which could hit them all through Korea, along its coast, from the mouth of the Han River to the Indo-China border?

Would the people of Korea back another struggle? I think they would. I believe there are still a vast majority of the people who have not given up, who will fight if given the opportunity to strike back at the menace that has dislocated their lives for so many years, that has brought ruin and desolation to their land.

But Syngman Rhee and his government is so difficult, we are told. How can we expect much from an ally who causes trouble, who threatens, who seems ungrateful for all that America has done for it?

Yes, Syngman Rhee is a difficult man, a man of single purpose. When I last talked to him in the fall of 1953 he spoke more of the menace of Japan than he did of other problems that might seem far more pressing and important. But is this not easily understood, just as we can understand the distrust of France toward Germany? In the case of Rhee and Korea, there is even more personal basis for hatred and distrust of the Japanese. For Korea suffered under forty years of Japanese rule, scores of its leaders were exiled, tortured, imprisoned. And Rhee is a smart man. He knows that there have been occasions when the U.S. government has forced inferior Japanese goods upon Korea, as in the case of the equipment for South Korea's power system. Syngman Rhee remembers too that even before the Communist invasion, Marshall Plan administrators forced Korea to accept Japanese ships, so inferior that at least one ship sank en route from Japan to Korea.

Certainly his stubborn opposition is wrong, just as France's failure to go along wholeheartedly with German rearmament has been wrong. At least it is wrong in so far as the total picture of Free World planning is concerned. But while wrong, it is also understandable. Korea, with all its troubles and problems, has a part to play in the liberation of Asia.

Militarily this may all be nonsense. But factors other than military will provide the final answer in Asia. And that answer will not affect only the peoples of Korea and Formosa. An effort to free China and North Korea, a bona fide attack by the Free World, would cause repercussions all through the nervous neutral lands. Burma, already stiffening a little, would be affected. The people of divided Indo-China would take heart. Little Thailand, probable next target in the Red push into Southeast Asia would be strengthened. And all through Asia the overseas Chinese populations would take their place on the side of the Free World.

President Syngman Rhee said all these things when he came to America in 1954. He urged the Congress of the United States to be realistic, to understand that the future of Asia was at stake. He was not applauded when he spoke to the Congress about war. Talk of war in an election year is most distasteful. But neither did any member of Congress or any official of the United States speak up with an alternative.

Of course it is wishful thinking to even consider such a two-pronged attack against Communism in Asia. For there is little time to prepare it, materially or otherwise. And given time, another year or so perhaps, Communism can repair its broken dykes in Asia. More "dissident elements" will be liquidated, more millions brainwashed until at last the spark of resistance is gone.

But equally important is what time is doing to the Free World's remaining allies. Years of war, years of uncertainty ahead, the breaking of ancient family ties, the awful insecurity that faces so many people is producing more and more Mr. Paks, who have given up the fight.

All of Asia is today in ferment. There is moral ferment and cultural ferment, brilliantly exploited by the Communists who offer an end to the uncertainty.

Near what was once called the 38th Parallel, I talked to a Korean Christian refugee, an old woman alone because her family was gone. One by one she had lost them to prison camps, to the army and death, to the unknown. The family had moved to escape the pressure; the father had changed business.

"How long will it last?" she asked me. "How long will we be always moving, always running, always escaping, always wondering?"

How long will it last, ask the young people, too, who have known only fear and uncertainty. War has broken the moral ties of the past. Uncertainty has brewed the greatest ferment in Asia's history. This too, is a part of the story of Asia in the aftermath of Panmunjom and Geneva.

BOOK FOUR

THE FAR EAST IN FERMENT

Chapter 1

THE old folks of Asia, whether it be in Korea, China or Japan are slow to change their ways. The pattern of existence is unchanging, men and women plant and harvest their rice fields in the shadow of great air bases just as they planted and harvested a thousand years ago. War devastates villages; rice fields are cratered with bombs and artillery; with infinite patience the people move elsewhere to claw and carve a new field, to build a new shack, to breed more children. War becomes just one more element which, added to flood and drought, must be contended with and reckoned with in the unceasing struggle for existence.

It is among the young of Asia that the yeast of uncertainty and the shadow of war has caused change and a ferment that is sweeping the continent. For the young there seems no out, no peace in sight, no future worth preparing for or waiting for, no place to go nor to hide. As they attempt to compensate for their restlessness, there is a bounteous sampling of strange fruit, an experimentation with the new, a vast cultural vacuum that is leading to moral and spiritual breakdown.

Riding through the streets of Tokyo one day, I noticed a theatre banner, in English. It read: "The Hottest Girlie Show in Town." Then below the main banner, reflecting the

Japanese difficulty with "R's" and "F's," another banner announced "It's Terrizic, Terrizic, Terrizic—Don't Miss It."

I was unable to take in the "hottest" show, but I did see a typical Tokyo girlie show, representative of the new "art" that is sweeping Japan. In the Nichigeki Music Hall, playing three times daily to standing-room-only crowds, I saw a show called *Women Prefer Locomotives*. There were dances and songs, a bilingual master of ceremonies with off-color jokes in two languages—and the most complete nakedness I have ever seen on the stage. A horseshoe-shaped stage projected well into the audience so that the nakedness could be viewed and appreciated at close quarters. As a part of the show, an attractive Japanese girl appeared dressed as a Catholic nun. She disrobed completely before the enthusiastic audience of United Nations troops on leave and Japanese from every walk of life.

The use of a nun's habit as a prop for a strip-tease surprised me. Could this be an indication of anti-Christian feeling, a slap at religion? The next day I questioned a Japanese newspaper friend.

"Oh no," he replied to my question. "There is nothing irreligious about it. That's just a gimmick—more clothes to take off."

The girlie shows of Japan are much discussed in the Japanese press. There are Japanese who lament the new art, others who praise it. One newspaper editorialized that the strip-tease Japanese style was a good thing, was bringing the theatre "back to the people" in simple, earthy fashion. Be that as it may, the girlie shows of Japan are but one aspect of the tremendous cultural change taking place in the Far East. One finds the change in Korea, in the mountains of Formosa, in Southeast Asia. The ferment is in part, but only in part, due to the presence of vast numbers of Americans. It is in part due to economic conditions and pressures. And it is also the result of spiritual and moral emptiness.

According to Japanese tradition, when the god Kamo Myojin descended to earth some 3,000 years ago he brought prostitutes with him. The girls have been a part of the Japanese pattern of life for generations, flourishing as licensed entertainers. But never before in Japanese history has prostitution flourished as it does today.

The Japanese government announced a census of licensed prostitutes recently. The number totaled 124,289. These are the girls who operate in the houses, under supervision, in districts like Tokyo's famed Yoshiwara where there is even a special hospital to serve the needs of the entertainers. Agents roam all of rural Japan, contracting for the services of girls long before they are ready to ply the trade. The parents often approve, for after all, "What other job can our daughter get that will support the whole family?"

The Japanese government census does not include the thousands who are unlicensed. To see them, one need only visit the streets that radiate out from the great open space in front of the Tokyo railroad system. Rain or shine, summer or winter, they gather, on the street that runs past the big U. S. Army Post Office building. Short skirts, high heels and lipstick are the style for these girls. In Tokyo alone their number is estimated at 25,000. They are a product of war and Americans, their very clothes gifts from American soldiers or bought at the end of the devious black market trail that began in an Army PX. Snappily dressed, many of them teen-agers, the girls have complemented their Western dress with ofttimes excellent knowledge of English.

It is not only on the streets and in the districts that the girls ply their trade. The nightclubs advertise blatantly that their hostesses are the prettiest and make it clear that services other than tending bar are available. One of Tokyo's plushest clubs reminds its patrons that the waitresses cannot live on tips and salaries, that they are available for other services when the club closes down.

It is estimated that the sale of women has brought an average of $85,000,000 a year to Japan since 1946, thus providing that economically unbalanced land a tremendous amount of foreign exchange. Women bring in almost ten times more money than does the tourist trade. Americans are of course the major buyers and contribute most to this flourishing trade, now one of Japan's biggest. Indeed, Americans have tried their hand at organizing it. Two astute young men, taking their discharges in Tokyo, set up a well-organized business that would have made them rich had not a Japanese newspaper exposed it. With American initiative and know-how, these technical-assistance experts gathered together a stable of Tokyo's most attractive maidens. A beautiful brochure was prepared, each girl's picture accompanied by vital and physical statistics. Advertisements, slightly camouflaged were placed in the English language newspapers.

The system worked nicely. A hotel guest needed only to call the number, and a runner would come bearing the brochure. The girl was picked out, headquarters was notified by number, and the fun began.

The changes in Asia range from the tragic to the ridiculous, have extended even into the high Formosan mountains. There the little mountain girls working in the tea plantations are well rouged and lipsticked—and nearly every girl has a fresh permanent. As I traveled the Formosan mountains and marveled at lipstick and hairdos, I noticed too that the young girls of China seemed of different proportions than those I had seen and known on China's mainland. It was Tommy Hsu who told me of the booming business in falsies that has swept the island. There is a definite boom in busts among all the ladies of Chiang's redoubt. And I picked up one other bit of incidental intelligence: riding the crest of the Formosan musical hit parade is the song, "On Top of Old Smoky."

Nowhere is the change that has come to Asia more apparent than in Korea, the land with an age-old morality in which the people once took pride. Literally thousands of prostitutes swarm that land. In Seoul alone there are 10,000 members of the Prostitutes' Union, known as the "Pure as the Lily Club." For many Koreans a new term has been added to the language. It is "Yang-Ki-Bal" and means "United Nations Madame," being a collective term for all the women who ply their trade professionally or as amateurs among United Nations troops and civilian personnel.

The Yang-Ki-Bals swarm the land, in a vast district near Pusan's railroad station, in Seoul's Banchang district and in the better homes on the slope of South Mountain, in hundreds of homes throughout the country where the more fortunate have been set up in modest housekeeping by their patrons. Each evening they gather on the wide avenue that runs past Seoul's Chang Duk palace, to be picked up individually or by Army truck load. Like their Japanese sisters, they too have abandoned traditional dress for high heels and smart American clothes. Nylon stockings and brassieres are in demand in Korea now, and there too figures have changed drastically as a result of war.

There have, of course, always been prostitutes, in every land. But in three years' residence in pre-war Korea I don't remember ever being propositioned upon the street, or hearing the chant of little brothers and other commission agents who swarm Seoul and Pusan: "Have nice clean sister, cheap," or "Nice young Korean girl, cheap."

The tragedy of Korea is that the Yang-Ki-Bals are being accepted, as a necessary, even advantageous part of life. One night I walked the streets of Pusan's teeming red-light district with newspaper friend Suh E Ton. Mr. Suh pointed out the various grade houses, those primarily for civilians, those reserved for soldier patrons.

"But how do the Korean people take this business?" I asked.

"A few of the old-fashioned people object," replied Mr.

Suh. "But after all we realize what an economic advantage these girls have. Why one successful girl can support twenty people sometimes! They help their families; they are of service to the nation."

I found girls who had once worked for me before the days of war, a little ashamed at first, then defiant. At the Eighth Army correspondents' billets in Seoul, the Yang-Ki-Bals paraded in and out, openly, without shame. It was a cozy and neighborly relationship. Prostitutes from a nearby district dropped in casually when business was light to attend the nightly movies showed for the correspondents and the military men who maintain the billets.

How many are there in Korea? Mr. Suh said 200,000 to 400,000—counting those who drift the streets as well as those who are kept in style and comfort. If this is correct and if we translate into terms of proportionate population here in America, it would mean that our nation would have a million and a half active plyers of the world's oldest profession.

"It's inevitable, it's something we can't stop," an officer told me. But how long can the moral fibre of a nation endure under such circumstances? Will there not be repercussions for generations to come? Already the results can be clearly seen in smaller places like Okinawa where the sale of teenage girls is taken for granted, by civilian population and U. S. Army alike. "We have reduced the people of Okinawa to a beer and prostitute existence," a disgusted American on Okinawa told me.

Of course the Communists are quick to seize upon the cultural vacuum, quick to capitalize upon spiritual and moral breakdown. Their approach is double-barrelled. They appeal to the old people by pointing out that imperialistic and corrupt America is responsible for the moral breakdown of the young. For the young there is a flood of propaganda, offering hope for the hopeless, a future for those now lost in uncertainty, security and stability for those who now have no moorings.

As thousands now seek to feed their bodies by selling their flesh, other thousands seek to fill their minds by sampling of the varied intellectual wares offered by Communism. In Asia's bookstores one can see how the Communists are attracted by the vacuum and how they exploit it.

In 1954 the Communists opened their first lending library in Tokyo; Communist books, in both hard-backed and inexpensive editions, are available throughout Japan. Prices are tailored to fit the pocketbook, for profit is not a motive. In a student district, handsomely bound books from Russia can be purchased for a quarter. The same book may sell for two and three times that amount in a well-to-do neighborhood. Through mid-1954 two big books, *The Works of J. V. Stalin* and *Problems of Leninism* had sold 50,000 and 60,000 copies respectively at a price equivalent to fifty-five cents a copy. Similar books about the United States or the men who helped to lay the foundation of our democracy would cost between two and three dollars. The U.S., worrying about copyrights, royalties and profits, does not make its story available to those who have little money. And U. S. Information Libraries cannot fill the gap, cannot compete with the enemy which makes it possible for the intellectual shopper to buy and own books.

What does this mean, translated into Communist Party membership, among the young? In 1954 the chief of Japan's security investigation board reported there were 100,000 party members in the country, organized in 5,470 known cells. Seventy thousand members were young men and women in their twenties.

In his frightening book, *Communism in Education in Asia, Africa and the Far Pacific*, Dr. Walter Eells reports the same picture everywhere, except in those lands ruled by terrible dictators like Chiang Kai Shek. Reporting on the huge University of Calcutta with 45,000 students in its 66 affiliated colleges, Dr. Eells states that about eight per cent of the students are card-carrying members of the Communist Party; forty per cent are fellow travelers; and about seventy per cent are anti-American. He notes that, "Students in the latter group in many cases differ but slightly from fellow travelers."

Dr. Eells devotes a chapter to the causes of Communist influence in the schools and notes that, "Normal economic and social conditions have been shattered in many countries." Writing specifically of Japan where he was advisor on higher education during much of the occupation, Dr. Eells paints the picture of what is happening to all of Asia's young people.

"The ideological vacuum has been particularly marked in the case of Japan. Its young people had been trained for generations to believe in the divinity and infallibility of the Emperor. . . . Then overnight all these ideals, so carefully built up in the minds of the youth, were rudely shattered. . . . Under such violent changes it is not surprising that many Japanese young people were bewildered. Many of them fortunately showed new interest in the teachings of democracy and Christianity; many drifted aimlessly . . . many others turned to the alluring promises of Communism."

The Japanese Education Reform Council, reporting on the causes of student disturbances, listed these as "social conditions subsequent to war, influence of international situations, and confusion of thought on the part of students."

Is it any wonder that the "influence of international situations" should cause "confusion of thought?" Consider Korea, after forty years of hated Japanese rule, then five years of supposed liberation while the nation became a pawn in international power politics, then three years of devastating war, followed by a truce that leaves the nation still divided.

Consider China. Just emerging from years of chaos, with good government in sight, she was suddenly plunged into an eight-year struggle against an alien invader, only to find the hoped-for peace then shattered by a civil war that has not ended yet.

Consider Indo-China, conquered and occupied by Japan whose defeat did not bring peace but only more war to end there too in a divided land. And so the picture goes all over Asia. Nations not touched by actual strife have felt the repercussions of strife. There is not a nation in Asia around which war or rumors of war have not swirled continuously for nearly twenty years.

Is it any wonder that the young people of Asia have a confusion of thought, that they seek desperately to find something to cling to, that they sample new ways of living?

This confusion and the cultural and spiritual vacuum which causes it is grist to the Communist mill. Whether it be a breakdown in morals or of the mind, the Communists are on hand to guide and direct and capitalize. The breakdown of old family ties and morality is to their advantage and is assiduously promoted. Visiting Guatemala just after the civil war in July, 1954, I was told how the Communists had brought in scores of prostitutes and party girls there, of how young and impressionable men in government were urged to "liberate" themselves from foolish bourgeois morality. And so even prostitution and the conditions which increase it, become a carefully used weapon. Not only can the moral fibre of a nation be warped; scores and even hundreds of the prostitutes are dope agents, adding narcotics as a powerful instrument of Communist policy. A steady stream of dope flows from Red China into Korea and Japan, to entrap Americans and native people alike, to find its way to America and the resulting foreign exchange that Red governments so badly need.

Dr. Walter Eell's description of Communist organization and tactics in Asia could be applied to all their tactics in capitalizing upon a continent in ferment. Writes Dr. Eells: "Even though only a minority of the student body belongs to a Communist cell, Communist students have often succeeded in gaining control of student organizations and activities . . . Communist student leaders know what they want. They are alert. They are on the job twenty-four hours a day. They are zealous missionaries for their cause."

With such alertness and zeal Communism is moving successfully into Asia's vacuum, may well win the battle without
recourse to war. Already the populations of every land are
dividing themselves: There are those who give up, physically
and mentally, to become physical prostitutes or "neutralists,"
the mental prostitutes who no longer care to whom they sell
their minds. There are those who hold fast, who hope, who
fight on and dream of a better day—the Tommy Hsus, the
Chen Shi Hos, the Chang Chows, the Walter Jhungs of Asia.
There are many who have turned to religion, as can be seen
in the Christian revival that has swept Korea, has penetrated
even into Japan and Formosa, or in the Buddhist revival in
Burma.

The heart and soul and mind of Asia is on the block, to be
won or lost by the democratic and Christian world. How Asia
came to be as it is must be better understood if the Free
World is to win the spiritual and intellectual struggle. It is
not enough to say that Asia's turmoil is inevitable because of
the combination of nationalism and the hatred of colonialism.
It is not enough to dismiss the problem by simply saying,
"The white man is finished, because he is hated."

Newsweek magazine has extended this "hatred of the white
man" theme to wishful thinking about the course of Chi-
nese-Russian relations, stating, in a review of Red China's
strength (all the magazines devote great space to Communism's strength in Asia, rarely mentioning the strength of
those who keep the rice growing green on democracy's side),
that "They [the people of China] regard the Russians, as
they do all foreigners, as barbarians."

This statement is worse than over-simplification; it is stupid. The Chinese and the Koreans are tolerant people, not per
se hating anyone or labeling anyone as barbarians. The average Chinese hates the American no more than the native
Taiwanese hates the mainland Chinese who tried to exploit
him. The typical native of Fukien has no more use for an

ill-mannered Shantungese than he does for an overbearing British businessman. South Koreans often have difficulties with their more aggressive refugee brothers from North Korea.

The white man may well be finished in Asia, but not because he is white, not because he is necessarily associated with colonialism. Even the French in Indo-China gave far more than they took. In his book *Report on Indo-China*, Bernard Newman states of the French: "In Indo-China they found countries devastated by internecine strife, very backward in administration, and with social services scarcely existing. But for the Viet Minh war, Vietnam could now be handed over as a civilized land."

The Far East is in ferment because of many factors. Certainly colonial powers were slow too often, confused even when they had good intentions. Diplomats are partly at fault. And Theodore White in his *Fire in the Ashes* neatly blames diplomatic failures on Joe McCarthy and senatorial investigators in general!

American churches must even share part of the blame. My own Methodist church, with a magnificent history of work in China dating back to 1847, turned its back on the land in 1949, could not believe that Free Chinese could hold on in Formosa long enough to make extensive missionary work worthwhile.

America's part in the tragedy of Asia must be shared by diplomats and churchmen and in particular by the men and women of the American press who have been reporting on Asia for the past quarter of a century. America's freedom of press may well have become, as far as Asia is concerned, our most dangerous freedom, its failures and dangers typified by the statement of an American newsman, returned to freedom after months of imprisonment in Communist China.

Richard Applegate, a reporter for NBC, was captured while cruising in a yacht in international waters off Hong Kong.

The story of Applegate's imprisonment was not a new story. There was the usual senseless questioning, the threats, the efforts to break the will by solitary confinement, poor food and constant fear. There was the usual effort to obtain a signed confession, and Dick Applegate signed one. I do not hold that against him; for I have no idea what I would do under similar circumstances.

But I was struck and startled by this statement, made by Dick Applegate when he was released. "Before this happened to me," he was reported as saying, "I was a reporter, and as a reporter I tried to stay neutral in the cold war between Communism and democracy."

Is the crime reporter "neutral" when he covers stories of murder and rape? Is it not possible to be objective and honest and still not be neutral? The sin of American reporting is that not only have there been many neutralists; there have been many who were not even neutral in Asia's struggle, who have been so lacking in an understanding of Asia's history that they have seen goodness only on the side of the enemy. By their reporting they have influenced American thinking and American policy just as much as have the diplomats, and so have contributed greatly to the confusion of this day.

Dick Applegate has seen the light. He followed his confession of neutrality with a forthright statement: "But now I'm not neutral any more. I'm going to get into it [the fight]. I'm going to fight that tyranny any way I can from now on."

Unfortunately for the people of Asia the other writers who cover the paddy field beat have not had the experience of spending eighteen months in the filth and horror of a Communist prison. There are still too many who maintain neutrality in the face of tyranny, and their story is a part of the story of Asia in the aftermath of truce.

Chapter 2

I WAS in Seoul during those hope-filled days of Operation Big Switch, when each day American boys came through from the living death of prison camps, to enter Freedom Village and to begin the long trip home. There were 180 correspondents, based at the Eighth Army's correspondents' billets but shuttling back and forth on the road to Munsan and Panmunjom. I was having a leisurely breakfast one day when the number of returnees was to be small and many correspondents had stayed in Seoul. There were five of us at a table, gossiping, talking of Korea and China and the problems of war and peace in Asia.

"What the Far East needs," said a UP reporter, "is three good heart attacks. One for Syngman Rhee, one for Chiang Kai Shek, one for Madame Chiang."

The others at the table nodded sagely at this unique solution of Asia's problems. Of the five of us, only I and one other had ever been in China, or Formosa. Of the five of us, only I had visited Kinmen or Matsu or Tungting Island. But thus, without knowledge or personal experience, American writers solved Asia's problems. The men at the table with me were not even neutral in the struggle between Free and Enslaved Asia. Their minds had been made up and closed, and it would

269

be naive to suppose that their reporting had not thereby become biased and lacking in objectivity.

It was two days after my breakfast with the experts that General William Dean was released. This was the big story for which scores of men had waited. It was truly a big story; for what had happened to Bill Dean had never before happened to an American general. But it was a story which had to be handled with care. Dean's statements and comments must first be carefully screened; for there were still others left behind who might be injured by premature statements.

The United States Army was quite correct therefore in demanding that the Dean story be carefully cleared by censorship. The rules were clearly set forth, and most men abided by them.

I was in the phone room of the correspondents' billets the afternoon the Dean story broke. It was mainly a wire story and I was writing only feature stuff, so I had little to do but watch and marvel at the efficiency of American reporters transmitting a big story to newspaper readers 10,000 miles distant.

Suddenly the enlisted man at the switchboard cocked his head in surprise. Quickly he pulled a plug and turned to an officer nearby.

"So and so upstairs is telephoning his story directly to Tokyo, in violation of your rules," the enlisted man reported. "I've just cut him off."

Almost before the officer could reply, a representative of one of America's great wire services stormed into the room fairly screaming in rage.

"Who cut me off?" he shouted. "Don't you understand this is the story we have been waiting for?"

The officer attempted to explain about the censorship rules but had no opportunity to complete his sentence.

"No son-of-a-bitch in the United States Army is going to mess me up; no damn censor is going to keep this story from getting to Tokyo. Open that line or I'll raise hell from here to the Pentagon."

With this parting shot a great newspaper reporter left the room. An amazed enlisted man was ordered to open the Tokyo line again. An officer of the United States Army shrugged his shoulders in shame and disgust, muttered, "What can you do?" and left the room.

So it was that a news agency, in the great tradition of American journalism, got its story through. The fact that some lonely American, still in prison camp, might have been hurt, did not matter. The fact that policy might be affected was of no importance. The story must get through!

I do not imply that all American reporters have become so calloused, so big for their britches. I do not even imply that all or even the majority of those who cover the Orient would solve Asia's problems with three heart attacks. I simply give these illustrations of the stupidity and arrogance that has become a part of reporting, that has contributed much to Asia's chaos and America's confusion.

For the past decade there has been a pattern of arrogant, biased, inaccurate and half-baked reporting, ranging from the tragic to the ridiculous. "Bulls in China's Shop," is the term I applied to reporters of this sort in an article in *The Freeman*.

In the fall of 1953, two bright young Americans, a world famous movie and TV camera team, arrived in Formosa, fresh from conquests in Korea. The truce had been signed; Big Switch was over; the young men sought new worlds to conquer. Their request of Chinese Nationalist authorities was simple; for after all, they had braved the enemy in Korea, and jumped with paratroopers. They wanted to be dropped, with equipment and interpreter, three hundred miles in the interior of Communist China. Then they would walk out, photographing and recording life under Mao, to be picked up by the Chinese navy at some prearranged spot.

The request was politely refused; courteous Chinese officials tried to explain the facts of life to the young Americans. Thereupon cables began to fly thick and fast to their New York headquarters. Uncooperative Chinese authorities were denounced. When American officials on Formosa refused to intercede, they too were denounced. Not only were Chinese and American authorities accused of being uncooperative, but they were also accused of committing that crime of which there is none worse: They were jeopardizing the *freedom of the press.*

The net result of the activities of this duo of bulls was that feelings were unnecessarily ruffled; all the guerrilla islands were for a time put out of bounds to all American correspondents; the already difficult task of reporting on this important sector of the Cold War front, a sector since become very hot, was made more difficult.

And who can say with certainty that this one incident did not contribute to the lack of knowledge in America about the importance of Kinmen, China's Golden Gate, that is called Quemoy in all our newspapers? I must confess at this point that the use of that name, Quemoy, irritates me. It is unknown except to educated, English-speaking Chinese; its use fails utterly to convey the importance of the island. Many years ago the ubiquitous British mapped the coasts of China, handing out remarkable names on the basis of supposed resemblance to local pronunciation. Kinmen (pronounced Jinmun in Mandarin) is as best I can render it phonetically *Gingmuong* in the local Fukien dialect, and from this the British achieved their Quemoy. Of all the newspapers and magazines reporting on the island, only *U. S. News and World Report* even mentioned the island's real name, its meaning in English, the magnificent activities that have been carried on there. Again consider briefly the confusion in the reporting on this small but vitally important spot. Conflicting statements on area: *U. S. News* reported 57 square miles;

Time reported 85 square miles. The UP described Kinmen as a flat sandpit; *U. S. News* remarked upon the remarkable fertility of the island; while Jim Lucas of the Scripps-Howard papers commented that "its soil is rocky and its weather dry, so it can't produce rice." And these descriptions are of the same place!

It has become fashionable in some quarters to blame the Nationalist government for poor public relations, thus causing confusion in reporting the news. The same persons who complain are also among those who accuse Free China of maintaining a vast "lobby" in this country to sway public opinion. But the Nationalist government is well aware of the importance of good public relations. It does make mistakes, fails to capitalize sometimes on events and personalities. However, the government maintains a Government Spokesman's Office in Taipei with the specific responsibility of helping visiting correspondents. The help is given generously. Interpreters are provided, transportation is set up, appointments are made quickly with top echelon officials.

But the poor Chinese are damned if they do, damned if they don't. It is commonly reported by American correspondents in the Far East that these services are used, not to help, but as a method of control. Flying from Okinawa to Taipei, I shared a seat with an American who gravely informed me that all Taipei hotel rooms are wired for sound, that every visiting foreigner is tailed wherever he goes, that baggage and rooms are searched, that all mail is censored. This is the story that every new correspondent in the Far East receives from the advance echelon of the anti-Chiang press forces in Tokyo.

Has anyone actually had evidence of tampering with his mail, or actually seen the recording devices, really caught a Nationalist secret agent in the act of searching his hotel room? No, it is always third and fourth-hand information, received from so-and-so who is now in the Balkans or back home, or dead. Yet the stories go on and on with variations applied for Korea and Syngman Rhee, and other great "dictator-menaces" of the Far East.

A few months ago I ran into a charming young American woman reporter in Taipei. I had known her briefly in Korea, and she was happy to see me, for she badly needed my assistance. Could I somehow arrange it for her to visit Sun-Moon Lake over the week-end so that "they" would not know it? Patiently I explained that it was only necessary for her to buy a train ticket, make reservations at the Sun-Moon Lake Hotel and be on her way. But no amount of explanation on my part could convince the young lady that she was not being tailed, that "they" were not watching every move she made, would stop her if she attempted to enjoy the mountain scenery. Gravely she informed me that her room and her baggage had already been searched.

"Did you actually see this being done?" I asked.

"No," she replied, "but I went back to my room suddenly and there was a man in there."

The fact that men or maids usually enter hotel rooms to make the bed, to clean up, or to repair seemed to have been forgotten in the mania of suspicion that filled her heart. When last seen she was slipping off to the railroad station, eluding the secret police of a government which had little interest in her week-end plans, or any plans of an unknown and not very successful writer.

My young friend will do no great harm except to add her bit to the body of anti-Chiang folklore that already has crippled American understanding and policy. But there are times when American writers do great harm, actually help the enemy because of sloppy or biased reporting. The United Press was guilty of such harm in the spring of 1954. The UP called attention to the possibility of a major Communist attack on the Ta-chen Islands, the northern anchor of guerrilla-land. In May and June, UP reported the situation so serious that all civilians were being evacuated from the islands. According to one UP story, the Ta-chen Islands form "the classic invasion route to Formosa."

The barren, rocky Ta-chens have never been an invasion route to any place, either in modern or ancient times. The total land area of all the thirty-odd islands in the group held by the Nationalists totals thirty square kilometers. The total population of *all* the islands is 18,576. Only a half dozen of the islands are of sufficient size to be of great importance; many are inhabited by only a handful of people.

As far as any student of China knows, the only invaders who have ever approached the inhospitable islands are the fishermen who settled there during the Ming dynasty. Yet this is UP's "classic invasion route" to Formosa.

The implication of the UP reports is clear. Loss of the Ta-chen Islands will be a major blow to Nationalist China. Formosa will be threatened. Having built up the importance of the Ta-chens, UP has made it almost mandatory that the Reds take over. And in so doing they will achieve a United Press-created victory of great importance.

"See," the anti-Chiang lobbyists will cry, "Chiang can't even hold the most important islands along the China Coast; he has lost the very approaches to Formosa."

The loss of any island along the coast can be serious from a psychological standpoint. But if the Ta-chens are lost, what should have been another battle among never-ending battles along the coast becomes instead an important Communist victory, thanks to the UP build-up.

Consider this curious twist in UP reporting: Kinmen, which *is* a "classic invasion route" to Formosa, which was used by General Koxinga as a staging area for attack on Formosa—which is important—is brushed off in UP's reports as a sandpit, is made unimportant!

It is an unpleasant statement to make, but it would be difficult to see how the Kremlin itself could improve upon the

275

manner in which the United Press has handled the news on Free China. Where battles are measured, not only in casualties and ships sunk but also in terms of psychological impact, the United Press makes the loss of the Ta-chens (which the Reds can take with ease) important. It then makes the loss of Kinmen, which will be taken only at great cost, unimportant.

The whole pattern of United Press reporting in the Far East has been negative and, to say the least, indicative of peculiar judgment. Rutherford Poats, chief of the UP bureau in Japan, author of *Decision in Korea,* published in 1954, makes this amazing evaluation of the Korean Truce: "We had reassured the many small and vulnerable nations living on the periphery of the Communist empire in both Asia and Europe." And commenting further on the effects of war and peace in Korea, Mr. Poats states that "We had thrown back the aggressors, inflicted terrible punishment on all North Korea, more than restored the violated border, and *brought the Korean Republic the greatest security it had ever known.*"

And in final vindication of what every military man of note considers a defeat, Rutherford Poats writes: "The final judgment on this question (effect of the war and truce) will not come from today's statesman or 'expert,' but from the actions of governments and peoples, particularly Asians, in choosing between nervous neutralism and boldly anti-Communist alignment with the democracies. In the first half year after the Korean Armistice was signed, *the verdict of opinion appeared to be on our side.*"

Just where does Mr. Poats get the facts to justify such a roseate outlook? I pass on without comment this statement by a bitter South Korean newspaperman who said: "The closest American newspapermen ever get to real Korean problems is the Korean girls they sleep with at night."

It is strange that the American correspondent, superbly courageous during battle, willing to take all manner of chances, has become so sloppy, so inaccurate in reporting the events which produce war. The big magazines, a half dozen of our largest newspapers, the big news agencies all have tremendous working staffs in the Far East. Men are available to seek out the news, to keep ears atuned to the murmur of coming events. Yet the UP, with a man resident in Taipei, never sent him to the guerrilla islands. The *New York Times*, with a half dozen men resident in the Far East, filed a feature story in the spring of 1954 on the fact that Chiang Kai Shek was losing the guerrilla islands, one by one. The story was written in Hong Kong, obviously based upon sources of information unfriendly to Nationalist China, and it did not mention a single island that Free China had taken from the Communists. The man who filed that story could easily have visited Kinmen or Matsu or the Ta-chens. But why leave the comfort and luxury of Hong Kong when you can get all the facts there?

I have already commented on the reporting of Joseph Alsop, who also prefers to get his reports from Hong Kong. When an American newspaperman with unlimited financial resources reports as Alsop does, it becomes apparent that objectivity has been thrown out completely, that the reporting is neutral or definitely negative, based upon information provided either by the British or by enemy agents.

While in Formosa a year ago, I met an old friend from China days, in Taipei to write a story for *The Reporter*. His was to be a report on economic progress. How long was he planning to stay in making his research? Seventy-two hours. Was he planning to inspect operations of JCRR? After all, Formosa's economy is based upon agriculture; any report thereon must consider advances in that field. No, he didn't have time for that; he couldn't travel outside Taipei.

My friend sensed my amazement and had the good grace to almost apologize. "But don't worry," he told me. "It will be an honest report—no smearing!"

Incidentally, an official of JCRR told me that as far as he could remember only one correspondent, representing a major American magazine, newspaper or news agency, had ever visited JCRR activities in the back country, had taken time to talk to farmers. This was a representative of *Time* and *Life*. The average stay of the American reporter in Formosa is forty-eight hours. During this time he lives in the swank Friends of China Club (wired for sound, of course!). He sees nothing of activities outside the capital city, indeed can see little of what takes place there.

If a Korean or a Japanese or a Chinese newspaperman were sent to the United States to write an interpretive story on life in America and spent forty-eight hours, all of it in Washington or New York, he and his newspaper would be damned by us who enjoy real freedom of the press. Yet almost every American newspaper and magazine carries stories on the Far East, based upon that amount of diligent research.

There are men who report honestly on the Far East, who chronicle events with sympathy. Jim Lucas of the Scripps-Howard papers, James Michener, Fred Sparks of *NEA*, Spencer Moosa of the *Associated Press*, Walter Simmons of the *Chicago Tribune*, the men of *U. S. News and World Report*, generally those who write for *Time* and *Life*. But they are only a handful out of the many who swarm the press clubs of Asia, who each day file scores of thousands of words of news.

The greatest single Communist victory in Asia has been in the use of the printed word in America to cause distrust of our only and logical allies in Asia. The typical American writer is proud of his American background, of the democratic way of life we have achieved. With the diligent prodding of the native and American fellow travelers, the correspondent sees inefficiency and corruption in Asia, all too often closes his eyes to either the good that is there or to the reasons behind the inefficiency and corruption. During the last days of World War II and during the days of the Marshall Mission in China, outright Communists had a large part to play in corrupting the news.

Vivacious and lovely Kung Peng, called the Communist public relations officer, was among the most popular Chinese in Chungking. She was invited to all the parties, was always available to give "background news." Her counterpart in Peiping was one Huang Hua, suave and intelligent, a "straight guy" as one American writer put it. Between them, Huang Hua and Kung Peng guided the keys on many an American typewriter. They were Communists, yes, but such nice, honest people!

What has happened to these two in the days since Nationalist collapse? Huang Hua turned up at both Panmunjom and at Geneva, a top Communist negotiator, hard as nails, adept at all the wiles that make negotiating with the enemy impossible. Kung Peng too was at Geneva, handling press conferences but no longer the lovely girl of Chungking days. Years of Communism have filled her face with hard and perhaps bitter lines.

With the assistance of these two excellent operators, helped along by a few American Communists among the writers, with our American predisposition to ferret out and write about that which is *evil*, Chiang Kai Shek and his government and, more lately, Syngman Rhee and the ROK's, have become the most disliked of the world's leaders and governments.

It is almost as if all corruption and evil was indigenous to the Chinese (Nationalists, that is) and the South Koreans—had been invented in those countries by special fiat of the leaders. Thus, in an article entitled "U.S. Backs a Dictator in Korea," appearing in *Pathfinder* magazine two years ago, I read with amazement this indictment of Syngman Rhee:

[He] ignored the legally elected National Assembly and arrested legislators who tried to block him.

Purged the courts of judges and prosecutors who wouldn't take his orders.

Killed and imprisoned opponents at a rate in excess of 10,000 a month.

Gagged the press and even the Voice of America.

Blocked land reform (foundation of all democracy in Asia) to win backing of wealthy land owners.

Overspent yearly (despite U.S. aid of $466 million from 1945 to mid-1950)—yet forgot to tax rich backers.

Waged undeclared war "to unify Korea"—curbed only by the U.S. cuts in arms shipments.

The author of this attack concludes with the statement that "Thus in the eyes of millions of Asiatics, the U.S. occupation saddled Korea with a corrupt, oppressive regime. . . ."

The catalogue of crimes committed by Rhee could have been lifted verbatim, from Radio Peiping. Although I could refute every charge, I comment on only one point, the charge that Rhee blocked land reform.

The simple truth is that South Korea, under Syngman Rhee's leadership, was the first nation in all of Asia to achieve real democratic land reform. The program has been continued, in spite of war and the natural opposition of landlords (a "wealthy landowner" in Korea is anyone who owns more than four or five acres), until it has almost wiped out land tenancy in the country. The program has been so effective that it was singled out by the National Planning Association in Washington for a special news release in 1953.

But I wonder how many people have read an article in any leading American magazine about Korean land reform? How many articles have appeared, anywhere, about the magnificent program of land reform in Formosa, or on JCRR? How often do we read of the development of constitutional government, either in Formosa or in Korea? Prior to the beginning of the China Coast "vest-pocket war," how many Americans ever had opportunity to know of accomplishments on Kinmen Island? How many American magazines have carried articles describing the Nationalists' enlightened program for the Formosan aborigines? Among all the recent attacks on General Chiang Ching Kuo, eldest son of the Generalissimo, what magazines noted that the young general has been responsible for raising the literacy of Free China's troops from almost nothing to approximately 90 per cent? Where, other than in General Mark Clark's memoirs, has the magnificent story of the Korean partisans and guerrillas been told?

The average American writer's deep-seated, almost pathological hatred of Chiang and Rhee has contributed as much as has any other single factor to the threatened loss of all Asia. It is one of the major Communist victories in the Far East. The pattern has improved, but it still exists, still clouds the real issues, confuses and divides American thinking on a whole continent.

During the ten year period in which our friends have been vilified, our enemies have been praised. Literally scores of articles have described the wonders of Communist land reform, the honesty of Communist administrators, the achievements of Communist governors. It is no longer fashionable to praise the enemy. Instead, our experts write of his "invincible strength," imply the inevitability of his victory. We are told that all Asia distrusts us because we possess and once used the atomic bomb in Asia. It is explained that Asia holds us in suspicion because of Senator McCarthy's activities. Gravely it is explained that Asiatics dislike us because of the way we have treated Negroes in America.

Every possible excuse is found for our predicament and Asia's predicament but the truth. And a large part of that truth, as unpleasant as it may be to admit, is that Americans have been victimized by their own writers and publishers until the truth has been lost in a maze of conflicting, inaccurate, biased and neutral reporting.

Last year I spent a long evening with a Chinese cabinet minister, a brilliant young man, graduate of one of our midwestern universities. He spoke of the difficulty his government had in getting its story told in America. He explained the situation in judicial terms.

"It has become like your court system," he told me. "Your judges base decisions upon precedent, the decisions of other jurists on similar cases, down through the years. Much of your law goes away back to the precedent of Anglo-Saxon law, set centuries ago. So it is with Free China, both as far as your editors are concerned and as far as your State Department is concerned. In the case of the former, there is a vast accumulation of anti-Nationalist reporting that the editor cannot forget, that sways his judgment when he selects articles. In the case of the latter, policy decisions of your government, whether it be under a Democratic or a Republican administration, are still made upon the basis of the volumes of anti-Chiang, anti-Nationalist reports that cram the State Department files. Every time a decision must be made, it is necessary to go back into the files, to see what went on before, to analyze the background. We in Free China will have a difficult time until the files are put in the archives and are replaced by new reports."

I had an experience with the editor of one of America's greatest weeklies which proved the Chinese minister's analysis to be correct. I met with him and outlined a story I wanted to write about the JCRR and Free China's new deal for its peasants. Hardly had I begun when he interrupted me. "But everybody knows," he exclaimed, "that all the farmers hate Chiang Kai Shek!"

Precedent was at work, the ghost of a former editor who was loudly pro-Chinese Communist, the influence of dozens of former pro-Communist contributors, were still so powerful that the judgment of an editor in 1953 was influenced. The editor of that magazine had never been to Formosa, of course. But *everybody* knows the true story of Chiang Kai Shek; so why change the story?

Upon the shoulders of scores of American writers, editors and publishers must be placed much of the blame for Asia's ferment and America's indecision. There have been too many "neutral" correspondents, too many who have in complete innocence, allowed themselves to become the enemy's mouthpiece. There have been arrogance and laziness and sloppy reporting, too. But the greatest failure has been failure to report on Asia in the light of its history, in the light of our own history.

No matter how facile he may be, no matter how large his expense account may be, no matter how efficient may be his communications channels back home, the American writer who has not read history cannot interpret the present. And if the total press corps in the Far East reads ten books a years, other than whodunits and westerns, I would be surprised. A study of history will show us that evil and venality did not originate with Chiang Kai Shek. It will show that there were events in Indo-China other than French incompetence that have caused the division of that land.

Reported against the background of Far Eastern history, the story of Formosa and guerrilla-land, of Syngman Rhee and his ROK's, become sagas of accomplishment easily understood by Americans who have gone through similar struggles to emerge as the most powerful, most truly democratic nation in the world's history.

Chapter 3

THERE was once a prosperous nation stricken by civil war which came only a few decades after other national wars had plagued the land. The civil war lasted for many months, preceded by months of bickering, and efforts at mediation and conciliation. But once war became inevitable, the nation abandoned hopes of settling differences. Other nations watched the civil war with interest; were wooed for support; did give some support; for the outcome of the civil war was of interest to all the civilized world.

The war turned neighbor against neighbor and brother against brother. Unbelievable corruption added to the problems of both sides. Eighty thousand troops deserted from one army because there were numerous generals who pocketed the money given by the minister of war for feeding the troops. Quartermaster supplies were funneled off by rapacious officers and sold. Some generals engaged in business on the side, even traded with the enemy. Desertions became a tremendous problem because men were so often forced to fight without food; the wounded sometimes went without medical treatment. Even in drugs and medicines there was a brisk traffic, with army doctors stealing and selling the very supplies provided for their wounded.

Civil liberties became a farce on both sides. The minister

284

of war for one of the belligerents boasted that he had power to place anyone in jail, to close down any newspaper, to arrest anyone he chose without warrant and to keep him in jail without judicial recourse. Newspaper correspondents covering the war were jailed, were held under suspicion and in several cases nearly executed. Lynching and mob rule were frequent. Vigilance committees were established to ferret out those with subversive sympathies. On one occasion a Christian minister was hung, without trial, on the merest suspicion that he was an enemy agent. On another occasion a twenty-year-old boy was hung as a spy, even though he was a regularly enlisted member of the armed forces of the other side.

This civil war occasioned heroic deeds and at the same time much corruption. One side sent a mission to another nation, and members of the mission could not account for tens of thousands of dollars of their government's funds. There was brisk trading with the enemy, even on the part of generals. Every device to escape conscription, to escape payment of taxes, to get along with both sides, was used.

One side employed a secret police with unlimited powers. People simply disappeared, suspected persons or those only vaguely suspected. Victims were placed in bleak confinement for weeks or months. Spurious confessions were secured through physical and mental torture. The head of the dread secret police was trapped in forgery, was accused of corruption, but his superiors kept him in power. His power became absolute, to be used for personal advantage and to throw fear into the hearts of thousands of innocent people.

Discipline among troops was a constant problem for both sides at first, especially later for the losing side. Looting could not be controlled. Sometimes what might have become a great victory was just another battle because the troops stopped fighting to loot. Straggling and deserting could never be controlled, even though hundreds of men were executed as examples. One soldier deserted and traveled through enemy and friendly territory for over a thousand miles to reach his home. In later years he wrote a book about his experiences, telling of the ease with which he forged passes, hoodwinked officers and men. On one occasion he traded a horse for a special pass.

Civilian support of the war, spirited at first, became progressively less enthusiastic. Citizens refused to pay taxes, young men did everything possible to escape military service. Inflation became a tremendous problem, with prices spiraling until the simplest necessities cost a fortune. And all the while there were hundreds of business men getting rich from the war, taking advantage of high prices to profit from friend and enemy alike.

As the weaker side began to lose battles, its leadership came under constant and sharp criticism. There were demands for peace at any price. There were occasions when generals simply gave up, refused to fight longer. One crucial battle was lost because the commanding officer of a key unit was drunk in his tent. Another general became enamored of a young woman, a spy for the other side, and allowed himself and his complete staff to be captured.

And so the war, dividing a civilized and prosperous nation, dragged on for months and years. Casualties were tremendous; economic chaos added to the confusion. Men and women of both sides became rapacious, lost all human dignity in the effort to survive. No complete account was ever kept of those unjustly imprisoned, those betrayed, executed without trial. When the war ended, the nation was still split ideologically, and many years were required for the wounds to heal. During those years the winning side took advantage of the loser in many ways. There was oppression, economic exploitation, liquidation of dissident elements. While constitutional government supposedly extended to all the land, victor and vanquished alike, there was widespread political corruption. Elections were conducted dishonestly.

286

Political favoritism was rampant. It was many years before decency again prevailed.

This certainly seems an accurate description of the years of China's civil war between Nationalist and Communist, does it not? However, the conditions and events I have described above took place, not in China, but in the United States of America. During our own civil war, just ninety years ago, every evil ever attributed to Chiang Kai Shek or Syngman Rhee or any other leader in Asia was found right here in the United States.

We who now pass judgment on peoples and leaders of other nations passed through the same stages of chaos before achieving our present vaunted stability and democracy. The chaos and corruption I have described is not a product of my imagination but has been culled from the books of a three-year period, written by some of America's most respected contemporary historians and authors.

What I have written of the civil war period can be amplified to other eras in our history. The struggle to develop Oklahoma, our youngest state, is another excellent example of the trials and tribulations of American democratic development. For in Oklahoma Territory there was thievery, political shenanigans, land stealing, bilking of the Indians that would even put Governor Chen Yi's exploitation of Formosa in 1946 to shame.

In the history of Kansas Territory, the struggle between anti- and pro-slavery elements just prior to the Civil War, we can also find all the evils ever attributed to any Asiatic leader. Kansas was ruled by gun and stolen ballot; a completely illegal government was installed and kept in power; men in opposition were ruthlessly murdered or imprisoned. A secret society flourished and held the people enslaved in a reign of fear and terror.

We can find similar stories in almost every section of the United States of the last century. Fort Worth, Texas, a great

287

and rich city, might now be a sleepy country village or even have ceased to exist had it not been for a cleverly managed vote fraud. Fort Worth became a county seat, emerged as a seat of government and trade, only because its residents stole the election in which the seat of government was decided. Illegal voters were brought in from a distant county by the score, their votes bought with money and liquor, and the opposition was thus swamped.

In a previous chapter I mentioned the treatment of the Cherokee Indians in Tennessee, a once great tribe forced into exile by Andrew Jackson in violation of solemn treaty. But Andrew Jackson was not alone in defrauding the Indians. The history of relations between whites and Indians is a story of fraud, stealing, dishonesty and broken treaties. It is a story that might be read and studied by all Americans with profit. For it too, shows how far we have traveled along the road to decent government and rule by law and order. Almost every treaty made with the Southern Indians during the first quarter of the nineteenth century was broken. Hundreds of Indians were massacred in cold blood. Thousands and millions of acres of land, legally owned by the Indians, were stolen from them. When the Supreme Court of the United States attempted to interfere, its decisions were flaunted. Andrew Jackson himself dared the Supreme Court to implement its decisions.

During the nineteenth century and even before, men in high places in America were frequently dishonest. Land speculation and land stealing were commonplace, engaged in by governors and senators. There were conspiracies to sell out young America to foreign countries, open trafficking with alien powers. William Blount, territorial governor of Tennessee, later that state's first senator, was expelled from the Senate of the United States because he sought to sell out his country to the British.

Stability and democracy in government did not develop in

the United States overnight, cannot develop in any land overnight. After one hundred and eighty years of the world's most successful democratic government, America is still imperfect. There is not a month passes that somewhere in our land corruption does not appear. Elections are still stolen, men in high places are still frequently dishonest, tax frauds are still uncovered, men and women still attempt to sell out their country, legislators can still be bought.

My first job after graduation from college was with the state government of Tennessee. That was but twenty years ago. I was idealistic, for I had studied American history as it is generally written, had no conception of the imperfections that still existed. I lasted exactly one year in my first job, for when a superior demanded a tremendous salary kick-back, I indignantly refused to pay up. I was fired, and when I sought to tell my story I found that no one would listen. Thousands of dollars were taken in by the department where I worked, but there was no system whereby the public's money could be accounted for, no supervised system of bookkeeping, no budgetary checks. It was possible to steal thousands of dollars of public money, and thousands of dollars were stolen each year. And that was just twenty years ago.

Communism's greatest victory in Asia has not been achieved by force of arms. It has been achieved because Americans, not knowing of their own history, have expected China and Korea and the Philippines and Thailand to automatically become stable democracies. The Communists have cleverly played upon American idealism, cleverly exploited American ignorance, to turn us against the very leaders who are our logical and only allies. The honesty and incorruptibility of Communist officials (achieved, of course, through fear and police state methods) have been cleverly compared with the chaos and supposed corruption of the Chiangs and the Rhees.

In March, 1946, I visited Chungking, China, as an inspector for the Department of State's information and cultural program. Chungking was still China's capital, the move back to Nanking being only then in progress. The evening of my arrival was spent at the home of charming Kung Peng, the same Kung Peng who handled Communist press conferences at Geneva in 1954. It was considered so important that I meet and talk with Kung Peng that I was literally whisked from the airport to her house. There were a number of Americans present that night, all officials of the American Embassy.

Miss Kung Peng was at her charming best as she told of her hopes for her people. China must have democracy just like America. There must be a decent deal for all. The freedoms enjoyed by Americans must also be enjoyed by Chinese. Her American audience sat enthralled as Kung Peng described the activities, the plans, the hopes of the Communists, as she told how real, honest-to-goodness democracy had been developed in Communist-controlled territory.

All through the years from 1945 until Chiang's collapse in 1949, Kung Peng's cleverly portrayed vision of hope for Asia colored the judgment of American diplomats and American writers. Beginning even in 1944 it became fashionable to journey to Yenan, Communist capital in the loess hills of China's Northwest, to see the great new experiment in democracy.

In Washington those who had made the pilgrimage were used to give lectures and indoctrination to employees and officials of the Office of War Information and the Department of State who had not themselves been privileged to go to Mecca.

Publishers began to vie with one another in publishing books and articles about the new democracy that had come to Asia. The flood of books had even begun several years earlier and continued unabated. The titles were exciting and provocative: *Battles for Asia, Unfinished Revolution in China, Thunder out of China, People on Our Side, Challenge of Red China.*

An article in the *Saturday Evening Post* described Communist General Chu Teh as having "the kindliness of Robert E. Lee, the tenacity of Grant, and the humility of Lincoln."

In a 1944 article on China in *Colliers*, the solution for China's misery was clearly set forth, including "immediate political reforms, including the democratization of the government."

There we can see clearly the trap into which we fell. What had required generations for America to accomplish as yet imperfectly, China was required to do "immediately"!

During this period I sat on several of the Department of State's "country committees." These were the committees of political and economic experts, set up to develop an American policy and plan for every nation in the world. It is interesting to look back, to see how naive we were. For every country policy statement was drafted with complete disregard for a nation's traditions and history. We always began those weighty pronouncements with a phrase about "democracy and freedom." Nations which were to receive our support must be "independent, united, free and democratic."

It was heady business indeed, grafting democracy into the body politic of nations still at war or floundering midst the traditions and thought and economic conditions of the middle ages. If a nation's leadership was not responding quickly enough, it was the function of the information agencies to send out some critical material for use by that nation's newspapers.

Thus it was official policy to search the American press, the magazines, the book lists for criticisms of Chiang Kai Shek and Nationalist China, to include the criticisms in a special "Editorial Comment" that was radioed to China and then distributed to all Chinese newspapers by the U. S. Information Service. With criticism and continual needling, we hoped to force China to vault across decades, to skip all the painful years of growing and learning we ourselves had endured.

All over Asia we began to establish wonderful American

libraries. There were pro-Communist books by the score in those early days. But just as damaging were the completely American books, the glowing accounts of America at its best, glossed-over histories, bright novels, anthologies. For by reading of democracy, people obviously would become democrats.

It was then too that we began to save the world by bringing more thousands of foreign students to America to study, to savor at first hand of our greatness. From China, Korea, Japan, the Philippines, from every nation in Asia they came, to study in American universities, to visit Washington, to study the Tennessee Valley Authority by the scores and by the thousands.

And then the students returned to their own lands, to find chaos and misery and little opportunity to use their new knowledge. For before TVA's can be built, there must be more roads and railroads. Before modern agricultural methods are accepted, ancient superstitions must be patiently conquered. Before progressive education methods learned at Columbia Teachers' College can be transplanted to China or Korea, there must be tremendous changes in the traditional teaching of centuries. Before people can intelligently vote and thus produce constitutional government, they must become literate.

So it was that the returned students themselves frequently became a disrupting source. No one had ever explained to them that the democracy they saw in America did not develop overnight. No one had ever explained that our development had been spotted with corruption and graft and greed. I doubt if any foreign student has ever been told that some 80,000 American soldiers of the Federal Army of the Potomac deserted because dishonest generals pocketed the money provided to feed and clothe the troops.

Faced with the unpleasant facts of life in his homeland, the foreign trained student became easy prey for the Communists who promised an easy short cut to Utopia. It need not have been so, but the unpleasant truth is that the United States has contributed scores and hundreds of men and women to the Communist cause through our well meaning exchange of students program.

For a quarter of a century the Communists have cleverly exploited our failure to understand the lessons of our own history. With the assistance of a few renegade Americans and scores of idealistic but naive writers and diplomats and economic experts, they have blinded us to the problems of a whole continent, have established that massive body of precedent that still shackles our diplomats and our editors.

And still the blindness prevails. In 1950, I watched the reporting of a New York newspaper correspondent in Korea, saw him assiduously dig out every disreputable aspect of Korean government, all with complete disregard of Korea's history, thus proving how the United States was supporting a reactionary government.

In 1954, I read an article in *The New Leader,* condemning the government of Thailand, a weak nation that now stands between the Communists and the rest of Southeast Asia, because that nation had not as yet allowed the development of labor unions in the image of organized labor in America. I heard Syngman Rhee roundly denounced as a dictator a month before the Communist invasion because the laborers of his land, faced even then with civil war and sabotage, did not have all the rights of collective bargaining American laborers enjoy after nearly two hundred years of struggle.

For five years we have read only of French inefficiency in Indo-China, have blamed the debacle there on the French without an understanding either of the good they did or of the history of the people they ruled. Writing in *Report on Indo-China,* Bernard Newman includes a chapter entitled "Honour Where Due" in which he shows what France did for its colonial subject. In answer to France's critics, New-

293

man writes: "Neither the French nor any other foreigners can give a soul to the Vietnamese army, or to any other organization. The point is important—the French can supply rifles to the army and ploughs for the rice fields, but nothing they do will touch the soul of Vietnam. This is a task for the Vietnamese alone."

Again, commenting upon the lack of democracy in Indo-China (generally attributed to the French, of course), Newman writes: "The fact is, of course, that democracy, while the most satisfying political system, is the most difficult. It demands restraints and common endeavours not always encountered in states which have adopted some new ideas and are rushing them forward in incomplete comprehension. Democracy thrives on traditions—and local traditions . . . are *not* democratic."

Sun Yat Sen understood that democracy must not be allowed to sprout up like a vast crop of untended weeds. He prescribed a period of "political tutelage" during which those traditions which Mr. Newman points out are absent, can be developed, a period when the illiterate can become literate and through that literacy begin to understand the world in which they live.

Any period of political learning is a period of great danger. Always there will be leaders who seek to perpetuate that learning period so that they may maintain personal power. Always there will be the lure of short cuts, offered by scheming Communists and naive, do-gooding Americans alike. But stability and democracy cannot be achieved by short cuts; and the sooner we learn that lesson, the better equipped we shall become to help the backward nations.

Only one nation in the Far East has ever achieved stability of government in the Western sense. Japan became stable and powerful. But the stability was not accompanied by democracy, was achieved through religious fanaticism and police control. The stability was paralleled by imperialistic ambition which in time shattered all the countries of Eastern Asia. We are still paying for that power-secured stability. We have replaced it with democracy and are learning unhappily that a few years of political tutelage under an American military occupation may not have been enough. For democracy, too quickly achieved, without tradition and understanding, can be an explosive and disruptive force.

If we are to help Asia out of its chaos and ferment, we must understand that generations may be required before nations are governed as we today are governed. We must understand that periods of political learning, dangerous to be sure, are a necessity, and that during such periods strong, personal leadership is a necessity. Instead of continually criticizing, we must understand that we ourselves went through generations of trial and error and still are not perfect. We must admit that every sin of omission and commission ascribed to Chiang Kai Shek and Syngman Rhee can be found either in contemporary American political life or in our past. We must be willing to understand that not all nations need our brand of democracy, that some nations will not be able to achieve stability for years, and all the technical aid we give will not materially hasten the process.

The peoples of Asia, South America, Africa have far more pressing needs than freedom of speech or the right to collective bargaining. Achieved too quickly, such basic rights as we take for granted can only result in chaos.

The great challenge to what we call the Democratic World lies in understanding these factors, in helping peoples through the dangerous periods of learning that are inevitable. It is a challenge as yet not met or even understood. The Communist world, with an able assist from American writers and publishers, has offered an enticing and dazzling short cut. More and more of the young men and women who flounder midst confusion and chaos are choosing the short cut.

The writer who blindly and continually criticizes Free

China or Korea or Thailand's leadership as it travels along the slow and painful road that must be followed contributes to the decisions of those who take the shorter path. Censorship of press and magazine and book in America is of course, intolerable. But somehow the publishers of our nation must understand the totality of Asia's war, must realize the use to which American writing is often put, must admit their contribution to Asia's plight. The glib young journalist, fresh from school, sent forth to Korea or Japan without the slightest background in either American or Oriental history, can become a potent Communist ally. I can name a score of American writers and a half dozen American newspapers and magazines that have contributed more to the Red conquest of China than has Russia.

If Asia is to be saved, unpleasant truths must be faced, old ideas abandoned. Perhaps I can illustrate the strangeness of the battle we face with two stories, one from Formosa, one from Korea.

Last year while I was in Formosa, the leading Chinese newspaper of Taipei, the "New York Times" of Free China, carried a picture and a story that would be in shockingly bad taste in the newspapers of any Western nation, would probably result in criminal prosecution. The picture accompanying the story showed a Chinese peasant woman, her skirts lifted high, her husband forced to practice upon her what we legalistically call in America a "pervert act." Around the pair stood Communist officials, watching in sadistic delight. The text explained that a dispossessed landlord and wife were being punished for their misdeeds. American residents of Taipei eagerly bought up that issue in which picture and story appeared. But most of the purchases were for the purpose of adding to pornographic collections. Few were the Americans who understood the implications of all-out war, of cultural change and ferment, of the vast chasm that separates America in its position of wealth and security from much of the rest of the world. Yet the Adlai Stevensons and Estes Kefauvers and Theodore Whites tell us that all the world distrusts and dislikes us because one U. S. Senator hunts Communists with too much vigor. Editors, radio commentators moan and groan because we attempt to legally circumscribe and condemn the very men and women who have brought sorrow to a third of the world. Can it be any wonder that Free Asia is confused, wonders just what America does stand for?

My other story comes from Pusan, Korea, where I sat one afternoon looking out over the lovely harbor. With me was a young Korean, frightened and bewildered, bitter too. Like my friend Mr. Pak, he too was disillusioned about his government and his leadership; for he had spent two years in America and expected to transplant American democracy to his homeland overnight. I tried to give my friend hope by telling him a bit of American history, by describing in particular our own civil war period of chaos. For an hour I talked, exhausting my knowledge of America's history. And as I talked, I could sense relaxation and hope coursing through the young Korean. When we parted that afternoon, the Korean almost begged me to do him a favor.

"Mr. Caldwell, when you get back to America," he said, "won't you send me an honest, unvarnished American history? You have told me things I never learned in America. I have never known the struggles you went through. There are many of us who could get hope from such a book."

There are American libraries in every nation, in almost every major city in the world, yet as far as I know none carry such a book.

Chapter 4

THE colonel was tired, almost sullen. It was his last day in the Far East and we had met, purely by chance, at a Chinese dinner party in Tokyo's Ginza district. The colonel was not a great admirer of Syngman Rhee, nor was he even what the American GI's term a "Gook lover," or one who thinks well of the Korean people.

It was his wife who told me the colonel had spent eight months as a member of the American negotiating team at Panmunjom, that his tour was over and they were returning to their California home on next morning's troop ship.

He was an Air Force man, a believer in the ships of his trade. He warmed slowly; but before evening's end he was talking vehemently of lost chances, of victory that might have been, of truce terms that could have been so much better, had America listened to the warnings of a wrinkled old revolutionist. The colonel blamed the truce terms, perhaps without justification, upon the Department of State.

"Each day," he told me, "those people in Washington would tell us exactly what to say the next day. Their directions even extended to what words should be used. Some-

298

times we would have an issue settled, we would know the Communists were giving in. Then would come word from Washington to 'explore' such and such a point further."

Then the colonel became angry. "Why anyone should know what happens when we start 'exploring' further," he almost shouted. "They see we are wavering, have not made up our minds. The gains of a week, a month may be lost. Time after time we had to back off from hard won points, had to begin all over again, had even to give in."

I was interested in all of the colonel's story. I know not whether his blame of the Department of State is justified. I was more interested in what he, as an intelligent American, would have done, had he had power to make the final decisions. I asked him.

"I'll tell you exactly what I would have done," he answered quickly. "I would have given the Communist exactly twenty-four hours to come to our terms. Maybe those terms would have been complete removal of Chinese Communist volunteer forces from Korean soil. That is not the important point. I would have made it clear that if our terms, whatever they were, were not met within the time limit, our air force would go into action. We would bomb the airfields across the Yalu, the manufacturing centers of Manchuria. If there was still hesitation, we would hit Peiping, then Hankow, Shanghai. We would use every weapon at our command."

The colonel then calmed down a little as he continued. "Of course they would have come to terms," he concluded. "That would have been the language they understand. Then we could have gone ahead and given the damn country back to the Koreans for Syngman Rhee or anyone else to rule or ruin."

I imagine Syngman Rhee would have liked the colonel. His angry words reminded me of the words of many Koreans, of the man who told me that there was no hope for his generation, that for his children there would be hope only because the children were going to college in America and would therefore escape the holocaust. I was reminded too, of the writers who sagely tell us that America is distrusted in Asia because we have used the atom bomb, because we imply by our atomic program that we may use it again. The colonel was actually speaking for most of Eastern Asia, at least for non-Communist and anti-Communist Asia. He obviously would be a poor representative of the Nehru view.

Fortunately or unfortunately, the colonel's ideas will probably never be accepted by America. Or if acceptance comes, it will be after many more diplomatic defeats. For the present our colonel's program is out because America's European allies would never agree to it, because so many Americans too, have been captivated by the lure of "co-existence." The fact that we could have won a victory is becoming academic, but it might still be worthwhile to remind ourselves of those who have in recent months clearly restated the facts. Of course, the views of General MacArthur are well known, but have again been forcefully restated in the book *MacArthur 1941–51* by Major General Charles A. Willoughby and John Chamberlain. General James Van Fleet, too, has restated his views, has recently commented in detail on the folly of the Korean Truce, on the fact that Asia can still be saved if we will allow the fighting men of Free Asia to do the saving. General Claire Chennault, of World War II fame, now head of the Civil Air Transport, has made his position clear and has added the interesting idea of a volunteer anti-Communist force in Asia, patterned after his famed Flying Tigers. General George Stratemeyer, who commanded our air forces in Korea and, before that, in China, has added his testimony to that of MacArthur, Van Fleet, Chennault.

It has always been an interesting point to me that the military leaders who were most successful in Asia, who were best liked, who were able to inspire confidence on the part of

300

Koreans and Chinese, are all in agreement that the Korean war could have been won, and more important, that we can still win in Asia.

On the other hand, balanced against the judgment of these men who inspire leadership, is that of the men who either have been failures in Asia or without experience there. Thus it was George Marshall and Omar Bradley, one a Far Eastern failure, the other completely without experience in Asia, whose military judgment has been followed in the Far East while the pleas of the MacArthurs and the Van Fleets and the Wedemeyers have been ignored.

A Korean official commented on this fact one day, saying, "It appears to us that any outstanding American leader who believes democracy can win in Asia, who begins to respect the Koreans or the Free Chinese, who can work with us, immediately loses favor in the United States, becomes another one of your voices in the wilderness."

Among the oriental proverbs there is none that is more applicable to the mess in Asia than the old Korean saying that, "When a man slips and falls into a stream, it is foolish to blame the stream."

It certainly is time to quit blaming Chiang Kai Shek and Nationalist China for Asia's continuing crisis. It is foolish to blame the Koreans as a people or individually. We slipped upon the slimy mud of Communist intrigue and treachery. Except as a lesson for the future, it is pointless now to continually blame individuals, who through treachery or misjudgment, supplied the push that landed us in the river. We are there; the problem is to get out.

Getting out of a Korean river is easier said than done. I well remember a duck hunting trip on the Han River below Seoul. My companions and I were in an Air Force surplus rubber boat, a handy craft for negotiating the muddy Han. The mud banks seemed safe, and two of us got out to take a short cut. We hoped to thus surround a flock of mallards, two of us by land, one by water.

I was in the lead when I began to sink deeper and deeper into the mud. My companion came to help, and he too went in—faster because he was a heavy man. We were both up to our waists when the man in the boat got to us, close enough to reach us with an oar. Then we slowly edged out of the sucking, sticking mud. Clinging to the oar, it was possible to slowly reach a horizontal position, to at last get clear of the danger. It was a frightening experience and a thoroughly dirty one. We were saved by a combination of circumstances. We were not alone. Had anyone of us gotten into the mud alone, the outcome would have been different. There were two of us in the mud and being together, we did not lose our heads, did not give in to hysteria. Then too, there was a man in the boat, and the oar.

In the Far Eastern river we Americans are not alone, and there are oars and other props to help us. But we must somehow learn to recognize the help that is available.

I have written little of Japan, even though it is itself an ultimate Communist goal in Asia. With Japan's industrial knowhow, the Communist empire would approach sufficiency. I have written little of Southeast Asia, more important by far than Korea, for with Southeast Asia's rice and mineral resources, Red China can quit worrying about floods and famine. Japan and Southeast Asia are far more important than Korea or Formosa. But in terms of Asia's salvation, both Southeast Asia and Japan must be disregarded; neither one can be considered the prop or the oar to extricate us from the mess.

If Asia is to remain free, Communist China's advance must not only be stopped. That much is obvious, and we seek halfheartedly to develop a roadblock through the organization of SEATO. But if Asia is to remain free, China must, in the words of the American diplomat in Taipei, "become friendly." Communist China will never be defeated (and therein lies the only solution) by rearming Japan or attempting to bind together the weak nations of Southeast Asia. Of what earthly value is backward Thailand, without a military tradition, its well-fed people completely unaware of the menace of Communism? Or the Philippines, isolated, with tremendous internal problems that must be solved? Or the divided French and the trade-minded, co-existence-dazzled British? Can anyone expect wobbly Japan, suffering the indigestion of too much democracy too quickly administered, to play an active role in keeping Asia free?

It has become fashionable to write off Asia, in terms of the white man's defeat. "The white man is finished in Asia," or "The white man is hated," we are told. Writing in *Human Events*, Garet Garrett stated that Communism is winning Asia because it holds out three things: the sweet taste of revenge (against the "hated" white man), nationalistic independence and expulsion of the white man from Asia.

In my opinion, Mr. Garrett over-simplifies the problem and is a bit off course. I have never seen evidence of hatred of the white man any place in Asia. Everywhere I have seen evidence of loss of faith, but revenge and the hope of expelling the white man play little part in the picture.

The white man is certainly on his way out, a matter of little importance in itself. But with the white man's exit will also go the foundations of democracy and decency that have been built over the centuries. In the final analysis, more Asians will remember the good works of America than will "hate" America because of our supposed support of colonialism.

But Asia is losing faith in America, of that there can be no doubt. For a century America lent a helping hand to the people of Asia. We, more than anyone else, built what foundations of decency exist. We, our churches, our foundations,

even our government itself through such activities as the
Boxer Fund, laid the foundations for the educational systems,
for medical facilities. It was America that supplied the vision
of better government that guided Sun Yat Sen and Syngman
Rhee and countless less important people in a half dozen
lands. It was a confused vision at times, but it was the first
real brightness to penetrate Asia's shadows. And if today we
and our influence are on the way out, it is because we have
refused to go the second mile.

When the chips were down, we have refused to help. Today we refuse to commit ourselves to those who can keep a
continent free. After providing the incentive, after laying a
bit of foundation, after making numerous pledges, we refuse
to hold out hope to the Tommy Hsus, the Allen Yehs, the
Kim Man Gus of Asia.

The tremendous change and confusion can be illustrated
by an occurrence that took place in Shanghai in 1949, soon
after the Communists occupied the city. Dr. Leighton Stuart,
last U.S. ambassador to the China mainland, tells the story
in his memoirs, *Fifty Years in China.* There were two for-
eign-owned newspapers which attempted to carry on after
Communist "liberation." The *North China Daily News* was
British-owned, the *Shanghai Evening Post and Mercury* was
American-owned.

Both papers soon got neck-deep in Communist-brewed hot
water. The British paper ran a story about mines in the
Yangtse River. Shanghai depends on sea-borne and river-
borne commerce, and the story caused fear, actually paralyzed shipping. Meanwhile, Randall Gould, editor of the
American paper, was having his troubles. Using a typical
Communist technique, all of the *Evening Post and Mercury*
employees had demanded tremendous wage increases and
had locked the paper's business manager up until the increase
was granted.

304

A British and an American editor were in trouble with the Communists, the one over a news story, the other because of a Communist-inspired wage dispute. The British editor extricated himself in a typically British manner, while Randall Gould's actions were of the type that have long inspired Asiatic respect for America.

The Britisher ran a page one, bilingual, apology. The apology was abject, humble and sincere, expressing hopes that the Communist military authorities would forgive and forget.

Randall Gould meanwhile went to his newspaper office, knowing that he too would be locked up by the employees. He was locked up, but he stood by his guns until a reasonable solution to the wage demands could be worked out. And then, since the dispute was newsworthy, Gould wrote a factual story describing what took place. When the paper's typesetters discovered the story, they went on strike. Randall Gould considered this Communist-inspired action intolerable interference with the freedom of the press. Rather than knuckle under, he closed down the *Evening Post and Mercury*.

There was one other American editor who stayed on. His publication, originally a weekly and later a monthly, had been an American fixture in Shanghai for years. *The China Weekly Review*, published for years by J. B. Powell, crusading editor in the best American tradition, had been a voice heard all along the China Coast and far inland. J. B. Powell was imprisoned by the Japanese, so tortured and broken in health that he died soon after the end of the war.

His son, John William Powell, better known as Bill, returned to Shanghai to reestablish the *China Review*. And like Randall Gould, Bill Powell stayed on after Communist "liberation." But he chose a path even different from that chosen by Gould or the British editor. Bill began to openly collaborate with the Communists, made the *Review* into a viciously anti-American publication filled with denunciations of America and stories of American troop brutality.

Repatriated American POW's report that Powell's magazine was must reading in all the prison camps, was used as a brain-washing textbook. For four years Bill Powell thus collaborated with the Communists and has been characterized by returned prisoners as a "murderer." In 1953, Bill chose suddenly to quit Shanghai, returning to America at the same time some 3,000-odd repatriated American POW's were returning.

Since his return Powell has been a witness before the Senate Internal Security Subcommittee, during which time he has taken refuge behind the Fifth Amendment *fifty-three times*.

Thus three newspaper editors chose three different ways to meet the challenge of Communism.

The Englishman chose co-existence. It did not do him a great deal of good, for no number of apologies saved his newspaper from either moral or actual extinction.

Bill Powell, son of a crusading American editor, chose collaboration. His paper too, is dead now; and Bill Powell leads a lonely life, branded as a "murderer," suspected by his government and his fellowmen.

Randall Gould chose to put moral issues above all else. He fought for what was right and went out of business when it became obvious that to continue in business he would have to forget moral principle.

Of the three editors, two Americans and one Englishman, only one can today walk among his fellowmen, head high, conscience clear.

The tragedy of America in Asia today is that Americans now infrequently follow the course set by Randall Gould. And the people of Asia who are on our side are losing faith. For they have learned the futility of compromise, they know that man cannot serve God and Mammon too, that it is but a short step from co-existence to collaboration.

It would be foolish to write optimistically of the future in Asia. The men of good will, the dreamers, those who have not given up, could prevail if we would but give them hope and renewed faith. But the sands are running out. A year or two more, perhaps, and Asia will be lost, to sink into a darkness that may last for generations. The tragedy will not lie in the fact that the white man will be driven out. Rather it will be in the fact that the good works, the moral principles which the white man brought along with his evils, will also be submerged and lost.

Those I have called the "lost Christians" will be truly lost. Chai Nam Soon who walked down the valley of death with a little brother strapped upon her back will again walk into the shadow of death. Tommy Hsu's dreams will end in nightmare. Captain Chang on Tungting Island will be engulfed without a ripple. For Tungting is such a small place, long unnoticed by the world we proudly call Christian.

A "heathen" Chinese, by his own admission, has written what well may be Asia's epitaph as far as America is concerned. Dr. Hu Shih, one-time President of National Peking University, one-time Chinese Ambassador to the United States, now at Princeton University, wrote an introduction to Dr. J. Leighton Stuart's memoirs, *Fifty Years in China*. Dr. Hu Shih wrote:

"When in 1949 I read Secretary Dean Acheson's Letter of Transmittal of the China 'White Paper' and came to these sentences: '. . . the ominous result of the civil war in China was beyond the control of the government of the United States. Nothing that this country did or could have done within the reasonable limits of its capabilities could have changed that result; nothing that was left undone by this country has contributed to it.'—when I read those sentences

I wrote on the margin: 'Mathew 27:24.' This is the text:

> When Pilate saw that he could prevail nothing,
> but that a tumult was made, he took water, and
> washed his hands before the multitude, saying,
> I am innocent of the blood of this just man: see
> ye to it."

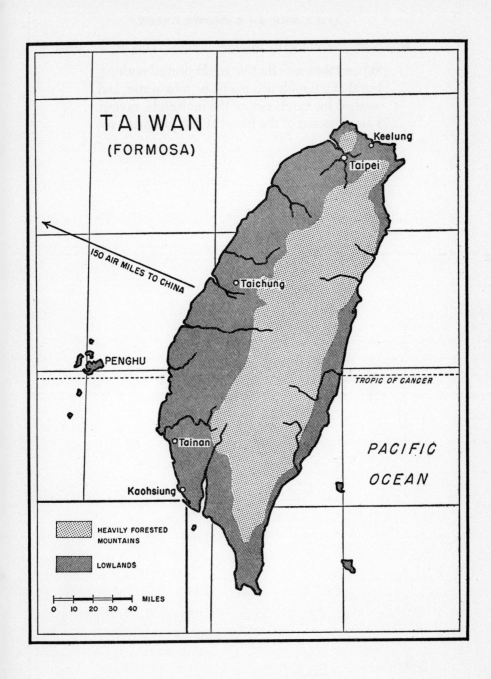

TAIWAN
(FORMOSA)

Keelung

Taipei

150 AIR MILES TO CHINA

Taichung

PENGHU

TROPIC OF CANCER

Tainan

PACIFIC

OCEAN

Kaohsiung

HEAVILY FORESTED
MOUNTAINS

LOWLANDS

MILES

0 10 20 30 40

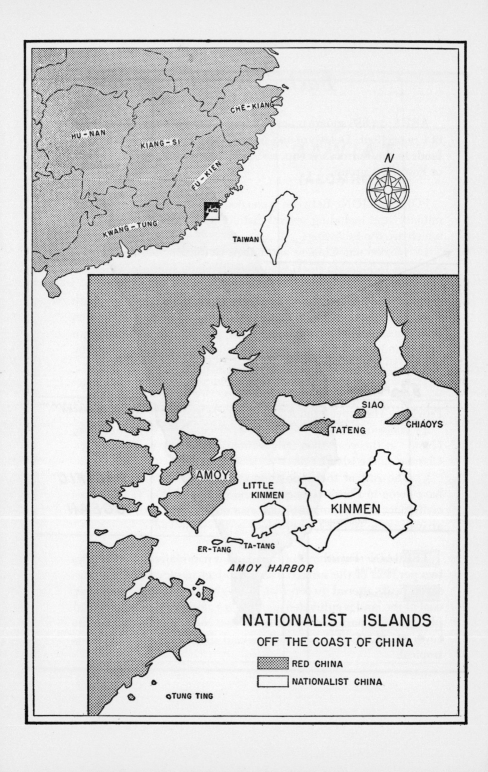

NATIONALIST ISLANDS
OFF THE COAST OF CHINA

RED CHINA

NATIONALIST CHINA

Facts About Formosa

AREA: 13,886 square miles or approximately the combined area of Connecticut, Delaware and New Jersey. There are fourteen islands in the Formosa group, and sixty-four islands in the Penghu or Pescadore group.

POPULATION: Between 9,000,000 and 10,000,000, including military, and including several distinct population groups among which are the following:

1) 150,000 non-Chinese aborigines, comprising eight groups of tribes, of Indonesian stock, who were living on Formosa when the Chinese arrived.

2) 1,000,000 *Hakkas,* descendents of immigrants from North China who first settled on the South China Coast then moved on to Formosa beginning some 400 years ago. They speak their own dialect and have retained a vigorous individualism as indicated by the fact that they resisted the Japanese bitterly.

3) 5,000,000 to 6,000,000 *Hoklos,* who came to Formosa between 200 and 400 years ago from the coast of neighboring Fukien Province. They speak the Amoy dialect of Fukien Province.

4) 200,000 Cantonese who settled principally in South Formosa. (Note: in the year 1600 it is estimated there were only 25,000 Chinese on the island.)

5) The rest of the population consists of "mainlanders" who have come to Formosa since the end of World War II and especially since the Communists took over on the mainland. These new arrivals come from every province of the mainland.

TERRAIN: Two-thirds of the island is mountainous, with forty-two per cent of the surface over 1,640 feet in elevation. Seventy-seven peaks exceed 10,000 feet in height. Only twenty-three per cent of the land is cultivated and this lies along the western coastal plain and in a narrow strip along the east coast. Jungles and forests cover two-thirds of the island. Lowland climate is tropical to semi-tropical.

311

AGRICULTURAL PRODUCTION: Formosa is one of the most fertile agricultural regions in the world. In 1953 the rice crop totaled 1,640,000 metric tons, highest in island history and providing an important export. Production of sugar in 1953 totaled nearly 900,000 tons, which also provided an important export, top foreign exchange earner with an income of nearly $70,000,000. Other important crops are pineapples, tea, bananas, citrus fruits, sweet potatoes and peanuts.

TWO OTHER FACTS TO REMEMBER:

1) Nationalist China controlled, as of late 1954, approximately 50 islands off the China coast. Total area probably approximately 1000 square miles, civilian population 65,000.

2) In spite of Communist pressure, most overseas Chinese will give allegiance to Free China. The principal overseas populations are as follows:

Thailand	3,500,000
Malaya	2,043,971
Hong Kong	2,000,000
Indonesia	1,600,000
Singapore	807,000
Vietnam and Cambodia . .	1,200,000
Philippines	141,000
North Borneo	220,000
Burma	360,000